When Hamlet complains that Guildenstern "would pluck out the heart of my mystery," he imagines an encounter that recurs insistently in the discourses of early modern England. The struggle by one man to discover the secrets in another's heart is rehearsed not only in plays but in legal records, correspondence, philosophical writing and contemporary social description. In this book Elizabeth Hanson argues that the construction of other people as objects of discovery signalled a reconceptualizing of the "subject" in both the political and philosophical sense of the term. She examines the records of state torture, plays by Shakespeare and Jonson, cony-catching pamphlets and Francis Bacon's philosophical writing to demonstrate that the subject was both under suspicion and empowered in this period. Her account revises earlier attempts to locate the emergence of modern subjectivity in the Renaissance, arguing for a more nuanced and localized understanding of the relationship with its medieval past.

Cambridge Studies in Renaissance Literature and Culture 24

Discovering the Subject in Renaissance England

Cambridge Studies in Renaissance Literature and Culture

General editor
STEPHEN ORGEL
Jackson Eli Reynolds Professor of Humanities, Stanford University

Editorial board
Anne Barton, *University of Cambridge*
Jonathan Dollimore, *University of Sussex*
Marjorie Garber, *Harvard University*
Jonathan Goldberg, *Duke University*
Nancy Vickers, *Bryn Mawr College*

Since the 1970s there has been a broad and vital reinterpretation of the nature of literary texts, a move away from formalism to a sense of literature as an aspect of social, economic, political, and cultural history. While the earliest New Historicist work was criticised for a narrow and anecdotal view of history, it also served as an important stimulus for post-structuralist, feminist, Marxist, and psychoanalytical work, which in turn has increasingly informed and redirected it. Recent writing on the nature of representation, the historical construction of gender and of the concept of identity itself, on theatre as a political and economic phenomenon, and on the ideologies of art generally, reveals the breadth of the field. Cambridge Studies in Renaissance Literature and Culture is designed to offer historically oriented studies of Renaissance literature and theatre which make use of the insights afforded by theoretical perspectives. The view of history envisioned is above all a view of our own history, a reading of the Renaissance for and from our own time.

Recent titles include

The culture of slander in early modern England
M. LINDSAY KAPLAN, Georgetown University

Narrative and meaning in early modern England: Browne's skull and other histories
HOWARD MARCHITELLO, Texas A & M University

The homoerotics of early modern drama
MARIO DIGANGI, Indiana University

Shakespeare's Troy: drama, politics, and the translation of empire
HEATHER JAMES, University of Southern California

Shakespeare, Spenser, and the crisis in Ireland
CHRISTOPHER HIGHLEY, Ohio State University

A complete list of books in the series is given at the end of the volume

Discovering the Subject in Renaissance England

Elizabeth Hanson
Queen's University, Kingston, Ontario

PUBLISHED BY THE PRESS SYNDICATE OF THE UNIVERSITY OF CAMBRIDGE
The Pitt Building, Trumpington Street, Cambridge CB2 1RP, United Kingdom

CAMBRIDGE UNIVERSITY PRESS
The Edinburgh Building, Cambridge CB2 2RU, United Kingdom
40 West 20th Street, New York, NY 10011–4211, USA
10 Stamford Road, Oakleigh, Melbourne 3166, Australia

First published 1998

Printed in the United Kingdom at the University Press, Cambridge

Typeset in Times 10/12 pt [CE]

A catalogue record for this book is available from the British library

ISBN 0 521 62021 X hardback

For Muriel and Ross Hanson

Contents

Acknowledgments

At last I have the pleasure of acknowledging here the many debts I incurred in the long process of writing this book. *Discovering the Subject in Renaissance England* began as a dissertation fertilized by the extraordinary teaching of Jonathan Crewe, who showed me a Renaissance far more disturbing and intellectually exciting than any I had hitherto imagined. It was shaped by the sympathetic, patient, and inspiring attentions of Jonathan Goldberg. The privilege of having learned from these teachers will support me throughout my life as a scholar. Marcie Frank and Joseph Harrison also offered invaluable encouragement and criticism in the early stages of this project.

Karen Sanchez-Eppler and Alexandra Halasz have read each draft of this book from its first inception to the form it appears in here. They have written sentences and paragraphs that the title page of this book would suggest are mine, shown me the implications of my ideas and saved me from my worst instincts. Their friendship has extended to every aspect of my life and by supporting its putative author has produced this book. Ian Morrison provided material and emotional support and a great deal of fun throughout much of the writing of this book. He also offered invaluable advice on legal questions. At Queen's University I have been sustained by a wonderful group of friends and colleagues whose humanity, intellectual seriousness, and sense of the professional absurd let me feel that I could write this book and still keep my soul. In particular, Paul Stevens provided constant companionship, intelligent commentary, and good-humoured sufferance of my murderous tendencies at some of the more difficult phases of the writing. Pat Rae was (and remains) my writerly fellow-traveller, confidante, and personal ironist. Mark Jones and Sylvia Soderlind offered friendship, hospitality, and inspiration. Sergio Sismondo guided me through the literature of seventeenth-century British science and taught me the difference between epistemic questions and epistemological ones.

I have presented parts of this book at the University of Colorado, Cornell University, Queen's University, the University of Toronto, and

York University, as well as at the Tulsa Conference on New Directions in Renaissance Studies, the Elizabethan Theatre Conference, MLA, the Group for Early Modern Cultural Studies, and the Canadian Society for Renaissance Studies. The audiences on all of these occasions asked questions which made a difference in the final form of this book. I am particularly grateful to Jonathan Culler, Lyne Magnusson, Ted McGee, Richard Streier, Olga Valbuena, and Ruth Widmann for making these opportunities available. In writing this book I have made use most especially of the collections of the Folger Shakespeare Library and of the University of Toronto libraries. I was supported in the earlier phase of writing by a Fellowship from the Social Sciences and Humanities Resource Council of Canada. I finished the project while a Visiting Scholar at the Center for Literary and Cultural Studies at Harvard University, and am grateful to Marjorie Garber for that opportunity. In different ways Margaret Ferguson and Jean Howard have given me practical advice and professional confidence that has helped me get to the end of this process. I am indebted to Stephen Orgel for his generosity and alacrity in supporting the publication of this project, to Josie Dixon for her work in guiding it through the Press, and to Chris Lyall Grant for careful and respectful copy-editing. Finally, I want to thank Patti Brace and Janelle Jenstad who at different times turned a messy virtual manuscript into clean, hard copy.

Ross and Muriel Hanson are ultimately responsible for this book, having brought me up in a household full of books, arguments, and ideas, and having then tirelessly supported the consequences of their actions. Kristin Hanson was my first interlocutor on intellectual matters and remains my most bracingly skeptical one. Erik Hanson built the desk on which I wrote this book.

I am grateful to the Regents of the University of California for permission to publish a revised version of chapter 2, which originally appeared in *Representations* 34 (1991) and to P.D. Meany Company Inc. for permission to publish in chapter 3 a revised version of material which appeared in *The Elizabethan Theatre* 14.

1   Introduction

When Hamlet rails that Guildenstern, formerly a school friend, now a spy recruited by the king, "would pluck out the heart of my mystery" (3.2.356–7), he assumes a position, as the resistant object of another man's scrutiny, within a scenario that recurs insistently in the discourses of Renaissance England.[1] The struggle to discover the secrets in another's heart, or to resist being the object of such discovery, is rehearsed not only in the drama but in the records of the Privy Council and state trials, and in correspondence, philosophical writing, conduct books, and literature of social description of the period. In fact, Hamlet's imagery here links his situation both to the actual culmination of many discovering operations of the Elizabethan state, the extraction and display of the traitor's heart at execution, and to moments of resistance to such operations, as when Catholic sympathizers wrote of the martyred Jesuit Edmund Campion that "one might sooner pluck his heart out of his bosom than rack a word out of his mouth that he made conscience of uttering."[2] The hostile discovery of another's innermost being, with its concomitant insistence on that other's secrecy, constitutes one of the most prevalent and historically specific versions of inter-subjectivity in Renaissance England. These discovering operations differ from other practices which make the heart the object of knowledge, such as the spiritual accounting of seventeenth-century Puritanism or the much later explorations of psychoanalysis, both in the presumed enmity of the participants and in the reification of the "mystery" of inner life they entail, the reduction which makes the "heart" susceptible to "plucking."

In this book I explore some instances of this Renaissance obsession with the discovery of the heart's secrets: the Elizabethan resort to interrogatory torture, particularly in response to the Jesuit mission to England; the revelation of secret iniquity in agents of the state which Shakespeare stages in *Measure for Measure* and *Othello*; the exposure of a criminal "underworld" in cony-catching pamphlets and in Jonson's *Bartholmew Fair*; and the discovery of nature that Francis Bacon envisioned, a project which will both replicate and depart in crucial ways from the discovery of the interior reaches of other people. The argument of this book is that the tendency to construe other people in terms of secrets awaiting discovery, which seems to have grown particularly intense during the period roughly defined by the reigns of Elizabeth I and James I, can be understood as a symptom of an epistemic change, of a redrafting of the terms on which the subject relates to the world in dominant political, religious, and intellectual discourses. The nature of this change is adumbrated in the very awkwardness which attends my use of the term "subject" in connection with this period, the jostling it produces between the modern meaning which designates the site of thought and experience, and the Renaissance meaning which proclaims the subordination of the governed. Implicit in these different meanings are two different grammars of knowledge. The first supposes that the subject knows transitively, taking the world as the object of his thinking. The second posits that to the extent that the subject knows (and this may not be his defining activity) he must do so self-reflexively, recognizing his place in a hierarchical order. The epistemic structure of discovery would appear to align with the first option. In the discovery of another's secrets, or, for that matter, of a new continent, truth lies outside the mind that would know it, masked by distances or surfaces which the discoverer labors to penetrate. This labor evinces the discoverer's freedom to act, the fact that existing authority cannot hold him for it does not as yet contain the truth he goes to seek. Thus the discoverer takes up a position that we might very crudely call modern. But our sense of the operative grammar is complicated in the scenarios with which I am concerned (Bacon's discovery of nature partially excepted) by the fact that the object the discoverer seeks to know is a subject: the site of thought and the origin of action. The intractable otherness which the discoverer encounters in his quarry arises, we shall see, because the latter possesses powers akin to those of the discoverer himself.

The self-reflexiveness of these discoveries suggests that they do not simply enact a modern epistemic stance but also defend against it. What is ambivalently at stake in them is the structure and meaning of knowing itself rather than the acquisition of specific information. More concretely, I would argue that in these discoveries of the subject we encounter a contradictory set of impulses and strategies arising from the new scope for individual action which an expanding royal administration, religious schism, new technologies, and economic arrangements – and their accompanying institutional fractures – had produced. As one man examined another, searching for signs of hidden motives or loyalties, struggling to place him in the social order (I will come presently to the reasons for my masculine gendering of this scenario), he confronted as in a mirror the idea of the subject, not merely as authority's subordinate but as the origin of discourse and action, as a practitioner who is not fully expressed in the structures which constitute the givens of his world. He saw, in other words, the possibility of a subject for whom certain claims, to authorial or to legal rights for instance, or to control over nature, might come to seem natural.

My purpose is thus to offer investigations toward a history of the subject, and in so doing to assist in the ongoing project, initiated by Michel Foucault among others, of de-naturalizing the relations between the subject and the world which have prevailed in the West at least since the eighteenth century. But my topic is not only the substance of epistemic change but also how it occurs. The conditions which underpin the Renaissance discovering operations – a distancing of the subject from his world and his reattachment to it through appropriating activity such as the methodical acquisition of knowledge – will receive philosophical exposition in the course of the seventeenth century by thinkers such as Descartes and Locke. However, in reading the Renaissance episodes in these terms, I do not wish to argue for backdating the emergence of their ideas by fifty to seventy-five years. The axiom from which this study proceeds is that by the time epistemic assumptions are held with sufficient consciousness and consistency to receive philosophical treatment they have long been used by people in highly contingent and untheorized ways to negotiate myriad local crises and opportunities in economic, social, and institutional life. In other words, new epistemic possibilities begin as improvisations around the fissures between the material conditions of life and the conceptual resources already in place in a culture. Therefore new ways of knowing are often profoundly at odds with the consciously held commitments of the people who begin to articulate them, emerging not as principles from which a world order can be derived, but as contradictions in discourse and social practice. The motives for the discovering operations I trace, as well as for some of the resistance to them, tended to be conservative, or at least stabilizing ones, desires to restore social legibility or to discourage doctrinal or political innovation. But the work both of discovery and of resistance to it necessarily exploited the very resources and opportunities which had disengaged the subject from his world in the first place, enforcing the discontinuities which it sought to close with the result that they could become, in time, the basis of positive claims. The place we are to look for signs of change is thus not the "thought" of a period, that is, the available systematic understandings of the world, but the institutional pressures and *ad hoc* strategies which come into play around particular social and political relationships.

Let me offer as an example both of this messy process and of the specific concerns of this book the development of the legal privilege against self-incrimination, a matter which I explore in greater detail in chapter 2. Enshrined in the American Bill of Rights as the Fifth Amendment, the right not to give evidence against oneself memorializes some of the discovering operations with which I am concerned here through the protection it affords against them. The right posits a subject in possession of a vital truth about himself, a truth which is also of interest to the state. But the state must refrain from forcing the subject (or "citizen" in the modern political context) to speak this truth, thereby demonstrating that subjecthood is a condition of freedom. At the same time, the state develops for itself the means to collect the evidence that will permit an objective reconstruction of this truth and its installation in the public domain. A typical architectural feature of modern democratic political structures, this right props up against each other a self-knowing, self-owning subject and a neutral administrative state; the prohibition which demarcates them serves also to maintain the mutual pressure which shapes both formations.

The principle that no one could be compelled under any circumstance to give evidence against him or herself was definitively established in English law during the treason trials between 1649 and 1653 of the obstreperous Leveller John Lilburne. The common law maxim that "no man is bound to accuse himself" (*nemo tenetur seipsum prodere*) seems to have originally meant that the Crown could only question the accused on a properly presented indictment. In the tumultuous half-century which preceded Lilburne's trials, however, it had been more and more frequently invoked as a global right in response to the increasingly inquisitorial legal procedures with which the Crown had met dissent.[3] But as Leonard W. Levy's magisterial study, *The Origins of the Fifth Amendment*, makes clear, the evolution of a legal right against self-incrimination is only one effect of a much longer process, beginning with the establishment of the Inquisition by the Fourth Lateran Council in 1215, which made the individual subject the target of a host of invasive ecclesiastical and political investigations and thus shaped his conscience as a potentially secret site of truth. In other words, the right is inconceivable without the idea of the subject as a private cache of truth, and this comes into being (as Foucault would have predicted) not at first as an oppositional strategy but as a disciplinary effect. During the late and, at least for England, particularly frenzied stage of this process with which my study is concerned, the multiplying occasions on which someone was compelled to utter his or her potentially incriminating thoughts to state authority also led to heated debate about the circumstances under which a Christian conscience could be compelled to answer interrogatories meant to ferret out dissenting opinion and activity. Thus the drive of the early modern state to secure uniformity of practice and allegiance was dialectically met by Reformation and Counter-Reformation notions of the authority of the conscience. Sometimes, but not always, these aligned with common-law opposition to inquisitorial procedures.

One of the most notorious instances of such conscientious resistance was the practice of "equivocation" or mental reservation of key details in the answer to an incriminating question, a strategy resorted to by recusants and Catholic priests who were caught between the need for self-preservation on the one hand and a deeply felt religious obligation not to lie on the other. Unlike Protestant claims for the conscience, the debate about equivocation did not explicitly intersect with the mounting common-law opposition to testimonial compulsion. It therefore tends to receive only passing mention in legal histories, although the same forms of investigation gave rise both to equivocation and to legal protests. Indeed such an intersection of legal and religious concerns was unlikely, insofar as the Catholic advocates of equivocation were often being prosecuted by the very common lawyers who were refining the privilege against self-incrimination – a project fueled notwithstanding by their distaste, as common lawyers, for the various inquisitorial devices the Crown had instituted to entrap Catholics. At the same time, the Catholics themselves rarely resorted to arguments based on common-law restrictions, focusing instead on the philosophical problem of what constituted a lie; in part, I would suggest, because their own institutional allegiances made them fundamentally sympathetic to inquisitorial modes of fact-finding. Yet it is precisely for this reason that the Catholic justifications of equivocation belong to the genealogy of the right against self-incrimination as much as do the more obviously pertinent arguments of common lawyers: in them we can see the idea of the subject which the disciplinary mechanisms of medieval Christianity produced, being recruited, under the pressure of the Elizabethan state's hostile discovery and against the ideological commitments of the Catholics themselves, for work in articulating new political and epistemic relationships between the subject and his world.

The Jesuit propagandist Robert Persons presents a fairly typical argument in *A Treatise Tending to Mitigation Towards Catholick Subjects* (1607).[4] Drawing on Aristotelian definitions of what constitutes a proposition, as well as on St. Augustine's treatises on lying, Persons argues that "a Catholicke being demaunded whether he have any Priest in his house, may answere by Equivocation that he hath none, reserving in his mind *that he hath none whome he is bound to utter or discover*"

(308), and this without lying, because utterances which occur only in the mind have the same ontological status as those which are spoken. For, he asserts,

> there is a voice in writing as well as in speaking, according to *Aristotle* himselfe, so is there an internall voice, as well as an externall, and an internall speach as well as an externall, which speaketh, affirmeth, or denieth to the inward eares as well or better then the voice, or letter to the outward. (329)

The connections between Persons's ability to imagine the inwardness of the subject and the institutional imperatives of Catholicism to interrogate and regulate the soul are evident in the way that inner life seems to be imagined as self-reflexive confession, internal utterance made to inward ears. The point is enforced by the fact that for Persons irrefutable proof of his argument lies in the consensus of

> all Devines [that] there may be mentall Heresy, when a man in his mind doth affirme, or give consent to any Heresy in his hart, for the which he may be damned everlastingly, if he repent not, though he should never utter the same in word or writing to any. (325)

The concerns of the inquisitor are glimpsed through the arguments of the martyr. But while Persons's commitment to Catholic authority leads him to imagine inwardness as always already open to inquisitorial probing, the historical circumstances of his writing compels him to make this inwardness a site of resistance to such probing. The completeness of internal utterance constitutes permission for the accused to thwart the magistrate by withdrawing into his own mind "as though he were alone and no man by" (342), not deceiving the magistrate (because the accused's desire is not to deceive but "to escape, and defend himselfe" [347]) but merely allowing him to be deceived should he fail in the task of interpreting "doubtful utterance" (346). In the protective self-enclosure of the accused, and the intellectually active position in which it places the magistrate, we can discern features of the relationship that will be established in the right against self-incrimination. That Persons does not endorse the idea of such a right and can perceive the threat it poses to Catholic authority appears not only in the anxiety evident in the example of mental heresy, but also in his insistence that his argument pertains only to situations where the magistrate is unjust. Where the magistrate is lawful, it is a mortal sin for an accused to resist interrogation, "either by willful[ly] holding his peace or by denying the truth" (414). And yet when Persons specifies examples of legitimate equivocations he offers "I have not stolne," with the unspoken qualification "so as I am bound to confesse it publickly, for that there is not witnesse, proofe or presumption against me" (421). Grounding the legitimacy of resistance in the state's lack of a proper indictment or presentment, Persons's justification of equivocation slides opportunistically into the common-law discourse of his adversaries which will lead to the establishment of the right against self-incrimination.

To read the Jesuit position on equivocation, or indeed any argument from this period as a harbinger of the post-Lockean rights-bearing subject, is to privilege a diachronic interpretation of culture, to analyze a particular historical moment for signs of the future rather than for the systematic beliefs and practices which distinguish a culture from its successors. In its emphasis on the emergent, my study departs from New Historicist treatments of the early modern English state in order to suggest the more tactical nature of practices that have been read as revealing the essence of the culture, and to invite consideration of some social conflicts and institutional pressures which such readings occlude. Thus I hope to make visible the potential for social transformation (although not necessarily liberation) evident even at moments of extreme repression.[5] For instance, against earlier claims about the theatricality of early modern modes of rule and subjection, which often note that England in this period lacked an extensive bureaucracy and police force, I emphasize the effects of the establishment of systems of royal administration, a point to which I will return below.[6] For while bureaucratic mechanisms of government in the inescapable forms in which we have come to know them were absent, the very fact that administrative apparatuses are *developing* in this period means that such arrangements possess a special salience, a capacity to provoke anxiety which their fully developed forms presumably lack. In other words, I want to indicate the ways in which cultural anxiety in the period is *historically* meaningful, the effect less of contradictions within a synchronic system than of new organizational possibilities – possibilities which are themselves multiplied and transformed in the attempt to manage the instabilities they produce.

At the same time that this study departs from some of the assumptions that drove cultural poetics, its more general argument, that discourse from this period offers evidence of a new separation between the subject and his world that is recognizably modern, invokes a familiar narrative of epistemic transition. This narrative received its clearest recent rehearsal in British cultural materialist work of the mid-1980s, such as Catherine Belsey's *The Subject of Tragedy* and Francis Barker's *The Tremulous Private Body*, although it is arguably implicit in every invocation of the period's new designation as "early modern."[7] As David Aers has noted, however, this narrative of the Renaissance emergence of something like modern subjectivity actually begins, although with opposite ideological investments, with Burckhardt's famous account of the individual's awakening in the Renaissance:[8]

In the Middle Ages both sides of human consciousness – that which was turned within as that which was turned without – lay dreaming or half awake beneath a common veil. The veil was woven of faith, illusion and childish prepossession, through which the world and history were seen clad in strange hues. Man was conscious of himself as member of a race, people, party, family, or corporation – only through some general category. In Italy this veil first melted into air; an *objective* treatment and consideration of the State and of all the things of this world became possible. The *subjective* side at the same time asserted itself with corresponding emphasis; man became a spiritual *individual* and recognized himself as such.[9]

Behind the cultural materialists' inversions of the Burckhardtian theme lies also Foucault's influential genealogies of modern deployments of power and knowledge. Most important of these is the account in *The Order of Things* of how, between the seventeenth and the twentieth centuries, Man emerged from the matrix of Discourse and temporarily asserted his priority to it only to become in post-modernity once more its mere effect. However, the story of the decorporealizing of punishment detailed in *Discipline and Punish* has also proved crucial to the cultural materialists' project. This narrative of a great epistemic shift has been powerfully criticized by medievalists, most notably Aers, who argues that it both attributes a false unity to medieval culture and wrongly identifies as "new" categories of thought and experience which had been in vigorous use in earlier periods.[10] Recent studies of medieval culture have supported Aers's contention, detailing practices of dissent and theatricalized punishment, and styles of self-presentation which both dissipate the Burckhardtian myth of medieval culture as dreaming corporatism and suggest a good deal of continuity with Renaissance cultural forms.[11] Certainly it must be conceded that the very repetition of the narrative suggests a formalism at work in these various accounts of epistemic change that embarrasses their historicizing claims – a problem, I should add, that is made particularly acute by the cultural materialists' rather reductive use of Foucault. But I also would argue that in focusing their criticism on the content of the cultural materialists' representation of the Middle Ages, the medievalists have to some extent missed the point about what makes that work so problematic. Meanwhile, they leave unaddressed the question of how we are to talk meaningfully about the process whereby new practices and concepts like experimental science, say, or legal rights, began to be thinkable. It will be useful then to consider some of the limitations which attend current versions of this narrative in order to suggest how we might more profitably recount the very real changes in what it meant to be a subject which took place in this period.

Any attempt to assess the validity of this narrative enterprise is complicated by the various filiations, revisions, grafts, misreadings, and shifts in focus that define the relationships among its various instances. Burckhardt posits a new consciousness of the objective nature of the world, and thus of the subject's subjectivity which results most crucially in a sense of individuality. These developments are articulated in the political and artistic registers. Barker likewise focuses on an emergent subject–object divide, which he denounces as "what was done to us in the seventeenth century," and follows Burckhardt in linking it to a loss of corporatism and to the emergence of an interiorized subjectivity (68). But he finds it most significant for the way it enforces a subjugation of the body to the mind, an argument indebted to Foucault's account in *Discipline and Punish* of a shift from the corporeal display of sovereign power in punishment to the decorporealized modes of surveillance which took hold in the Enlightenment.[12] Catherine Belsey also echoes Burckhardt's concern with nascent individualism in her account of the emergence of the "subject of liberal humanism" (ix). But if Burckhardt's individual flourished in the despotic political culture of Renaissance Italy, Belsey's subject, "unified, knowing, and autonomous," seeks "a political system that guarantees freedom of choice" (8), in other words, bourgeois liberal democracy. Moreover, Belsey identifies this subject not with Burckhardt's individual but with Foucault's Man, invoking at the beginning of her project the narrative frame of *The Order of Things*, the tale of how this "discursive hero of a certain class" (Belsey's phrase) emerged as the inevitably temporary effect of certain "arrangements of knowledge" (Foucault's phrase) (14). But Foucault himself, it should be noted, is concerned not so much with the emergence of this "discursive hero" *per se* as with the "arrangements of knowledge" that produce him. And he describes these arrangements with such attention both to their internal complexity and to the details of their evolution from the seventeenth century to the present that any sense that there is a single more-or-less coherent version of the subject operating in discourse over this period becomes untenable. In fact, the epistemic shift which Foucault locates in the earlier seventeenth century – a dissolution of knowledge based on the recognition of similitude within the Creation and the emergence of a new knowledge based on the accurate description of the discrete identities of things and their relation to each other – initiates a dispensation that will last only until the end of the eighteenth century.

What this palimpsest of epistemic histories reveals is the wide array of personages, issues, timetables, and models of change that can be adduced for what sounds, at a certain level of abstraction, like the same narrative. In each of these accounts we find that the "subject," the placeholder for human consciousness within discourse and material relations, meant something drastically different after the "Renaissance" than before. Moreover, this difference seems to have to do with an increasing sense of the subject's detachment from what we would now call the objective conditions of his existence. This process culminates in philosophical projects, such as Descartes's, which make that detachment the primary meaning of subjectivity, although that condition may be construed in terms of a range of possible relationships, between mind and body, inner self and outward show, individual and state, mind and nature. If the thematic concerns of these accounts echo each other, however, their chronological plotting varies drastically. For example, the epistemic shift which Foucault posits in *The Order of Things* as the beginning of Man's emergence occurs in the early seventeenth century, between what he calls the Renaissance and the Classical periods, while the displacement of the spectacular display of the body by more internalized modes of subjection which he describes in *Discipline and Punish* occurs in the later eighteenth century. But Barker's analysis conflates these events, locating the key transition between *Hamlet*, in which "the spectacularly visible body [. . . lies] athwart that divide between subject and object, discourse and world that characterizes the later dispensation" (24), and the bourgeois regime he reads out of Samuel Pepys's mid-seventeenth-century (i.e. Classical age) diary.[13] Moreover, while both Barker and Belsey find the beginning of the bourgeois subject's lamentable emergence on the Jacobean stage, the awakening of the individual with which Burckhardt is concerned starts in the fourteenth century with Petrarch. We might well ask whether the Renaissance is in fact early modernity, as Burckhardt (ironically enough) would suggest, or, as Foucault argues, the world which "the men of the seventeenth and eighteenth centuries, [who] do not think . . . in terms that had been bequeathed by preceding ages," had left behind.[14]

The incoherence which these chronological variations threaten to produce in the narrative of epistemic change is partly the effect of mapping what I have already suggested are the oversimplifying appro- priations of the cultural materialists back onto the works of their progenitors, although the problem is also compounded by conflating projects which deal with developments in Italy, France, and England. But it would be a mistake, I think, to treat oversimplification only as a characteristic of weaker versions of epistemic history, rather than as a methodological feature of the exercise in general. If this statement sounds dismissive it is intended as a recognition that what even strong epistemic history such as Foucault's offers is not a transparent account of the way things were but a specific kind of *writing,* characterized by the imposition of narrative tropes (of shift, departure, loss, birth) onto the discursive residue of cultures, in order to make discernible the extremely elusive forces that shape human consciousness differently over time.

This distinction between trope and positivist assertion is also valuable in understanding the nature of the medievalists' masterful response to the narrative of early modern epistemic change. The new work on medieval culture demonstrates that a culture can embody innocent wholeness only as long as it is not examined in detail. Train one's critical sights on a specific episode or practice, a Lollard's strategies of resistance to his interrogators, say, or a village's penal practices, and the culture will appear conflicted, heterogeneous, and continuous with later cultures, if only in its heterogeneity and proneness to conflict.[15] But the point here is not so much that the medievalists have done their homework while the early modernists have not as that their writing, often in the format of the micro-historical essay, foregrounds a particular trope, the local detail, which jams, as it were, tropes of historical change. Invited to look at the way in which the Lollard clergyman's ostentatious intellectuality under interrogation distinguishes him from the people he purports to speak for – in other words, to examine the subtle fractures within a community – we do not see his interrogation as one event in a centuries-long trail of interrogations. Nor do we ask what it signifies that 175 years later religious dissidents increasingly claim to have answered their interrogators with stoic silence rather than skillful argument, nor consider how this development might relate to the articulation another 70 years later of a legal right to remain silent when charged with any offense. Similarly, I would argue that one reason the cultural materialists' narratives seem so reductive is that they (notoriously) tend to favor synecdoche, the trope in which the part stands for the whole, particularly as an efficient way to establish the pre-history of their own subjects. This rhetorical choice interacts unfortunately with the content of their argument that certain kinds of divisions, between subject and object or between mind and body, which are epistemically important in the seventeenth century, do not especially characterize medieval ways of knowing. In other words, a tropological effect (the organic unity of the thing represented) tends to return as the attribute of the object described and the Middle Ages come to stand, problematically enough, for Wholeness itself.

An awareness of the rhetoricity of our own practices of cultural description is important so that we can choose our tropes wisely, conscious of the theoretical implications they carry. But, more crucially, it is necessary if we are to grasp the nature both of the phenomena which such work addresses, that is, cultural formations themselves, and of our own relation to them as objects of knowledge. The various slippages or repetitions that seem to beset the telling of the history of the subject testify to the impossibility of specifying when an epistemic formation is latent or burgeoning or fully achieved, or what its constituent elements are. If we go looking for the modern subject we will find signs of his "emergence" everywhere, but will be hard pressed to seize upon either the time and place of his birth or his definitive full-dress instantiation, because at any given moment in discourse the subject is situated within a unique, non-systemizable network of material pressures and intellectual filiations. Some of these elements will survive into the future, as intellectual tradition, ideology, or economic or political structure, but others will not. Those elements which do survive will then manifest themselves in relation to other forces and will therefore bear a different meaning. My point is not, however, that the relationships which determine what it means to be a subject at any given moment are all *ad hoc* ones; what makes it possible even to locate a subject in discourse is the intelligibility produced by some clear or well-established alignments, mutual dependencies, and conflicts among the ideas and forces that construct his position. These formations can endure across time, acquire additional applications, and be rendered obsolete. In telling the subject's history as an eventful narrative replete with emergences, ruptures, and shifts, we are trying to make visible the semi-autonomous life of conceptual resources. But the rhythms and chronologies of this story can never fully synchronize with all the repetitious, idiosyncratic instances of these resources' actual use. Thus the historicity of such a narrative depends on the maintenance of dialectical pressure between the necessarily abstracting and stabilizing tropes of epistemic transformation and the excessive, contingent complexities which attend any given appearance of the subject in discourse and material practice.

This approach to the history of the subject permits us to heed the medievalists' justifiable demand that we attend more carefully to earlier periods and to the continuities with modernity they present, but without our having to abandon the work of discerning epistemic change. At this juncture then I want to offer my reader not an account of the subject's late-medieval condition and how it differs from his Renaissance incarnation, but a consideration of two pre-Renaissance episodes which anticipate the concerns of this book and so might challenge the special claims it makes for the Renaissance. Certainly these episodes demonstrate the extraordinarily long (if intermittent) history of some of the ways of thinking which contribute to the discovery scenarios I describe. But I offer them because they also suggest that the meaning of those ways of thinking can change radically depending on the circumstances of their use. Thus they force two methodological recognitions: that the narrative of epistemic shift is an heuristic device and that epistemic formations are more profitably understood as complex re-weavings of conceptual resources rather than mental continents adrift from one another in time.

I have chosen to embed my discussion of the discovery scenario within the story of the Renaissance emergence of the modern subject, in part because, in the histories of the various institutions and practices which impinge on the discoveries of the subject, the distinction repeatedly asserts itself between an earlier corporatism and a separation and enclosure of the subject that gathered momentum in the sixteenth century. For instance, until the mid-fifteenth century English juries could be counted on to know the accused and the facts of the crime already, and they viewed their task as meting out justice. By the mid-sixteenth century the jury was becoming a fact-finder, assisted by the Justice of Peace, who had been reconstructed as a Crown investigator by Act of Parliament.[16] Similarly, at the turn of the sixteenth century auricular religious confession seems to have functioned, at least in part, to alleviate tensions within communities; we know this from manuals instructing priests on how to make penitents look inward and confess their own sins rather than those of their neighbours.[17] An interiorized notion of confession was promulgated at the Council of Trent in 1551, and, by the turn of the seventeenth century, penitents had begun to have their self-enclosure more thoroughly enforced through the new penitential technology of the confessional box.[18] Thus the Renaissance histories of legal proof and religious discipline offer both terms of analysis (the subject and his increasing separateness, inwardness, and so forth) and point to a critical time period (the later sixteenth and early seventeenth centuries), thereby encouraging us to speak in terms of a radical change in the meaning of subjectivity. And yet, in relation to these same topics, the Fourth Lateran Council of 1215 also seems to mark the advent of an interiorized and epistemically problematic subject. In addition to establishing the Inquisition (up until this point heretics were simply excommunicated), this Council forbade the participation of the clergy in the administration of trial by ordeal, a form of proof in which the guilt or innocence of an accused was revealed in, for example, the healing rate of a burn inflicted on him or her for this purpose.[19] A practice which implies a unity of body and mind, the immanence of God's and the soul's truth in the flesh, the ordeal was supplanted on the Continent by inquisitorial procedure in which a judge functions both as discoverer of fact and dispenser of justice, a system which gave rise to the use of judicial torture as a mechanism for evidence-gathering, and which therefore makes the subject a focus of epistemic concerns. (Of course, the transition takes on a different meaning in England where the result of the ordeal's suppression was the establishment of the communally based jury system.) The Council also instituted for the first time the requirement of an annual individual confession and stressed the inward nature of sin, a concept which nevertheless had to be redebated and re-enforced over three centuries later at the Council of Trent.[20]

If the Fourth Lateran Council troubles the narrative within which I wish to install the Renaissance obsession with the discovery of others, consider the difficulties posed by the argument Page duBois advances in a book bearing the same title as my first chapter: *Torture and Truth*.[21] Dubois explores the use of judicial torture by the Athenian state in the fifth century BCE, and argues, as do I with regard to the English resort to torture, that the practice is connected to a particular kind of epistemology, one which imagines that "truth [is] eternally located elsewhere, either hidden in the body, or hidden in the earth, or inside or beyond human existence" (102–3), and therefore that its acquisition or "dis-covery" (120) constitutes "a passage through a spatial narrative of some sort" (105). DuBois opposes this epistemology of discovery to one she associates particularly with Heraclitus, which makes truth relational and non-essential, "implicated in the practice of daily life," a pragmatic way of knowing akin to the one I would associate with the English jury system.

But while the similarities in duBois's analysis and my own might seem to problematize the historical claims implicit in both of our arguments, it is also important to note that in our respective accounts the practice of discovery is affiliated with quite different epistemic and political arrangements. DuBois argues that torture, which was inflicted only on slaves as a kind of supplement to their testimony, was predicated on the assumption that "slaves are bodies; citizens possess *logos*, reason" (52). Slaves are tortured *as* bodies; the truth is hidden in the slave's corporeality, but it does not belong to the slave, either as something he knows or as a truth about him. If there is a subject position articulated in the Greek discourse of torture, it belongs only to those who acquire knowledge as a result of the torture. The stark distinction between subject and object, torturer and tortured in duBois's account also maps precisely onto social hierarchy, connecting the ways of knowing embedded in torture to an anti-democratic strain in Athenian politics. In contrast, I argue that in Renaissance England people were tortured as subjects. Not only were victims deemed to know the information the torturers sought, but often that information had to do with the commitments and beliefs of the victim. Moreover, this symmetry in Renaissance torture, which is under-scored by the frequent absence of significant social distinction between torturer and victim (a matter I discuss in chapter 2), indicates that what fueled the practice was, in part, competition for authority within the early modern state. In other words, torture in the period with which I am concerned is both deeply inflected by the processes of subjection that had developed in Christian Europe and prevailed for centuries, and implicated within specific institutional developments in early modern England.

Attention to the chronological awkwardness these situations produce in the narrative of the subject's emergence suggests the wisdom of disarticulating, for analytical purposes, elements that a critic or historian may intuitively feel belong to a single epistemic formation. For example, instead of assuming that a sense of inwardness necessarily means a mind–body scism, the objectification of nature, and an ethic of possessive individualism we would do well to ask *under what conditions* inwardness comes to entail any of these other possibilities. Or more generally, how do a particular epistemic stance and a set of political relationships come to be interdependent?[22] Such questions are theoretically important, ensuring that diachronism does not become full-blown teleology, or inversely that the study of a formation's beginnings does not turn into the revelation of (often scandalous) intrinsic meanings. This latter propensity, in particular, characterizes some otherwise valuable historical critiques of our own epistemic assumptions.[23] For example, duBois's account of Athenian torture is intended in part to expose the violence she finds underlying deep traditions in Western philosophy which reify truth and locate it in secret and inaccessible places. Thus she concludes her study with a dizzying leap from Plato's anti-democratic arguments to Heidegger's fascism. This procedure is problematic because it elides the role which historically specific factors such as economic pressures, institutional traditions, and technological developments play in shaping the political meanings which an epistemic stance will bear at any moment in history. But, more importantly, such a procedure also embarrasses her own critique, insofar as it too partakes of the discovery mode, stripping away the idealizations of the academy in order to reveal the violence at the heart of the West's noblest traditions.[24] By hypothesizing a looser connection between the ways of thinking, the social and political relationships, and the material forces which may be involved in each of the situations with which I am concerned, I want as much as possible to maintain a provisional epistemic practice. In other words, I want both to make the process whereby the act of knowing acquires certain meanings the object of my study and to keep the inevitable reductiveness in our discernment of that meaning palpable.

More simply, the procedure I am recommending here, of separating out the various conditions or relationships that may be impacted within an epistemic formation, helps to hone our understanding of what may have distinguished the period in question from its successors. In particular, I want to argue that what is new and catastrophic in the Renaissance is not, as Barker and Belsey assert, a sense of interiority, but the usually fearful, even paranoid recognition that interiority can give the subject leverage against his world. David Aers is undoubtedly correct in insisting on the absurdity of any account of the mental world of pre-Renaissance Europe which denies it the experience of inwardness, that does not acknowledge the importance of the Augustinian tradition that makes the heart its own place and the site of self-reflexive knowledge – the tradition that provided the Jesuits with the casuistical foundation for equivocation (182–3). But we would be mistaken to conclude, as Aers seems to, that inwardness bears the same significance in the early modern period as it does in earlier centuries.[25] After all, the arguments for equivocation also reveal the slide of a spiritual interiority into a strategic one; Christian ontology affords a platform for acts of resistance that were perceived, at least by the Elizabethan authorities, as fundamentally political. This slide from the spiritual to the strategic is in fact ubiquitous in the period and will ramify in increasingly secular ways.

Consider, for example, the case of William Scott's *Essay on Drapery* (1635), published some thirty years after the height of the equivocation controversy.[26] The pamphlet offers, in the words of its editor, "the first substantial piece of writing that exalts business as a career" (1). Scott, who apparently was a draper, undertakes to produce "the Compleat Citizen" through instruction on the various ethical problems that confront a man of business. Utterly earnest in its attempt to make commercial practice conform to copiously cited religious and philosophical authority, the pamphlet is nevertheless inadvertently prone to suggest the inverse: that Scott is appropriating the letter, if not against the spirit then not exactly with it either, in order to legitimate worldly self-interest and shrewd practice. Thus reminding the Citizen that "God is *totus oculus*, all eye and must see all his Actions," and exhorting him therefore "to dip the penne of the Tongue in the Incke of the heart," he adds "Lying then is to be banisht: but this rule must bee observed; as wee may not lie, so we need not speake all the truth" and offers a paraphrase of the Augustinian texts on lying which formed the basis of the Jesuit defense of equivocation (23). In fact, it is precisely the same argument, right down to the example of the strategic omission that protects a friend from discovery by his enemies, although Scott betrays no consciousness of the earlier application of this line of thinking and denounces the Jesuits in passing for "retain[ing] nothing of Jesus but his name" (20). [27] It is not clear just what truth the Citizen may withhold: "he must never turne his back to honesty; yet sometimes goe about and coast it, using an extraordinary skill, which may be better practis'd then exprest" (35). He is also admonished to take few apprentices and not to talk to his wife about business lest his secrets get out; moreover he is to dissemble his own distrust, appearing open in order to disarm other's desires to deceive him (36), a piece of advice that installs the Citizen in the dizzying circularity of the discovery scenarios with which I am concerned.

Scott's pamphlet reveals not only an appropriation of the Augustinian tradition in the interests of an emergent secular interest, but its connection to a tentative sense that a man might make the conditions of his existence. I say tentative, because what is striking about Scott's pamphlet is the degree to which, in contrast to later capitalist ideology, it presents economic life as something to be stoically endured rather than shaped by the energetic entrepreneur.[28] And yet he ponders the question, "Is the maine thing which raiseth a mans estate without him, or within him? *Quaeritur*" (29). Momentarily the answer seems to be "within":

There are than open vertues which bring forth praise; but hidden and secret ones which bring forth fortune.

Certaine deliveryes of a mans self, which have no name; like the milkie way in the skie, which is a meeting of many small starres, not seen asunder, but giving light together, for there are a number of scarse discerned vertues, which make men fortunate. (30)

The mysteriousness of these inner qualities, the fact that Scott cannot specify them or elaborate on them, suggests the novelty of the possibility he is propounding here. But the language of hiddenness and secrecy also works to associate these qualities with secrecy itself, the virtue in which Scott instructs his citizen at length, and which he also anxiously seeks to limit in his prohibitions against lying. In short, what emerges in Scott's pamphlet is a connection between inwardness and the capacity to act upon one's circumstances, a sense that these conditions might, in fact, mean each other, and that their conjunction served legitimate self-interest.

This alliance between inwardness and agency in the service of self-interest is the specter which haunts the Renaissance discovery scenarios. When one man sought to discover the interior reaches of another, it was because there lurked "intent," to borrow a word from the Elizabethan torture warrants, the will behind potential action. Scott's pamphlet is later by thirty to sixty years than most of the material my study is concerned with and differs from it in describing this alliance in ideologically positive terms. For the Elizabethans and early Jacobeans the mysterious inner power which Scott wonders at was more likely to represent a subversive or even demonic quality, the ability to operate secretly beyond the constraints of constituted authority – hence Robert Persons's anxious comparison of the equivocator's withheld truth to internal heresy.[29] Clearly, Scott's work is significant not only for its valorization of this strategic inwardness but for the connection it draws between that quality and success in business. It is therefore tempting to ascribe Scott's fascination (and by extension the period's obsession) with strategic inwardness to emergent capitalism. Certainly, economic changes in the period contributed both to the loss of social legibility and to an increased range of economic activity which made such strategic inwardness imaginable, as the conycatching material I deal with in chapter 4 attests. Moreover, the canny businessman who can make himself fortunate has a long career ahead of him as capitalist hero. But Scott's own vision of economic life is rather old-fashioned; he never mentions finance, price fluctuations, or market pressures of any kind. This, as well as the intertextual relationship between the pamphlet and the equivocation debate, suggest a more complicated possibility: that Scott is importing into commercial discourse a way of thinking about the subject that had already developed elsewhere, particularly in connection with problems of state authority, but which now seems useful to him for thinking about his own position. Indeed, other debts the pamphlet discloses, to conduct literature and Stoic philosophy, for example, suggest an effort in translation from the sphere of counsel, political struggle, and gentlemen aspiring to preferment, to the sphere of trade.[30]

Historians have long noted that one of the greatest accomplishments of the Tudor monarchs was their consolidation of power through the development of systems of royal administration. This achievement required above all else the creation of a pool of educated men who could serve as councilors, secretaries, clerks, Justices of the Peace, and spies. It required, in other words, a distribution of intellectual resources among a minority of the male population and the delegation of its authority to a segment of that minority, allocations that produced an elite masculine culture organized around the interplay of ambition and knowledge. The discoveries which litter the discursive field of Renaissance England are for the most part phenomena of that culture. Thus, while I would insist that the discovery of the subject was determined by many different social processes I also want to privilege the administrative consolidation of royal power as an explanatory context. The career of Francis Bacon, which fuses service to the state (including espionage and interrogations during torture) to a philosophical project of discovery that proclaims itself as revolutionary, embodies the connection between more narrowly political activity and profound epistemic change. But the point I would make here is not simply that the work of discovery was aligned with a particular political project or that its practitioners were engaged in government surveillance. In the early modern state, the power the monarch comes to "hold" is founded, paradoxically, on the dispersal of authority among a portion of her/his male subjects. The question this paradox raises – on whose behalf does a man really act once he has been equipped to serve the state? – impinges on all the discovery scenarios with which I am concerned, producing the self-reflexiveness which I have suggested is endemic to them.[31]

Lest my focus on the development of royal administrative apparatuses seem surprisingly restrictive, I should emphasize that, insofar as equipping a man to serve the state overlapped to a considerable extent simply with educating him, questions about the Crown's control of its own agents (or potential agents) tended to crystallize more general concerns about political and social authority. The Renaissance obsession with discovery develops as knowledge begins to compete with status as the basis for that authority; but discovery, which, after all, was intended to produce more knowledge, only exacerbates that competition. Thus while the subject who emerges in discovery would seem to belong to an absolutist politics, the ambiguity as to whose authority is consolidated when he speaks, or writes, or discovers suggests how easily he might be recruited for a republican regime. Moreover, while this subject position may in the first instance have been articulated by political pressures, insofar as knowledge rather than status comes to be its defining feature it will quickly become meaningful in relation to other domains of experience, as Scott's pamphlet demonstrates.

My book begins with an extreme example of how the consolidation of royal power produced an epistemic crisis around the subject. The use of interrogatory torture in England coincides with the period of Tudor state-building. Torture was an administrative procedure, executed under warrant from the Privy Council, in order to procure information for use both in treason trials and in the more general control of potentially subversive activity. At the same time, however, this use of torture differs drastically from reforms such as the establishment of parish record-keeping or the regularization of the functions of Justices of the Peace insofar as it was never systematically practiced, never had nor acquired a foundation in English law, and completely disappeared by the end of James I's reign. In short, torture was a desperate measure, marking the outer limit of the state's knowledge and control of its subjects during a critical period of its development. In this first chapter I chart the intersections that occur around the use of torture between the administrative discourse of judicial investigation and the religious discourse of conscience, particularly as it was employed by English Catholics in their struggles with the Crown. My analysis reveals the conceptual inter-dependence that emerges in torture between two apparently oppositional modes of knowing, the discovery of secrets and the stoic experience of inward truth. The subject who is fixed at this crux is the state's "other," that which the state defines itself through knowing and that which it can never know. Torture thus offers a paradigm of discovery, one that, insofar as it also constitutes a limit case, reveals the contradictions which drive it.

Chapter 3 takes up the representation of discovery on the Renaissance stage through an analysis of *Measure for Measure* and *Othello*, both of which offer revelations of the secret iniquity lurking in the heart of a man who represents himself as honest, the latter recapitulating with extraordinary precision the epistemic crisis of the torture chamber. My readings focus, however, on two key differences between the scenario I delineate in the previous chapter and the stories these plays tell: here the state's "other" is its own agent, and sexual desire rather than treason forms the manifest content of secrets. Depicting political worlds in which power moves through a chain of command rather than inhering in a consecrated ruler, discovering secret subversion in the heart of a subordinate officer but ambiguously implicating his superiors as well, these plays suggest that the epistemic anxiety driving discovery is the effect of an undecidable play of differentiation and identification between hierarchically related men. In the intersections between sexuality and state business both plays present, women serve as a ground of representation for men's secrets; they become a means for recasting power relations as knowledge but are themselves specifically excluded from the processes of subjection that concede interiority and some degree of power to the men in the chain of command. In my account neither the discourses which impinge on torture nor Shakespearean mimesis offer a definitive version of the discovery scenario. Each is shaped by a particular representational context and offers a lens through which the other may be re-seen. This chapter concludes by returning to the conflict between Catholic martyrs and the Elizabethan state which figures in chapter 2, and re-framing it in terms of gender and status concerns which the plays bring into view.

Both in the discourses of torture and in these plays of Shakespeare, the domination inherent in the work of discovery is qualified by a latent reversibility in the positions of the discoverer and the discovered. This potential for reversal, for the subject under discovery to be revealed as the discoverer's confrere, arises because the contents of the secret – the will to constitute one's own authority – is ultimately what is also driving the discoverer. In chapters 4 and 5 I consider the self-reflexiveness of discovery in relation to the initial articulations of two opposing but complementary positions within modern knowledge-making arrangements: the author and the scientist. Chapter 4 focuses on the somewhat unlikely figure of Thomas Harman, whose *A Caveat for Common Cursitors* fathered that popular Elizabethan genre, the conycatching pamphlet, which purports to discover the secrets of a criminal underclass. Harman's work of discovery coincides to some degree with the duties he had fulfilled as a Justice of the Peace but it also exceeds them, particularly as it offers him a platform from which to become a published author. Harman's frequently remarked affinity with the rogues whose deceptions he claims to discover arises because the rogues' duplicity and opportunism figures his own position as he constructed himself as an author, grafting self-promotion to the work of maintaining public order. The complexities of Harman's position arise not only because of royal administrative reforms but also because of economic changes which have produced both masterless men and the new platforms offered by the print market. Thus my analysis moves out from questions of state power and knowledge toward a more general consideration of efforts to imagine a subject capable of authorizing himself as an agent and as origin of discourse. In this connection I take up pamphlets by Thomas Dekker and one S. R. from the first decade of the seventeenth century. These texts mockingly discover the secret of their plagiarism from Harman to pose the question of whether in the print market the writer's labor could become the basis for an authority comparable to that of the discovering Justice of the Peace. The answer would appear to be "no." However, Ben Jonson's treatment of some of the material's topoi in *Bartholmew Fair*, with which my discussion concludes, suggests ways in which the contradictions of Harman's text can be transumed in a mystified notion of authorship.

The book concludes by looking at Francis Bacon's vision of a scientific discovery of nature. Many scholars have noted that Bacon explicitly aligns the discovery of nature both with espionage and with inquisition; in short, with the methods by which the absolutist state sought to know its subjects. My argument is that the scientific project offers an imaginary resolution to the problem of the subject which bedevils the work of political discovery, but in so doing fulfills the threat against the sovereign that the discovering subject has posed all along. Bacon's philosophical writing repeatedly envisions a discoverer who resembles the state's subjective "other" in the scenarios of discovery I deal with in earlier chapters: secretive, self-interested, willfully departing from all constituted authority. At the same time, however, Bacon insists that the discoverer must be transparent, no more than a recorder of the facts of nature, in the same way that the state's agents must do no more than transmit its authority. This contradiction ensures that the discovering subject remains a site of crisis in Bacon's vision. But in commanding submission not to the sovereign but to the as-yet-undiscovered facts of nature, Bacon also permits the policing of the subject to be reframed as epistemological self-discipline. For Bacon, the research project is a great and long work, requiring the organization of discovery on a scale as yet unattempted by the Crown. He thus installs the discovering subject in a community of similar subjects, whose work regulates the excess of will or desire which also endlessly fuels it, and who therefore have rendered the sovereign irrelevant.

Like Bacon's aphorisms, the chapters which follow offer broken knowledge. They are essays rather than units in a historical survey, explorations of a few situations in as much detail as possible rather than a comprehensive account of the early modern discourse of discovery. I have chosen to write in this fashion because historical survey, no matter how much evidence it marshals or how supple its analysis, tends to flatten out phenomena, making them reveal the widespread availability of a particular concept or the dominance of a given ideology in a period. Such a procedure potentially obscures the way in which the meanings of a discourse depend on the contingencies of its individual deployments, which are myriad and can never be exhaustively described. More particularly, historical survey can mask the politics of a discourse's circulation, the way in which a discourse uses kinds of people differently, and is differently used by them. My topic itself already works to obscure this phenomenon. For the subject is an abstract thing, not a person, but a placemarker for personhood within discourse that seems devoid of demographic markings. Spoken of in the singular, the subject is necessarily hegemonic, a default position in discourse. My effort to situate the discovery of the subject in relation to particular institutional and material pressures is an attempt to resist hegemonic abstraction. These essays seek to recognize the way in which the dispositions of power and knowledge which, from one point of view, define the "subject" can also be seen as producing masculinity and femininity, ruling elites, and incommensurate kinds of knowledge. However, to the extent that I am concerned with the discovery of the subject as a recruitment process, the focus of the book will necessarily be on those who for one reason or another could contribute their subjectivities to the formation whose history I trace. It will be concerned with men more than with women, and with highly educated men more than with artisans or laborers. Thus, I want to bear witness at the outset to what can only perhaps be glimpsed around the edges of my analysis, the vast array of subjectivities in Renaissance

England which could not be compassed within the epistemic structure of discovery. Desdemona's sadness and bewilderment, for example, hardly signifies within the problem which she is temporarily made to embody. Invoking the exclusionary effects of class or gender does not do justice to the variety of ways of knowing the world which my account of Renaissance England will leave unaddressed, although my hope is that in localizing the emergence of the discovering, discoverable subject, the view from other vantage points will become more available.

2   Torture and truth

To know our enemies minds we rip their hearts;
Their papers is more lawful.   *King Lear* (4.6.257–8)

Scratched on a wall in the Tower of London there is an inscription:

Thomas Miagh which lieth here alone
That fayne wold from hens begon
By torture straunge mi trouth was tryed,
Yet of my liberte denied.   1581 Thomas MYAGH[1]

It was Myagh's misfortune to find himself suspected of complicity in
Irish rebellion during the relatively short period, roughly the last half of
the sixteenth century, when English authorities resorted to interrogatory
torture in criminal investigations, as Sir Edward Coke was to write,
"directly against the common lawes of England."[2] An aberration in
English juridical practice, the use of torture in Elizabethan England was
a brief departure from a legal tradition that abhorred and ridiculed the
highly organized practice of judicial torture on the Continent. The
immediate purpose of much English torture was political repression.
Like modern torture, it was a form of official terrorism, used to crush
perceived dangers to the Elizabethan state, particularly, although by no
means exclusively, the persistence and spread of Roman Catholicism.
Nevertheless, the goal of torture was characterized in the official warrants as the acquisition of knowledge; its purpose was the "discoverie of
the truth," "manifestacion of the truth," or, most frequently, "the
boultinge forth [sifting out] of the truth."[3] These characterizations of
torture are not merely official euphemisms, for, as I shall argue, the
appetite for knowledge of the Elizabethan torturers was intimately
related to their agenda of repression.[4]
    What is striking about Myagh's account of his situation, however, is
that he too interprets his torture as a procedure whose goal is truth. But
if Myagh shares the language of the warrants when he characterizes
torture as a trying of truth ("try" is a synonym for the warrants'
"boult"), he signals his resistance to the state's coercion by styling the

24

truth that emerged from his torture as his own.[5] In so doing, he subtly re-characterizes the nature of the truth at issue in torture. Where "the truth" the torture warrants seek is information about Myagh's actions (names, times and places of rendezvous, reports of conversations) "mi trouth" suggests at once a protestation of loyalty to the Queen ("my troth"), and a condition of soul, a spiritual self-possession in contrast to the thralldom of his body. Whatever Myagh intended, though, his torturers' efforts to discover treasons confer a special urgency on the second, stoic meaning of "mi trouth." The position from which he writes, lying alone in the Tower, affirms not his place in the polity but his self-enclosure.

Myagh's pathetic inscription locates him at an epistemic crux. "The truth" the Crown wanted from him was an account of his activities; "mi trouthe" emerged in the frustration of that account's production. Myagh's "troth," his bond to the community of the realm, was the ground on which this struggle occurred. But this same struggle also obscured troth as a mode of knowing, marking its transformation, on the one hand, into the imperative to discover the facts of treason, and, on the other, into the truth of the inviolable soul. The epistemic overdetermination of Myagh's situation is typical of episodes of torture in this period, and suggests that underlying the practice was not just the fear of subversion, but the contested establishment of a particular regime of knowledge. The various truths implicated in torture were, however, seldom explicitly distinguished in Elizabethan writings on the subject, and occupied overlapping conceptual and discursive space, as the similarities between Myagh's and the Crown's characterizations of torture suggests. Their differences were not established but burgeoning ones.

The circumstances of the English resort to torture suggest that it may have been conceptually allied to other knowledge-producing practices of the period, such as the anatomy lesson or the voyage of discovery, which locate truth in the material world but beyond the limits of common perception.[6] Torture occurred within the context of the developing practice of criminal investigation, which had begun to make the facts of the crime the object of methodical inquiry in a manner unprecedented in England. Moreover, the structure of interrogatory torture posits a victim in possession of hidden information that the torturer must struggle to uncover, and therefore produces a narrative of discovery, a movement from unknowing, through labor, to an encounter with truth. The dual role of Francis Bacon, as a champion of the discovery of nature's secrets and as a persistent practitioner of torture, apparently the only English lawyer who actually asserted that torture was permissible in English juridical practice, is also suggestive. His roles overlap in his philosophical writing when he exhorts his reader not to think "the inquisition of nature is in any part interdicted and forbidden," or when he proposes "to examine nature herself and the arts upon interrogatories."[7]

If torture shares an epistemic stance with other more respectable Renaissance projects of discovery, however, it also presents an extremely primitive version of that stance. In the voyage of discovery or the anatomy lesson, the discoverer's stance may reframe the meaning of the body or the world, but the materiality of these things both supports the claim that they are knowable as objects and enforces methodological refinements. The truth at issue in torture can be manifested materially, in the actions that constitute treason, but it is not literally to be found in the body on which the torturer operates. Torture is like the anatomy lesson or the voyage of discovery more because of a metaphorical reduction, produced by the torturer's positioning and enforced in the ferocious materiality of his method, than because of properties belonging to the truth sought, which remains at least in part metaphysical. Thus the truth at issue in torture is objective primarily because it is *thought of* as an object, something that can be covered and therefore dis-covered. In other words, the torturer's operations on his victim enact a fantasy of epistemic mastery and appropriation but do not plausibly lead out toward a world of knowable objects.

Catholic opponents of Elizabeth's government, who were the most visible and vocal victims of English torture, went further than this, insisting that the claim that torture was a method of discovery was simply fraudulent. "Is not your rack used or threatened," demanded William, Cardinal Allen, head of the English College at Douai, "to force men by the fear thereof to speak things against truth by your appointment?"[8] The Jesuit missionary and poet Robert Southwell accused Francis Walsingham of having himself instigated the Babington plot to assassinate Elizabeth and place Mary Stuart on the throne, and of then having "proved" it by torturing and executing English Catholics.[9] Elizabethan torture, Catholics asserted, was intended literally to verify lies by forcing people to "reveal" treasons that would justify the government's further repression of Catholicism. In short, the Catholic accusations of fraudulence suggest that the torturer was actually manufacturing the hidden "truth" that the interrogatory nature of torture suggested he was struggling to uncover. The torturer's violent intervention on the body of the victim could disclose the torturer as the origin of a "truth" whose authenticity, the rhetorical structure of interrogatory torture would insist, lies in its independence from and initial inaccessibility to him.

But the accusation of fraudulence leveled at the Elizabethan torturers by Catholics was, in fact, twofold. The charge that the torturers were forcing their victims to confess to treasons the torturers had themselves invented merged with the significantly different complaint that the torturers were attempting to discover matters that had to do, not with the alleged treasonable activities of the victims, but with their spiritual experience – matters which were by nature radically inward and therefore not susceptible to discovery. Allen's accusation that torture was used to force men "to speak things against the truth" embraces both charges. In the Catholic accounts, the lie perpetrated by government torturers was to treat a realm of experience that the victims increasingly defined as interior, private, and subjective *as though* it were external, discoverable activity.[10]

The Catholic critique of torture as a mode of investigation suggests that the difference between "the truth" of the torture warrants and "mi trouth" of Myagh's inscription is, at least initially, more a matter of epistemic stance than of substance. "Truth," which both perpetrators and victims make the issue of torture, is not so much a specific content as a sign for the validity of the competing ways of knowing in the torture chamber: Truth is that which is susceptible to discovery versus Truth is that which is felt in resisting discovery. In other words, the Elizabethan resort to torture reveals that the state used its power to inflict pain to verify not just dubious treasons but a way of knowing that would make those treasons, as discoverable forms of action, constitute the truth. Thus the torturer's aggression manifested in Bacon's philosophic writing emerges not in accounts of specific investigations but in exhortations to begin investigating.

This chapter will consider the epistemic dualism I have described, as it manifests itself in the discursive practices that impinged on English torture: law, criminal investigation, martyrology, and religio-political controversy. In the discursive economy of English torture the body functioned amphibiously, giving truth a basis in material reality that made it susceptible to discovery, while, in the intense subjectivity of its ordeal, making truth inaccessible to all but the sufferer. These meanings of the tortured body were determined both by the irreducible experience of the human nervous system, and by the collision of a new sense of the material location of truth with religious training that found in the body's torment the making of the soul.[11] But if torturer and victim were often locked in fierce ideological opposition, the epistemic dualism that defined the scene of torture arose not from these differences but from a method of investigation that served more than one kind of truth. Nor does the choice of such a method reflect the incompetence of Elizabethan investigators, for we shall see that while they desired that truth be that which could be discovered, the truth they sought was nevertheless to be found deep in the souls of their enemies. It is therefore insufficient to speak of the scene of torture, as I have done, in terms of competing, and by implication, separately constituted ways of knowing. We must consider why discovery and Christian stoicism needed to be articulated together, in the hideous intimacy of torture.

"Not in time of Judicature, but when somebody bids"

After the Fourth Lateran Council abolished the trial by ordeal in 1215, English and Continental methods of criminal prosecution diverged significantly.[12] On the Continent, the adoption of Roman-canon standards of proof, which required either the testimony of two witnesses or the accused's confession in order to secure a conviction, made torture for confession an integral part of criminal prosecution and the subject of an extensive jurisprudence. In England the development of the jury system, whereby determinations of guilt or innocence were made by twelve representatives of the community according to their own knowledge of the case, meant that a law of evidence and an apparatus for producing proofs did not begin to develop until the seventeenth century, when the role of the jury had radically changed. Juries could convict without a confession and acquit in the face of one they knew to be involuntary, and so torture never gained a role in common law.[13] The English were proud of this difference between their law and Continental procedures; it was a juridical commonplace that, as Sir Thomas Smith claimed in *De Republica Anglorum* (1565, published 1583), "torment or question which is used by the order of the civill lawe and custome of other countries to put a malefactor to excessive paine, to make him confesse him selfe, or of his fellowes or complices, is not used in England, it is taken for servile."[14] Coke, discussing the law of treason in his *Third Institute*, asserts that "So as there is no law to warrant tortures in this land, nor can they be justified by any prescription lately brought in."[15] However, Coke's complaint against "prescription[s] lately brought in" suggests an important difference between his position, writing in the 1620s, and Smith's: while Smith asserts that torture does not occur in England, Coke only claims that it ought not to.[16]

Smith's and Coke's assertions that torture is contrary to English law demarcate roughly the period of torture's limited use in England. Between the composition of *De Republica Anglorum* and the *Third Institute*, Smith and Coke both participated in the interrogation of accused persons by torture, Coke on a number of occasions, Smith only once and under protest. Although there is evidence that torture may have been used occasionally in England from the reign of Richard III, it was during Elizabeth's reign that interrogatory torture became increasingly a recognized, although always unusual, part of the prosecution of important cases of felony. By the time Coke wrote the *Third Institute*, however, the use of torture had apparently again become infrequent; the conciliar records disclose only five episodes of torture between the Gunpowder Plot and the Civil War.[17] Coke's proscription of torture was in fact more in accord with actual practice than his complaint about "prescription[s] lately brought in" might indicate.

Attempts to account for the peculiar career of torture in England in terms of the development of legal institutions have been notably unsuccessful.[18] The phenomenon appears to have had neither origins nor ramifications in English law, and the pattern of its use makes it difficult to specify causes for its occurrence. Torture was used in the context of the developing practice of the criminal investigation, and in connection with offenses ranging from theft to treason, but in only a tiny fraction of prosecutions. As interrogatory torture was central to the highly developed practice of criminal investigation on the Continent, it has been supposed that both were Continental imports, brought in to fill the need for evidence-gathering mechanisms which had failed to develop under the jury system. But while Continental torture was governed by an elaborate set of rules and was practiced throughout the judicial system, English torture remained an exclusively executive function used only in cases where the Crown had a special interest – a very small percentage of the total criminal investigations.[19] Moreover, although the pre-trial investigation steadily gained importance in English criminal procedure during the seventeenth century, torture quickly disappeared. Another avenue of explanation, that the use of torture was tied to the doctrine of the royal prerogative, is frustrated by the fact that the use of torture actually declined and ceased as the doctrine was expanded under James. Although its use was carefully restricted by the monarch, no positive legal right to torture was ever asserted by the Crown. Torture in England remained an *ad hoc* practice remarkable for its discontinuity from the legal discourse to which it presumably should have belonged.

The political context yields no more satisfactory explanation than does the legal one. After the promulgation of the bull *Regnans in Excelsis* in 1570, which declared Elizabeth a heretic and absolved her subjects of their obedience to her, the incidence of torture increased as the government struggled to detect the alleged treasonous activities of Catholic missionary priests, and other sympathizers of the Catholic cause. With the accession of James and peace with Spain in 1604, the use of torture rapidly subsided. But while clearly related to the threat posed to

Elizabeth's government by Catholicism both at home and abroad, the use of torture was by no means coextensive with it. Although the majority of cases of torture touched the safety of the state, not all of these involved Catholics. Moreover, suspects were tortured in connection with burglary and ordinary murder. Before the promulgation of *Regnans in Excelsis*, while torture was rarer, its use was confined principally to ordinary felonies. At the same time, however, it is noteworthy that the English failed to resort to torture in connection with other serious threats to constituted authority. Protestant sedition was met by torture only rarely, as in the case of the Marprelate printers. Neither the Henrician Reformation, the Marian persecutions, nor the conflicts leading up to the Civil War involved significant recourse to interrogatory torture.

Torture thus cannot be understood simply as an especially harsh repression of especially serious threats, at least not without resorting to the circular argument that what proves the seriousness of these threats is the resort to torture. The pattern of its use does suggest, however, that the threat posed by Catholicism was relevant to the goals of torture as a means of investigation in a way that other threats to Elizabethan authority by and large were not. Thus, without attempting to specify causes, we need to locate our discussion of torture at the intersection between the new practice of criminal investigation and the specific resistance Catholicism offered to the Elizabethan state, and ask why the one should be so relevant to the other.

The difficulties Elizabethan torture poses for the legal historian arise from the fact that torture seems to have had no proper discursive ground. Its legal foundation was the lack of an express prohibition against it and the immunity of the sovereign from prosecution. Its language was borrowed from Continental jurisprudence, but not its institutional context. Its justification as a political tool was borrowed from its *de facto* status as a tool in some criminal investigations. An aberrant, quasi-juridical, quasi-political phenomenon, it occupied a discursive space opportunistically fabricated from absences and borrowings. This discursive homelessness of torture in England was identified by John Selden who, comparing English to Continental practice, complained, "but in England they take a man and rack him I do not know why, nor when, not in time of Judicature, but when somebody bids."[20] Selden's critique, which opposes a deliberate system of discourse and authority to arbitrary actions based on power, bespeaks his common lawyer's interests; "somebody," after all, spoke in the monarch's name. But what seems significant is that to Selden the monarch's resort to torture is heinous not because of its obvious cruelty, but because it cannot be located discursively.

A search for contemporary legal commentary on torture reveals the justification of Selden's complaint. There are Smith's and Coke's statements quoted above, asserting that torture has no place in English law. There is also the trace of writings by Robert Beale, clerk of the Privy Council and one of Edmund Campion's torturers, whom Archbishop Whitgift accused in 1584 of authoring "seditious books, written and published against the hierarchy," that, among other things, "condemneth without exception of any cause racking of grievous offenders as being cruel, barbarous, contrary to law and the liberty of English subjects."[21] The seditious books themselves do not appear to have survived. Finally, there is Bacon's assertion in a letter to King James in 1603 that, "By the laws of England no man is bound to accuse himself. In the highest cases of treason torture is used for discovery and not for evidence."[22] Although Bacon's statement defines a place for torture in English juridical practice, it does so by placing it outside of legal discourse *per se*, in a field of activity identifiable 250 years later as police work.

The charges brought against Beale suggest that there were persuasive political pressures to prevent lawyers from discoursing on the evils of torture while it was practiced with any kind of regularity. What this sparse catalogue of legal formulations also indicates, however, is that despite the government's repressions, it was in fact easier to say that torture had no place in English law than to say that it did. Smith, Coke, Beale, and Bacon all took their turns as "rack-master"; none (though Bacon is something of a special case) chose to write about the method, the goals, or the legal justification of the practice in which they had engaged.[23] The point is not that these men were hypocrites. In fact, they represent a range of moral response; Smith and Beale found the procedure repugnant and their legal statements are protests, while Bacon seems to have been more cooperative, as was Coke until he stepped into his role as champion of the common law. Collectively, however, these men constitute a phenomenon. The gap between their practice and their theorizing suggests that while torture could be used as a method of investigation, it was available to its practitioners as a subject for discursive formulation primarily in terms of negation and exclusion.[24]

Elizabeth's government did make some effort to place its use of torture in "Judicature," or at least to link the practice to the authority of the monarch. Warrants from the Privy Council were issued in most cases and on one important occasion the government attempted to account for its actions in print. In answer to Catholic accounts of the torture of the Jesuit Edmund Campion and his companions, the government brought out a pamphlet called *A Declaration of the Favourable Dealing of Her Majesty's Commissioners, appointed for the examination of certaine traitors, and of tortures unjustly reported to be done upon them for matters of religion.*[25] It contended that torture was applied only as a last resort in dealing with the stubborn refusal of the Jesuits to speak the truth, that torture was with regard to matter of treason, not religion, and only where "it was first knowen and evidently probable by former detections, confessions, and otherwise, that the partie so racked or tortured was guilty and did know, and could deliver truth of the things wherewith he was charged" (48). Finally, it adverted to "the more general law of nations [by which] torture hath been and is lawfully judged to be used in lesser cases, and in sharper manner for inquisition of truth in crimes . . . whose conspiracies and the particularities thereof it did so much import and behoove to have disclosed" (49).

This attempt to place torture "in Judicature" in fact clumsily places English torture in Roman-canon law. The claim that torture was applied only when partial proof had been gleaned from other sources (a requirement in Roman-canon law) could be meaningful only in the context of a jurisprudence that assigned probative value to various kinds of evidence, which English law did not do.[26] The assertion that it is necessary to make the suspect himself "deliver the truth of the things wherewith he was charged" similarly supposes a legal system which depends on confession, and is at odds with the trial by jury that awaited the accused in these cases. Indeed, such a proposition was widely held to be directly contrary to common law. Hardly designed to have comforted John Selden, this cobbling together of Roman-canon law phraseology and assertions of political necessity reveals the temporizing discursive foundations of English torture.

To shift our focus from the discourse of the practitioners to that of the Catholic victims, however, is to turn from poverty to plenitude of evidence. Catholic polemicists presented again and again the scene of torture – the pain inflicted, the interrogations and strategies of resistance of the imprisoned priests – as evidence of the cruelty, desperation, and dishonesty of English Protestants. Works such as Allen's *A Briefe Historie of the Glorious Martyrdom of XIJ Reverend Priests* (1582), Robert Persons's *An Epistle of the Persecution of Catholickes in Englande* (1582), and Richard Verstegan's *Theatrum Crudelitatum haereticorum nostri temporis* (1587) represented, both in text and picture, racking, disemboweling, and other cruelties. Even the chapel walls of the English College at Rome were decorated with scenes, some rather improbable, of the torture and execution of English priests.[27] Concerned with torture as a technique of persecution rather than as a juridical problem, these representations placed the racking of Catholics firmly within the discourse of martyrology; the function of torture became the vindication of the truth of the Catholic faith. Thus Robert Southwell exhorted the English authorities, "Go on you good Magistrates, racke us, torture us, condemne us, yea grind us: your iniquity is proofe of our faith."[28] This proliferation of representations of torture as a trial of faith forced Elizabeth's government to retaliate by attempting in the *Declaration of Favourable Dealing* to re-place torture "in Judicature." Torture was a tool, acknowledged by the "more general law of nations" for use in the investigation of treason.[29]

In this controversy torture itself, either in its merits as a method of evidence-gathering or in its morality, was never at stake, for the Catholics were ultimately committed to the right of the church to use such methods in the extirpation of heresy. On both sides the charge was that torture occurred because the other side had cast the conflict in terms of the wrong discourse: the English authorities were treating matters of religious conscience as treasonable action, or the Catholics were treating matters of treason as religion. *Regnans in Excelsis* and subsequent papal support of Spanish and Irish military actions against Elizabeth had made the problem of Catholic loyalties acute. While the missionary priests were forbidden by their vows to engage in political activities, and there was little evidence that they did so, their work had considerable political implication and their superiors were indeed conspiring with papal and Spanish forces.[30] Curiously, Elizabeth's government did not respond by pointing out that under the circumstances the distinction between religious and treasonous activities was spurious, but by insisting on exactly the same distinction. Although Elizabethan statutes had in effect made performing the duties of a missionary priest (hearing confession, saying mass) a matter of treason, the government claimed that the priests were prosecuted according to the treason statute of 1352, which defined treason as, among other things, open rebellion against the monarch, as well as compassing, imagining, or causing his death. Elizabeth's government thus placed itself in an extremely awkward position, as it could glean little evidence of traditional treasons against the missionary priests and had to rely on evidence pertaining to religious practice and "conscience," a term that embraced both the knowledge of the religious beliefs of others and privately held answers to hypothetical moral and religious questions. It had, in other words, to reveal in religious matters material for criminal investigation. The English authorities found Catholics so compelling as victims of torture, I would argue, because, in the peculiar political problems with which they presented Elizabeth's government, they articulated the limits of investigative discourse.

Thus the *Declaration* argues that torture was avoided where the victim claimed not to know the truth:

But if [the victim] said that his answer in delivering truth, should hurt a Catholic, and so be an offence against charity, which they said to be sin, and that the queen could not command them to sin, and therefore, howsoever the queen commanded, they would not tell the truth, which they were known to know, or to such effect; they were then put to the torture, or else not. (49)

Torture was a result of the victim's refusal to acknowledge that what was going on was an investigation for treason and not a trial of faith. To the Catholics, torture was the government's attempt to prop up "newe laws by which matter of religion is made treason," an attempt that, as far as they were concerned, actually produced demonstrations of the invincible truth of the Catholic faith.[31] Both sides, then, construed their work in the torture chamber as the establishment of torture's proper discursive ground. Torture was conceived as a self-consuming process, a struggle to annihilate the discursive duality that structured the relation between the torturer and his victim. Both sides called this goal the "truth."

Although the goals of both the Elizabethan torturer and the Catholic victim can be framed symmetrically, their strategies obviously cannot be. The torturer exercised an horrific power over his victim. But the point at which he applied force to the victim's body (the point at which he broke with English legal traditions) marked the limit of his discursive hegemony. Here he became inarticulate, dependent on the rack, the manacles, and the "scavenger's daughter" to "command" the prisoner as the Queen could not, dependent on the victim to supply him with information, and, most importantly, dependent on the victim to speak in the discourse in which this information constitutes the "truth." Often this inarticulateness was dramatized by the interrogator leaving the room while torture was applied, as in the case of the Jesuit John Gerard, who was left to hang for several hours in manacles, filling the empty space with forbidden Latin prayers, until his interrogators, Bacon among them, returned for the answers to their questions about his activities.[32] As long as the victim could refuse to speak in the torturer's terms, either by praying instead of answering, or by directly asserting the religious nature of the struggle ("the Queen could not command [him] to sin"), he could protract the inarticulateness of the torturer, widening the gap between his enemy's discourse and the truth that both sides agreed that the victim possessed. Elizabethan torturers sought to establish discursive hegemony by forcibly appropriating their victims' speech. Their victims, in struggling to maintain religious discourse in the torture chamber, sought the same end by holding their enemies' discourse at the frontier marked by torture.

The extent to which Catholic resistance actually succeeded in the torture chamber is certainly open to question. It was at the level of representation that Catholics mounted a formidable resistance, exposing in their pamphlets the violent silence on which English accusations of Catholic treasons depended. If the English authorities had the power to torture their victims to appropriate their speech, Catholics had the power to appropriate the scene of torture as a subject of representation in their pamphlets. Although the infliction and the representation of torture are events of different phenomenological orders, their functions are more or less symmetrically opposed to one another. For the practitioners, torture is a violent extension of an insufficient discourse; for the victims, its representation is the discursive extension of a (probably impossible) bodily resistance. To understand torture as an epistemic phenomenon, then, we must consider the meaning of torture both as a rupture within the discourse of the practitioners and as a sign within the discourse of its victims.

"For discovery and not for evidence"

In 1565, Thomas Smith could write of the English trial by jury that "for the most part. . . they [the jurors] are unknown to [the accused] nor they know not him. . . ."[33] Nor were they merely unacquainted; while the jurors were "substantial yeomen that dwell about the place where the felonie is supposed to be committed," the accused were "idle menne," the shifters and masterless men who formed the newly defined criminal class of Elizabethan legal and literary imagination.[34] Smith's statement signals a moral and epistemic as well as a demographic change. The medieval jury trial had been an occasion for twelve members of the accused's community to mete out justice, to "render verdict according to con-science," an action that could involve the suppression of the facts of the crime if mercy was called for, as, for example, when murder was committed in self-defense and the jury concluded the assailant was unknown. It would be anachronistic to describe such verdicts as a misrepresentation of the crime, for only when the tasks of representing the crime and deciding guilt or innocence are distinguished is such a perception possible.[35] The trial that Smith describes, however, involves just such a distinction; its function is to make the previously unknown accused and the facts of his crime known to the jury.

A decade before Smith wrote, the pre-trial investigation had acquired legislative authority in the Marian bail and committal statutes that specified the examination and deposition procedures the justice was supposed to follow, and ordered him to bind over witnesses for trial, making him a sort of Crown prosecutor.[36] As Michael Dalton suggested in *The Countrey Justice* (1618), however, he "should take and certifie, as well such information, proofe and evidence, as goeth to the acquitall or cleering of the prisoner . . . for such information, evidence or proofe taken and the certifying therof by the Justice of peace is onely to informe the King and his Justices of Gaole deliverie, &c. of the truth of the matter."[37] (The accused himself did not have the right to subpoena witnesses or to testify under oath in his own defence.)[38] In short, the production of an account of the crime was now supposed to be in the hands of the investigating justice rather than the jury. Torture occurred in the most assiduous pre-trial investigations, that is, when the Crown was most anxious to make its new methods for the discovery of the truth of a crime before trial succeed, usually because its interests were directly at stake. But success entailed not just the acquisition of enough information; it also required the reconstitution of the juridical subject as an object of inquiry.

Dalton's book is a late example of a literature that developed in the sixteenth century devoted to instructing justices on their duties, including proper methods of investigation. It is here, in the context of investigation rather than of trial, that rudimentary ideas about evidence began to emerge in the common law. The investigating justice was concerned principally with testimonial evidence, the depositions made by the accusers and by the accused himself. Both Dalton and William Lambarde, author of *Eirenarchia* (1581), the most famous of these handbooks, argue that it is important that the justice take all depositions on oath, save that of the accused, in order to compel witnesses to speak the truth who otherwise might, in Lambarde's words, "speak coldly agaynst a Felon before the face of the Justice, when as they have first made their bargaine with the offendor."[39] If Lambarde regards the oath as sufficient to prevent such misrepresentation, Dalton feels compelled to provide a reminder of why this should be so.

And here let me admonish all such as are to informe or beare witnesse against a prisoner, or any offendor, before a Justice of Peace, or other Magistrate, That they be well advised what they testifie upon their oathes, knowing that in such cases if either they should not speake the truth, or shal conceale any part of the truth they should offend against God, the Magistrate, the innocent, the Common wealth, and their owne soules. (264–5)

The sworn deposition was juridical speech that derived its truth value from the religious faith of the speaker; the name for faith as it related to true speaking was "conscience." Dalton's admonition suggests, however, that if in the methodology of investigation conscience provided access to truth, it also became itself an object of suspicion.

While the justice must take care to secure the witness's conscience with an oath, Lambarde implies and Dalton explicitly argues that to swear the accused himself is to violate the common-law principle that *nemo tenetur seipsum prodere* – "no man is bound to accuse himself."[40] Indeed, both see the Marian statutes, which required the examination of the accused (albeit not on oath) as a departure from this principle. The accused's deposition was central to the investigation, but it had to be verified, not by his conscience but by "other meanes and men."[41] Thus Lambarde provides a table of circumstances to be considered in weighing the truth of the suspect's deposition. These include matters "precedent" (revealing the "will to doe the fact"), such as "Parents: as if they were wicked and given to the same kind of Fault," and matters "subsequent," such as "witnesses that proove it," and "signes, which discover him: as by having blood, or the goods about him . . . the measure of his foote: the bleeding of the dead body, &c" (220). In short, the investigator was to look for the truth of the accused's statement in reference to its surrounding circumstances.[42]

In arguing that "torture is used for discovery and not for evidence," Bacon places the issue of torture in relation to the problematic role of conscience in investigative methodology. His concern, shared by Lambarde and Dalton, is with the privilege against self-incrimination: "By the laws of England no man is bound to accuse himself. In the highest cases of treason, torture is used for discovery and not for evidence."[43] Bacon's statement occurs in a letter to the King protesting the use of a particular investigatory procedure, the oath *ex officio* in the ecclesiastical Court of High Commission.[44] The oath *ex officio* allowed for a person under suspicion but not yet charged to be compelled to swear the oath and then questioned about anything the Court chose, usually until it found something to charge him with. Common lawyers found this inquisitorial practice extremely objectionable and from the 1580s to 1641 when the Court of High Commission was finally abolished there were frequent protests against it.[45] Bacon formulates his complaint by noting the protection afforded the accused in other jurisdictions:

In capital matters no delinquent's answer upon oath is required, no not permitted. In criminal matters not capital, handled in the Star-chamber, and in causes of conscience, handled in the Chancery, for most part grounded upon trust and secrecy, the oath of the party is required. But how? Where there is an accusation and an accuser, which we call bills of complaint, from which the complainant cannot vary. (III:114)

Bacon thus favorably contrasts the practice of torture for "discovery" with the wholesale invasion of the accused's conscience and knowledge practiced in ecclesiastical investigations.

That Bacon should couple the legitimation of torture with the protection of the rights of the accused seems nothing short of astonishing. As Bacon's letter reveals, however, the rule that "no man is bound to accuse himself" seems to have coexisted with all sorts of testimonial compulsion. In addition to the cases of Star Chamber and Chancery that Bacon mentions, there was the requirement of the Marian statutes that the accused at common law make a deposition to a Justice of the Peace.[46] A statute of 1593 required a suspected Jesuit to answer on oath to officers of the Crown, as to "whether he be a Jesuit or no."[47] And while an accused felon could not be sworn at trial, he was compelled to answer questions put to him by the Crown. A global right against self-incrimination was not recognized in English law until the 1640s, when the Courts of Star Chamber and High Commission were abolished, and accused persons could refuse to answer questions in jury trials "because they were not bound to accuse themselves."[48]

Bacon's is a conservative formulation of the principle. He proceeds by distinguishing the impugned practice from other examples of testimonial compulsion, including torture, to which it might be compared. Other lawyers seem to have framed the issue more broadly. The charges Whitgift brought against Robert Beale twenty years earlier link Beale's arguments against torture to similar protests against the *ex officio* oath.[49] Moreover, as we have seen, Lambarde and Dalton both contended that the statutorily required pre-trial examination of the accused constituted a departure from the principle, and that the examination of the accused on oath, even upon proper presentment, would be a further violation. The law eventually endorsed their positions.[50] Indeed, all of the practices Bacon distinguishes, and thereby tacitly legitimates, came to be regarded as violations of the right against self-incrimination.

To some extent Bacon's allowance of practices the Crown was already engaged in must have been politically motivated; he frames the problem restrictively in order to avoid raising other sensitive issues. But his formulation of the principle is not merely opportunistic. Contrary to Lambarde's claims about statutory departure from common-law principle, both the practices against which lawyers invoked the maxim regarding self-accusation – torture, the *ex officio* oath, the pre-trial examination – and the interpretation of the maxim in terms of a limitation of the Crown's access to the accused's speech were innovations of the late sixteenth century. The new laws and practices made the accused's speech crucial in the proceedings against him at the same time that lawyers were defining that speech as privileged. The relation between these innovations, however, cannot be understood in terms simply of increasing oppression and resistance to it; Lambarde's application of the principle to pre-trial examination occurs, after all, in the context of a manual on examination techniques. Rather, the effort to "protect" the accused's conscience can be seen as an attempt to replace it in the judicial process with data procured by new methods of investigation. For, if the accused's conscience could force him to yield the truth, it was also an authority potentially in competition with that of the Crown. Thus when Dalton asserts in *Countrey Justice* that the justice was to take evidence that would exonerate the accused, he adds the proviso, that it is probably not possible to take evidence against the Crown on oath (261). But before the accused's self could be excluded from the process of accusation and conviction it had to become the central object of the process, so that its truth could be absorbed, as it were, by methodologies that would displace it.

The distinctions Bacon draws between impugned and permissible practices represent a variety of quite inconsistent strategies to address the problem of the relation of conscience to judicial process. He distinguishes the *ex officio* oath from the oath used in Star Chamber and Chancery on the grounds that the latter binds the accused's conscience only in respect of specific charges rather than in respect of anything the Crown happened to be interested in. The objection to the *ex officio* proceeding would thus be the lack of presentment or indictment; it in effect compels the accused to discover to the Crown grounds for charges against himself. However, Bacon distinguishes the compelled answers of an accused at trial by jury on the ground that there the accused is not sworn at all; although he may have to answer incriminating questions relating to specific charges, he is not bound by an oath. The objection would thus seem to be as much to forcing the accused to speak against himself *on oath*, as to at-large questioning. But the basis on which Bacon distinguishes torture (it is used "for discovery and not for evidence") would appear to be precisely that it is used not to produce answers to a particular charge, but to discover possible offenses. To be sure, much interrogation by torture seems to have been aimed at forcing the victim to "discover" accomplices and their activities, rather than his own crimes.[51] But the famous "bloody question" devised by Burghley "to try the truth or falsehood of any such seditious person" – if papal or Spanish forces were to invade England, whose cause would you support? – which figures prominently in accounts of torture, seems to exemplify precisely the kind of probing of the accused's conscience that lawyers found so objectionable in the *ex officio* proceeding.[52] What Bacon would seem to object to is the oath, rather than the lack of a specific charge.

The shiftiness of Bacon's formulation derives from the fact that while he acknowledges at every turn the deep dependence of the judicial process on the availability of the accused's speech, he nevertheless seeks to diminish the role of the accused's conscience which confers on the speech its truth value. Insofar as he makes the lack of a specific charge the basis of self-accusation, he retains the accused's speech, guaranteed by his conscience, but contains it within the charge. Insofar as he makes the swearing of the accused the basis of self-accusation, he retains the accused's speech for the Crown but divides it from conscience which he excludes from judicial proceedings. His back-handed legitimation of torture, "it is used for discovery and not for evidence," similarly divides speech from conscience, suggesting that the information extorted through torture comes from a different place than does testimony. Following the convention established by Fortescue and Smith, Bacon frames his statement on the law of torture in terms of a distinction between English practice and Continental judicial torture for statutorily required confession. But in using it to *include* torture in English practice, he also uses it to attenuate the connection between the accused's tortured speech and the traditional, ritualized procedures of trial. Torture belonged to a different arena: it took place in the Tower or Bridewell, under executive control. Its object was not to make the accused confess his guilt, but to gather information which could be used for a variety of purposes: to gain more information, to discover more activities, and, eventually, to aid in prosecutions. In the arena of torture, Bacon implies, the Crown does not compel the accused's conscience, as it does in forcing him to swear an oath *ex officio*. Bacon thus grants the Crown the accused's speech but denies it the guarantee of his conscience. Instead of conscience, Bacon gives the Crown his body.

When Bacon impugns the oath and legitimates torture, he implies that the conscience belongs to the "self," while the body is in the public, or, more accurately, the royal domain. In drawing this distinction, he also implies a difference in the kind of truth at issue: torturing the body provides information, while binding the conscience with an oath yields confessions of guilt or innocence, revelations in fact of the condition of conscience itself. But the efficacy of torture as a method of discovery also depends upon the equivalence of body and conscience, the ability of the body somehow to stand in place of the conscience as the guarantor of speech. The torture warrants, in which claims that torture is for the "discovery of the truth" are juxtaposed to orders "to wreste from him the truthe," or "to wringe from them the truth," "to withdraw from him the knowledge of his wicked entente," show that this equivalence is more than just formal. The physicality of the struggle to "wringe" the truth from the victim imagines the truth as a thing, a substance contained in the victim's body. The torturer's control of his body thus makes the victim's "entente" susceptible of transfer to the torturer's possession. But the struggle to extract it also points embarrassingly back to the tortured man as a site of resistance to the transfer, subverting Bacon's implicit claim that the truth the tortured body yields is not part of the "self" he seeks to protect.

The need for a body that could mediate between the investigator's methods and the conscience wherein resided the truth he struggled to discover arose not only from the fraught political circumstances of the cases in which torture was involved, but more generally from the epistemic instability of the investigation itself, the inconsistency between the kind of evidence it yielded and the truth it ultimately sought. This is evident if we turn from legal discourse to accounts in the popular press of crime and its discovery, that is, to writing in which the pressures to stake out jurisdictional and methodological territory, although not interest in questions of evidence, are in abeyance. I want now to consider a case with no link to religious controversy and which did not involve torture, but which nevertheless furnishes an uncanny allegory of the problematic role of conscience in the investigation. There we will find that the relation between investigative methodology and the representational agenda of martyrology is not oppositional but supplementary.

The story of Dell's Case exists in two versions, *The Horrible Murther of a Young Boy (by a Woman Called Mother Dell)* and *The Most Cruell and Bloody Murther Committed by A. Dell on the Body of A. James*, both published as chapbooks in 1606.[53] The case concerned two children, Anthony and Elizabeth James, taken to Dell's Inn by strangers who paid the hostess and her son to do away with them. The Dells cut Anthony's throat and threw his body into a pond. Then Mother Dell cut out Elizabeth's tongue and forced the girl to throw it into the pond with her brother's body, after which she was left to wander and beg. Three weeks later, the boy's body was discovered by some hunters still wearing "a greene coate with nine skirts about the wast," that had been remarked by a tailor, one of the "signes . . . that this was the childe who three weekes before was seene in *Dels* house." Mother Dell was examined by the Justices but denied "that which was so manifestly prooved against her," and sufficient evidence was not found to bring her case to trial. At the end of four years, "by the hand of God" Elizabeth wandered back, and when she saw Dell's Inn began to cry and point. The neighbors, putting two and two together, took her before the Justices, who showed her a variety of children's coats to which she did not respond, and then produced her brother's, which caused her to cry out. She was now recognized as the sister of the murdered boy, but there was still not enough evidence against the Dells. Then, upon the crowing of a cock, her speech was restored, "that by her the wonderfull workes of God might be glorified and the Murthers discovered." The Dells were convicted on the testimony of the girl, the tailor, and others, although they denied the crime to the last, and were hanged at Hertford, on August 4, 1606.[54]

In both versions of the story the focus is the complex process whereby the truth of this crime was established. Until the girl speaks, the story unfolds in terms of the careful consideration of signs that refer to a historical truth, the action of the murder, and the disposal of the body. The mystery begins to unravel because of the coat. We are told what interested the tailor about it, how he came to see it again and thereby identify the dead child, how the Justices used it to link the dumb girl with the murdered boy. *The Most Cruell and Bloody Murther* discovers Mother Dell's motive, noting that "the lease of her Inn was (at the time of this action) at pawne for 250 L." But despite the clues and the ingenuity of the examining Justices (one even dresses up in a devil costume and accuses the child of lying) the investigation literally requires the assistance of a "mightie miracle" in order to establish the truth. The truth arrived at, which embraces not only the Dells' actions but the child's spotless conscience and Divine Providence, is not susceptible to the methodology which obviously fascinates the pamphlet writers. *The Horrible Murther* calls attention to the epistemic seam within the story, prefacing the miracle with the caveat that "in this next succeeding action, which if wee looke into but with the eyes of naturall reason and humane sence, it will be thought incredible and impossible. But with God nothing is impossible." Nevertheless, the reader is to take the text itself, not on faith but on the testimony of supplementary evidence which the reader is invited to search out: the writer continues, "and this ought not to be thought incredible because it was so lately and so neere unto us done, and for that the Childe is yet living in Hatfield, to affirme for truth all that is been written of her."

The Most Cruell and Bloody Murther makes clear that the epistemic oscillations in the story derive from the problematic relation between speech and truth in the investigation. When Mother Dell was examined the first time, we are told, she denied ever having seen the children, "and being offered her oath hereupon she was as redy to sweare and resolute to deny, but who knowes not lying and swearing are partners and as inseparable companions as a theefe and a retriever, and (as I may say) sworne brethren." Sworn speech, as the infinite regress set up by the little joke about "sworne brethren" reveals, is inherently ambiguous. The very interiority of the conscience from which sworn speech derives its truth also provides for the withholding of truth from speech in lying. Thus, the Justices respond as though the little girl's speech were indistinguishable from lying, resorting to various stratagems in order to test its credibility. The warning one Justice addresses to the child, reminding her that she would be "a lyer and a murtherer both . . . (by the death of *Dels* wife and her sonne) if she persevered in this testimony" suggests that she is the double of lying Mother Dell. The child's response to all her interrogators, including the one in the devil suit, is "I must not lye, I have that within me bids me tell truth." Clearly, the child's assertion of a compulsion to speak the truth opposes her to Mother Dell. But her insistence on the interiority of that compulsion places her truth, like Mother Dell's falseness (swearing and lying are sworn brethren), beyond the reach of the investigators. Thus every time she refers to "the thing within me," the Justices invent a new way to test the truth of her speech.

There is, of course, never any real doubt as to the truth of the child's speech. The account of the Justices' tricks seems almost a pretext for the writer to repeat the child's thrilling claim about what she has within her. But the power of this claim to break the mystery derives from what the child does not have; it is the absence of her tongue that guarantees the truth of her speech. In one sense, the story transfers the child's conscience to her body, making the truth of her speech visible in her flesh. In *The Horrible Murther*, the last thing the jury does before going out is to look into the child's mouth; her speech thus becomes part of the same order of evidence as the green jacket, what Lambarde called "signes which discover." But what the jury sees is nothing, "not so much as the stumpe of a tongue." The mutilation of the child's body is what makes her conscience visible to the jury; paradoxically, however, what they see is that the thing within her cannot be found in her flesh. It is this possibility that the mutilated body will elide the difference between the truth of conscience and of material "signes" that brought the Crown to torture in circumstances demanding the most thorough investigation.

"The truth of martyrdome"

At Edmund Campion's execution for treason the executioner, dismembering Campion's body in the name of the state, got into a scuffle with Catholic relic-seekers. Someone managed to cut off a finger and another attempted to bribe the executioner 20 pounds to do likewise for him, before Campion's severed quarters were carted off for display around London.[55] If the meaning of martyrdom and the staple claim of martyrology is that the soul's truth cannot be found in the flesh the oppressor torments, this incident gruesomely reveals that the Catholics nevertheless shared with the English authorities a need to imagine a corporeal location for a person's truth (or treason). Martyrology is, in fact, an intensely corporeal genre, and accounts of the Catholic persecutions abound with the customary manifestations of truth in the martyrs' flesh: chains spontaneously falling off holy ankles, blood miraculously bespattering the hands of iniquitous judges, the smell of eviscerated bowels indelibly staining the hands of executioners.[56] Examples of such stories can be found even in the writings of sophisticated Jesuit polemicists like Allen and Southwell. But the martyrological writing of this period also reveals a contrary agenda, a tendency to call into question the representational economy both of martyrology and of martyrdom. The meaning of martyrdom comes to depend not on the immanence of the soul's truth in the flesh, but on the same division that Bacon's statement on torture posits between the truth of conscience and the truth the body yields.

In the *Epistle of Comfort to the Reverend Priests* (1587), seeking to assure the victims of the English persecutions that they "have the truth of martyrdome," Southwell confronts the problem that the religious conflicts of the sixteenth century have made true martyrs hard to distinguish from heretics.[57] Southwell initially suggests that the difference is one between faithful and fantastic representations. A heretic is "as one taking the King's image ferforth with exquisite cunning and with most choice pretious stones, a rare workman . . . [who] change[s] it from mans shape and the seemely fashions that it had, to the likenesse of a Foxe or Dogge, using still the same metall and the same pretious jewels though rudely and grosly disposed" (161). But the clarity of this difference is lost as soon as Southwell considers what the actual visible signs of the truth are. Protestants also suffer torments for their religious beliefs: Anabaptists die "as though they had bodies of steele that felt no payne or torment" (360). "But," admonishes Southwell, "let not this move anyone to think the truth on their side (360). For even to this day doe the Jewes die in defence of the fables of their Talmud, which is to them as our Byble is to us" (360). Suffering for religion cannot be proof of martyrdom, "for if all were Martyrs that die for their Religion, then many heresies both contrary amongst themselves and repugnant to the evident Doctrines of Christ should be truthes; which is impossible" (358).[58] Even heroic silent suffering, so important in Catholic accounts of torture, can signify not the one truth, but the multiplicity of heresy. Thus he must now present the difference between true and false martyrs as, not between true and false representations, but between truth and representation. A Protestant or Jewish martyr is

as one that in a hot sommers day walking in a dry and barren field and being sore parched with the Sunne and extreame thirsty, [and] though he settled himself to paint or grave in the earth most pleasant fountayns or delightsome and shadowy bowres, shold be nevethelesse much annoyed with heat and as little eased of his thirst as before. (364)

In place of a picture of true martyrdom, Southwell offers a rhetorical question: "How is it possible, for them to have the truth of Martyrdome that want the truth of Christ?" (357). The "truth of Christ" it would appear, is supplemental rather than intrinsic to the fleshly act of martyrdom.

As it emerges in Southwell's argument, martyrdom is dual, both a truth and a visible sign. But, he admits, the devil can "by inveigling and deceiving our sense or imagination . . . make that appeare a miracle which is none" (170). Nevertheless, he dismisses it as "extreme folly . . . to doubt whether miracles be true . . . being written by so grave and authenticall authors, and only to allow that whereof our owne sight and sense doth acertayne us" (174). The dualism of martyrdom thus necessitates an epistemic choice. The fact that the visibility of miracles which invites captious empiricism (one thinks of the jury looking into the child's mouth in Dell's Case) also facilitates the devil's inveigling, suggests that textual authority is a more reliable avenue to the truth than "our owne sight." Southwell struggles to preserve the martyr's body as a site where "the truth of Christ" is made manifest, but the effect of his argument is to divorce "the truth of Christ" from the modes of knowing to which he thinks the body is susceptible.

If Southwell's epistle founders on contradiction, Allen's *A Briefe Historie of the Glorious Martyrdom of the xii Reverend Priests* (1582), describing the torture and execution of Edmund Campion and the priests tried with him, furnishes an example of how the act of martyrdom could be inscribed within an opposition between the truth of martyrdom and the spectacle of the suffering body. Occasionally there are scenes of miraculous spectacle, like the execution of Alexander Briant, "who after his beheading, himself dismembred, his hart, bowels and intrailes burned, to the great admiration of some, being laid upon the block his belly downward, lifted up his whole body then remayning on the ground" (48). To this description, however, is appended the caveat "this I adde upon report of others, not mine owne sight" (48).[59] Allen's treatment of this incident exemplifies the problem which can be discerned in Southwell's *Epistle*. Confronted with the spectacle of the martyr's suffering body, Allen privileges the evidence of the senses, claiming the foundation of the book to be eye-witness reporting. But he establishes this authority for his narrative by witholding it from the account of the martyr's miraculous body. In so doing, he puts slightly but surely into question the capacity of the visible body to act as a vehicle of God's truth.

Allen begins his account of Briant's martyrdom with the doubtful incident at Briant's execution; the remainder is devoted to an account of his torture. The theatricality of public execution demands that the martyr's truth (or the traitor's treason) be manifest in the suffering body. The representational economy of execution, if not the meanings it produces, is a given. But in the hidden struggle between torturer and victim what is at issue is precisely whether the body will yield access to the truth; Briant's torture allows Allen explicitly to divide the truth of martyrdom from the problematic spectacle of the body. This is Allen's account of Briant's torture:

He was even to the dismembring of his body rent and torne upon the rack, because he would not confess where *F. Parsons* was, where the print was, & what bookes he had sould and so was returned to his lodging for that time.

Yet the next day following, notwithstanding the great distemperature and soreness of his whole body his senses being dead, and his bloud congealed (for this is the effect of racking), he was brought to the torture againe, and there stretched with greater severitie than before (supposing with himself, that they would plucke him in pieces, and to his thinking there was a vaine broken in his hand, and that bloud ishued out there a pase) he put on the armor of patience, resolving to dye rather than to hurt any creature living, and having his minde raised in contemplation of Christ's bitter Passion, he swoond, so that they were faine to sprinckle cold water on his face to revive him againe, yet they released no part of his paine. (49–50)

On the next page Allen appends his source for this account, a letter from Briant to the Fathers of the Society of Jesus in England which had been smuggled out of the Tower by a sympathizer. Briant describes his experience as follows:

Whether this that I will say be miraculous or no, God he knoweth: but true it is, and thereof my conscience is a witnesse before God, and this I say, that in the end of the torture, though my hands and feete were violently stretched and racked, and my adversaries fulfilled their wicked lust, in practisinge their cruell tyranny upon my body, yet notwithstanding, I was without sense and feeling well nigh of all greefe and paine: and not so only, but as it were comforted, eased and refreshed of the greeves of the torture bypast, I continued still with perfect and present senses, in quietness of hart, and tranquilitie of mind. Which thing, when the commissioners did see, they departed and in going foorth they gave order to racke me againe the next day following after the same sorte. Now, when I hearde them say so, it gave me in my mind by and by, and I did verily believe and trust, that with the help of God I should be able to beare and suffer it patiently. In the mean time (as well as I could), I did muse and meditate upon the moste bitter passion of oure Saviour, and how full of innumerable paines it was, And while I was thus occupied, me thought that my left hand was wounded in the palme, and that I felt the blood runne out, but in very deede there was no such thing, nor any other paine then that which seemed to be in my hand. (53)

The experience Briant describes is clearly that of receiving stigmata. But where Briant tells of a private miracle, Allen offers an unimpeachably factual account of the effect of torture on Briant's body. He describes

Briant's painlessness as one of the bodily effects of torture (his blood was congealed) rather than as a supernatural suspension of those effects. Where Briant's declaration that he felt he was "wounded in the palme" makes clear the religious significance of his sensation, Allen's statement that he thought "there was a vaine broken in his hand" presents Briant's experience as a simple misunderstanding about a physiological consequence of his racking. Indeed, in separating Briant's meditation on Christ's wounds from the sensation in his palm, Allen's account assists the reader in missing the meaning of the event which Briant clearly intended him to find.

Briant does well to consider whether this experience "be miraculous or no." The stigmata are visible, corporeal signs of God's favor. But while his experience feels corporeal, it is also wholly private. His "conscience is a witnesse before God" to the truth of this experience, but his body bears witness to nothing. If a miracle is a manifestation of spiritual truth in the material world, in Briant's account of his experience he redraws the boundary which miracles are supposed to transcend. It is an event transpiring entirely in the mind – and in narration, a point to which I will return. But to Briant, oddly enough, the fact that "there was in very deede no such thing" seems to enhance, rather than diminish his experience. What is miraculous is intense psychic experience that cannot be seen in the body. Not surprisingly, one of Briant's torturers challenged the accounts of Briant's miracle by reasserting the body as a site of evidence, insisting that he had seen in Briant's body "open signes of peine."[60]

Allen's double presentation of this story, in which the miraculous nature of Briant's experience is first unavailable and then apparent to the reader, duplicates the structure of the miracle itself. There is no actual contradiction between the two versions of the event; it is simply that the religious meaning of Briant's experience is dissociable from the facts of what happened to Briant's body, including the sensation in his palm. In fact, such a dissociation is necessary if the representation of the miracle is not to undermine its significance, for part of what rendered Briant's experience miraculous was the failure of the soul's truth to be represented in the body.

Catholic polemicists repeatedly charged the Elizabethan authorities with using torture to violate their conscience, to penetrate an interior spiritual knowledge. What we can trace in Briant's experience, however, is the retreat of his truth, before the probing of his torturers, from his available, tortured body into the privacy of the conscience.[61] This enclosure of the victim's truth in turn provoked the torturer's zeal for discovery. An exchange between Campion and Queen's Counsel at the former's trial exemplifies how torture defined this circle of secrecy and discovery. Campion, having admitted to confessing during torture the names of some people who had sheltered him, declared "yet in this I greatly cherish and comfort myself, that I never discovered any secrets there declared, and that I will not come Rack come Rope."[62] Queen's counsel retorted "it must needs be some grievous matter and very pernicious that neither rack nor rope can wring from him" (1060). Campion's response was to proclaim that the secrets he withheld were:

... not such as concerned State or Commonwealth, whereunto my authority was not extended, but such as so charged the grieved soul and conscience whereof I had power to pray for absolution. These were the hidden matters, these were the secrets, in concealing of which I so greatly rejoiced, to the revealing whereof I cannot, nor will not be brought, come Rack, come Rope. (1060–1)

What is striking about this exchange is the rhetorical cooperation it reveals between Campion and Queen's Counsel. It is Campion who presents the contested truth in the vocabulary of the torture warrants when he claims that he has not "discovered any secrets," and it is Queen's Counsel who emphasizes the inseparability of Campion and his secrets in Campion's own language. In defining his knowledge as "secrets" Campion announces its susceptibility to discovery, which Queen's Counsel recharacterizes as intractable resistance. The repeatedly invoked "rack and rope" acts as a rhetorical hinge, signifying the truths the body will and will not yield, marking the boundary that defines both discoverer and withholder of secrets.

Campion's revelation at the conclusion of this exchange is framed as a kind of conceptual pun: the secrets he would not "confess" to the Elizabethan authorities were those that had been confessed to him. He asserts the incommensurablity of the secrets of the confessional and matter of treason, but he does so in terms of an analogous relation between religious and juridical confessions that legitimates both practices. The irony of Campion's rejoinder is enabled by the religious and political vicissitudes that made these analogous practices hostile to each other, and thereby produced Campion's career as martyr and traitor. But the irony is greater perhaps than he intended, revealing as it does how intimately entwined were the processes of subjection which Campion sought to defend with those he struggled to resist.

The analogy between juridical and religious confession is taken as given in Allen's treatise on confession, where he defines it in terms of a jurisdictional division established by Chrysostom: the earthly prince has power to bind the body, while the priest has power to bind "the verie soule" of the penitent.[63] Having established this ground of difference, Allen goes on in his argument to depend on the analogy with juridical practices to explicate religious confession. Thus, for example, he argues that it is necessary for the penitent to be specific in naming his sins because, in hearing confession, as in hearing civil and criminal causes, no one would want to give sentence until he knew the details of the offense (198). In suppressing confession, Allen suggests, Protestants have desta-bilized the analogy, collapsing the distinction between bodily and spirit-ual jurisdictions, and making "temporal laws to cover their ambitious usurpation" (97).

The jurisdictional dispute with the Protestants tends to emphasize the difference between religious and juridical confessions and thus obscures the significance of Allen's invocation of the analogy. As Allen's deploy-ment of the analogy makes clear, religious confession, like its juridical counterpart, entails the detailed accounting of the speaker's secret iniquity to authority. Confession is to ease the terror which arises from the "continuall close keping [of sin] in the covert of oure conscience" (247). It is an opening of the conscience through speech, bringing "truth in minde" into conformity with "practise in outwarde facte" (247). The bashfulness of penitents, however, requires that "the covert of the conscience" be replicated in the act of confession, which is made to "one man's most close, secrett, meek and mercifull judgement" (189). As its proliferation of terms for psychological interiority indicates, Allen's account of confession locates sin in the mind (just as, it should be noted, the "bloody question" placed the Jesuits' treason in their "verie thoughts") rather than in the sinner's deeds and his relations with his community. In this respect, his version of confession belongs specifically to the Counter-Reformation, as does the invocation of the model of juridical confession, which was a rhetorical strategy frequently used by advocates of an interiorized notion of the sacrament.[64] While the jurisdictional distinction between body and soul was of use in underlining the interiority of sin, the asserted similarity of procedures was in fact of greater importance in this regard, casting the confessor as a compassio-nate inquisitor probing hidden iniquities from his own position of secrecy rather than as a mediator between the transgressor and the Christian community. The recourse to the juridical analogy, in other words, was a step in the invention of "the covert of the conscience," the construction of spiritual experience (and transgression) not merely as inward but as secret. The process whereby confessional methodology could produce the soul's secrecy was given concrete form in Cardinal Borromeo's invention of the confessional box, which was first introduced in northern Italy in the 1570s. (Hitherto confessions had been properly conducted in full public view.) To Borromeo, one of its virtues was that it made the analogy between religious and juridical confession explicit: here the priest was to speak, "like a judge from the seat of judgment" (*tamquam pro tribunali judex*).[65]

The juridical procedures Allen and Borromeo invoke are, of course, those of Roman-canon, rather than the common law. But if, as Allen complains, Elizabeth's heretical government had ambitiously usurped the spiritual jurisdiction of the church, their usurpation was enforced, as we have seen, by methods (torture, inquisitorial oaths) which to common-lawyers like Smith and Beale looked suspiciously like Roman-canon legal practice, and which were justified by appeals to "the more general laws of nations." The new practices made the analogy between religious and juridical confessions meaningful in an English context. At the same time, however, they invested the secrecy of religious confession with a new meaning. The making of a confession signified a person's reconciliation to the church and therefore implicated him in activities against the government, while the hearing of confession was itself matter of treason. The names of other Catholics was information eagerly sought in inter-rogations by torture, information which Catholics had the most compel-ling humanitarian reasons to keep secret. The ritual performed by confessor and penitent thus became less an opening of secrets than itself the secret to be opened in juridical confession. The tension discernible in Allen's account between the ostensible purpose of confession, which is to discover the secrets of the conscience, and the desire to maintain the "covert of the conscience" by reproducing it in the confessor, was thus resolved. The "covert of the conscience" was now defined by its absolute resistance to inquisitorial probing.

According to the Catholics, the interest of their interrogators went beyond the identity of the participants in the sacrament to the very contents of confessions. In Campion's exchange with Queen's Counsel, the distinction between juridical and religious confession is carefully preserved. He suggests that his torturers were either misguidedly searching for treason where there was only religion, or deliberately attempting to break the bond between penitent and confessor for their own political ends. Thomas Cottam's statement at his arraignment collapses the distinction. According to Allen, "he avouched in the presence of the rack masters":

Indeed you are searchers of secrets for you would needs know of me what penance I was enjoined by my ghostly father for my sins committed. And I acknowledge my frailty that to avoid the intolerable torment of the rack I confessed (God forgive me) what they demanded therein. But when they further urged me to utter also what my sins were for which that penance was enjoined me (a loathsome and unchristian question), I then answered that I would not disclose my offenses saving to God and to my ghostly father alone. Whereupon they sore tormented me and still pressed me with the same demand.[66]

In Cottam's claim that his torturers actually demanded that he confess his sins to them, torture unites the two forms of confession in a single iniquitous interrogation. Cottam presents this "confession" as an enactment of the Elizabethan government's "ambitious usurpation," an attempt by illegitimate authority to "discover" and thereby appropriate the truth of religious confession. Yet all this "confession" does is literalize the analogy that defines the interiority of sin and repentance in comparison to the exteriority of earthly crime. The effect, paradoxically, is to turn analogy to absolute difference, to produce a fissure within the structure of the confession itself. Thus Cottam's interrogation, as he recounts it, only confirms the radical interiority his torturers sought to violate.

Cottam's and Campion's "confessions" bespeak the fact that the inviolable truth of conscience is a product of discovery, even as they also reveal that this truth escapes its way of knowing. Thus while Campion's announcement at the conclusion of his exchange with Queen's Counsel is framed as a dramatic revelation – "these were the hidden matters, these were the secrets . . ." – it is also an anti-climax, and therefore, a brilliant exit from the discovery–secrecy circle. Campion makes the narrative the trial is supposed to produce fall flat by substituting spiritual concerns for treasonous conspiracy as the object of discovery. The secrets he will not speak are utterly opaque because they have no meaning as truth in the context of the trial. The boundary defined by rack and rope thus divides not just the discoverer's desire to know and the withholder's secret knowledge, but two incommensurable concepts of truth.

Although the secrets both Cottam and Campion refused to speak were the same (the sins spoken and heard in confession), their accounts of their torture suggest that the truth they defend with their silence is defined not by its contents but by the power of the rack to force the discovery of other truths. Neither Campion nor Cottam assert that they met all of their torturers' questions with silence. Both admit that "the intolerable torment of the rack" brought them to confess matters of conscience – in Campion's case the names of people who sheltered him and whose confessions he heard, and in Cottam's the penance enjoined him by his confessor – before they resolutely refused to speak the contents of confession. The rack produces the hybrid confession; it opens the secrets of the Catholics' consciences to the juridical interrogator, who appropriates their historical truth. But these secrets open only to reveal a deeper secret "that rack and rope cannot wring" from the victims. What

Cottam and Campion speak becomes falsity, words of betrayal; what they refuse to speak remains truth, its integrity guaranteed by its separation from speech.[67]

In their resistance to torture, Catholics defined the truth they defended in terms of its discontinuity from utterance and representation. Paradoxically, however, instead of silencing its defenders, the enclosure of this truth enabled a copious discourse. For, if the Catholics' truth was silent and immovable, the struggles of their enemies to discover their secrets were themselves susceptible to discovery. If the purpose of torture was to produce a narrative discovering the victims' activities, in the case of the Catholics, to expose those who "steal secretly into the realm . . . [where] the whole scope of their secret labors is manifestly proved to be secretly to win all people with whom they dare deal," what the Catholic writers produced in their accounts of torture was also, ironically, a narrative of "secret labors" and their discovery.[68] Thus Robert Persons charged that "our adversaries bestowe no small diligence in this point, that the afflictions and torments which are there practiced within doores, be not brought to the knowledge of them that are withoute: but buried rather in darknesse, and cleane hyd in blynd and obscure dungeons . . . Yet at lengthe the truthe of the matter came to light when maister Campion himselfe did utter it in an open audience."[69] The truth both these accusations discover is the fact of the secret laborers' contrivances, of their tampering with an original and essentially metaphysical truth – that of Elizabethan authority, or of the Catholic faith. The original truth itself is inert, its existence marked only by the illegitimate operation of its enemies upon it. Thus Southwell's proclamation to the English authorities, "your iniquity is proof of our faith," describes a representational economy; the narrative of discovered "fact" (in Elizabethan usage, literally "doings") speaks for a truth no narrative can contain.

In this representational economy meaning emerges not so much from a moral opposition between secret laborers and truth's guardians, as from the disjunction between discovery as a mode of knowing and inert truth. Indeed, the moral opposition can disappear altogether without impairing the functioning of this economy. Thus the narrative of Jesuitical secret labors and the narrative of torture not only imitate each other but become, on occasion, the same story. In Persons's *An Epistle of the Persecution of Catholickes in Englande*, for example, Alexander Briant's letter recounting his experience on the rack is printed again, here with an account of its history that reveals the letter to be implicated in a network of secret activity. Persons writes that:

Althoughe it be true, that Catholiques imprisoned in the tower of london, are kept so straitlye, and uncourteouslie in warde: as neyther friends maye have accesse unto them, nor they permitted eyther to have company or to speake with other men, and muche lesse to have books, paper, or penn and ynke: Yet during the late disputation there with father Campian the prisoner, some of them whiche were entred in to heare the disputations, finding oportunitie, stepped a syde unto the holes of some seclused priests, to visit and salute those servants of Christe: by whiche means, as by gods holie providence, some thinges were under stoode and knowne, touching their state . . . And among other things this epistle foloweing, written in haste (even foorth of the mouth dowtlesse, as it semeth, of the holy ghooste) by a good priest, which had bene miserablie tormented and sundrie times racked, came to my hands frome the reverend fathers of the Societie of Jesus, to whome it was sent. And here I thought good to place yt woord by woord taken oute of the Authors owne handwriting. (L5r)

In the throng assembled to hear Campion dispute, Catholic sympathizers, indistinguishable from loyal Englishmen, "step a syde" and assist in the production of secret writings which are then sent by Catholic agents to centers of Jesuit activity on the Continent. There they are printed in books, presumably to be smuggled back to England. (It will be recalled that Briant was interrogated as to "where the print was.") Having discovered the history of the letter's production, Persons opens the letter to public view. (Queen's Counsel did likewise with Campion's correspondence at his trial, gleaning from it Campion's assertion that while he had named names he could not be brought to confess "secrets . . . Come Rack come Rope.") "Taken out of the Authors owne handwriting," the letter offers proximity to the author's "verie thoughts." And the contents of the letter, as we have seen, do take the reader into the sanctum of conscience. Even as he tells the story, however, Briant signals the limits of the reader's penetration; the truth of the experience lies in Bryant's "conscience [which] is a witness before God." Persons's narrative places the (presumably sympathetic) reader in the torturer's position. The reader discovers ever deeper secrets until the narrative brings him up against the point where it verges on pure self-reference. This "discovery" of the impossibility of seeing further reveals, as it were, the impregnable sanctum of truth.

In torture, the object of discovery and the site of its failure was the subject – in both the political and ontological senses of the word. The epistemic anxiety that attached to the subject in Renaissance England is suggested in the Privy Councilors' use of "truth" and "treason" as interchangeable terms in the torture warrants to designate what the torturer was to discover. The subject's truth was susceptible to discovery only in its betrayal, in the secret labors of treasonous conspiracy. But the ability of discovery to reveal only treason also bespeaks the fact that every project of discovery, "successful" or not, revealed that impenetrable sanctum it had created. Thus the victim's positive assertions of his truth were never treated as a discovery that he possessed no subversive secrets. There was no redress for Thomas Myagh's complaint, "by torture straunge mi trouth was tryed / yet of my liberte denied." It was precisely because his truth had been tried and, he claims, proven that his ordeal had not ended.

3   Brothers of the state

> Shepherds of the people had need know the calendars of tempests in
> state, which are commonly greatest when things grow to equality, as
> natural tempests are greatest about the *Equinoctia.*
>
> Francis Bacon, "Of Seditions and Troubles"

The Renaissance English stage is notorious for its violent corporeality,
its display of stabbings, dismemberments, eye gougings, boilings, and
other atrocities. But there is, to my knowledge, no scene of interrogatory
state torture in the drama of this period. Like the spectacle of execution,
official torture apparently could not be played at, its motions divorced
from the power they proclaim, its deadly force mocked through representation.[1] The rack, that potent symbol of the state's compulsion to wring
truth from the subject, does appear on stage on at least one occasion,
however, in Chapman's *Bussy d'Ambois* (1604), when the jealous
husband Montsurry uses it to interrogate his adulterous wife Tamyra.
The scene presents a bizarre overlay of state violence and domestic crisis,
one which entails a double displacement of social reality, for, with
apparently only two exceptions, victims of interrogatory torture in
England were men, while wives suspected of adultery were rarely of
interest to the state and generally met with more banal forms of domestic
violence.[2] The introduction of the rack into the scene of marital crisis
thus produces a semiotic disturbance which signals that whatever we are
looking at here, it is not simply mimesis, either of domestic strife or of
state power. The incongruity of the scene brings to our attention what
cannot or will not be shown, making us aware of the displacements,
repressions, and analogies on which representation depends. In other
words, the wife's body here signifies metadramatically; she is not herself
a repository of secrets so much as the vehicle through which otherwise
unrepresentable matters of state can be brought to light.

I take this strange tableau as an emblem for the issue which this
chapter will explore: the intertwining of the state's discovery of the
subject with marriage plots on the Renaissance stage. While no other
play goes so far as to place a wife on the rack, *Bussy d'Ambois* is not

unique in this period in using women, and men's desire to possess and control them, as the medium through which the vexed relation between the subject and the early modern state can be articulated. Two other plays of the same year, *Measure for Measure* and *Othello*, which will be my focus in this chapter, enact this procedure full scale, bringing the discovery of the subject to the stage in marriage plots which, as we shall see, also arrive at a threshold where a representational exchange between torture and marriage bed is explicitly performed. Indeed, I would argue, the well-known generic problems which beset those plays – *Othello's* indecency and triviality, *Measure for Measure's* darkness and distasteful coerciveness – arise from the same splicing of the marital and political that produces the incongruous effect in the scene from *Bussy d'Ambois*. This generic instability reminds us that what we confront here is not institutional practice (except for that of the theatre) but representation, which is subject to pressures as hard as censorship or as soft as generic convention or cognitive deficiency. This is not to say, however, that the marriage plots are a mere distortion of or code for a problematic that is more authentically enacted in torture. Rather, in this chapter I will argue that the theatrical grafting of the marriage and state plots actually articulates aspects of the epistemically resistant subject and the conditions which produced him, which other representational contexts such as legal and religious controversy, or torture itself, either suppress or leave invisible. In these plays, I want to suggest, the marriage plot furnishes resources for figuring relationships – gender difference, sameness, and hierarchy, rights of possession, bodily desire, and events – which supply deficiencies characteristic of situations such as torture in which a subject inviting discovery emerges. In other words, marriage provides a sort of grid through which the problems surrounding the subject, so tightly impacted in torture, where the world contracts to torturer and victim and a man to body and soul, can be given social definition.[3] In "plotting" the epistemc crisis of the subject, these plays reveal historically important features of that crisis which we would not glean from reading the State Papers Domestic: that it is not the effect of an "Other's" resistance to the state so much as an endemic feature of the expansion of state authority itself, and that it concerns the contradictory construction of masculinity as both a hierarchical arrangement of men and a collective domination of, desire for, and differentiation from women.

The terms in which the discovery of the subject will be reformulated on Shakespeare's stage can be discerned in the exchange of marriage for torture which both plays perform at their conclusions. As the Duke's plot begins to come to light near the end of *Measure for Measure*, Escalus accuses "Friar Lodowick" of slandering the Duke and orders,

"To th' rack with him! – We'll touse you / Joint by joint, but we will know his purpose" (5.1.309–10).[4] This event is forestalled by the discovery of the "friar's" identity, and therefore "his purpose," in the struggle to drag him away to prison and torture – the discovery that authority already knows and controls this schemer's secret intent. With the re-establishment of the Duke's authority, the deputy, Angelo, becomes the object of the state's threatened violence. But the rituals of juridical discovery are again pre-empted as Angelo admits quite readily his transparency before the Duke, who, "like power divine [has] looked upon [his] passes" (367–8). The Duke sentences him along with the wag Lucio to execution following their marriages only to remit all torments but marriage itself.[5] If this gesture might be moralized as an act of mercy, Lucio's shrewd complaint that "Marrying a punk . . . is pressing to death, / Whipping and hanging" (520–1) insists on another possibility, that these marriages furnish not so much a reprieve from state violence as an equivalent to it. The intent of Lucio's sentence is quite clear: marrying him to a whore ensures that he will be a cuckold. But the comment with which the Duke hands Mariana to Angelo, "I have confessed her and I know her virtue" (524), with its insinuating intimacy and hint of prior possession, and his intended appropriation of Isabella, the object of Angelo's desire, suggests that it is not only marriage to a punk that can procure this result. However chaste Mariana and Isabella themselves may be, the marriages with which the play concludes serve not so much to regulate sexuality as to install the men in a hierarchy of (imaginary) control over a sexual common ground.[6] In the "comic" resolution of *Measure for Measure* the power over the subject, so ferociously concentrated in torture, is diffused through marriage into male sexual rivalry.

The conclusion of *Othello* suggests how precarious such a resolution must be. Lodovico and Gratiano, senators and emissaries of "the Venetian State," give orders for Iago's torture three times in the last seventy lines of the play, responding to his declaration of epistemic impenetrability, "Demand me nothing, what you know, you know, / From this time forth I never will speak word" (5.2.304–5), with the assurance that "Torments will ope thy lips" (306).[7] These orders reproduce an effect that Iago has been manipulating throughout the play as he conjures up scenes to be played in the mind's eye, beyond the boundaries of theatrical decorum. Now before us on the marriage bed lie the remains of these fantasies, the black ram and the white ewe, Desdemona "topp'd," even, insofar as Emilia lies there too, Othello twixt Iago's sheets – only to be displaced by another scene it is impossible we should see in Lodovico's final commands, "The object poisons sight, / Let it be hid" (365), and (to Cassio) "the torture: Oh enforce it" (370).[8] The scenes of Desdemona "topp'd" and Cassio enforcing the torture of Iago thus form a kind of palimpsest, each adumbrating and repressing each other – an effect that Iago has helped to create in the fantasy he feeds Othello of Cassio "kiss[ing] me hard / As if he plucked up kisses by the roots" (3.3.438–9). At the end of *Othello* we are induced simply to shift our focus, to avert our eyes from the detritus of marital jealousy and imagine the new lord governor enforcing the torture of the ensign.

Framed thus the ending of the two plays mirror each other, the move into/away from torture away from/into marriage structuring an opposition onto which can be loaded a host of binaries: comedy and tragedy, on-stage and off, heterosexual and homosocial pairing, live brides and dead wives, a knowing Duke and a duped general, a transparent subordinate officer and an eternally opaque one. In other words, what we see as we focus on the torture/marriage exchange is the similarity in the sexual and political configurations the plays present – and the apparent ease with which they resolve themselves in generically and epistemically opposite directions.

Let us suspend for the moment the question of marriage and its role in these different conclusions and consider just the patterns of relationship the plays share. At the center of both is a pair of men, a commander and a subordinate officer or deputy, locked in unilateral intimacy, and a woman of great chastity, temporary eloquence, and a powerful capacity to arouse men's desire, who furnishes the occasion for one man's operations on the other's heart. (It might be added that this woman is paired with another, also "good" although less absolute in chastity, and that the male couple maneuvers around a third intermediate male figure who remains innocent of their entanglement.) These configurations are not however merely symmetrical. Placed side by side the male couples form a chiasmus, the superior in *Measure for Measure* showing the propensity for scheming and preternatural knowledge of the other's heart that characterizes the subordinate in *Othello*. This inversion, inconceivable in the diads themselves, nevertheless makes explicit the possibility that haunts them in both political and sexual registers, that each man can somehow occupy the place of the other.

This necessarily reductive account reveals that the structural similarities in the men's relationships arise from a political vision the plays share, of the state as a chain of command. Leonard Tennenhouse has argued that *Measure for Measure* and other comedies of the same year which exploited the disguised ruler motif constitute a "remarkable moment" when, just after the succession of James (a succession determined not by the previous monarch's procreation but by the judgment of her Privy Councilors) a number of playwrights were able, for the first time, to imagine the state "as a mechanism run by deputies or substitutes."[9] In fact both *Measure for Measure* and *Othello* present worlds in which the consecrated center of power has been superseded by a structure of delegated authority – in *Measure for Measure* because that center has absented itself from the polity, in *Othello* because the action has absented itself from the center (where, in any case, the patriarchal privileges of the oligarchy are subordinate to the desires of one who has "done the state some service" (5.2.340).[10] Tennenhouse reads the disguised ruler motif conservatively, as offering a glimpse of a proto-bureaucratic state only to resuscitate consecrated authority by staging the ruler's return to right the wrongs inevitably committed in his absence. But the residual ambiguities of *Measure for Measure*'s conclusion, not to mention the ending of its tragic contemporary, *Othello*, which is literally administered by a representative of the Venetian state, suggests that in 1604 Shakespeare's interest in the proto-bureaucratic vision of the state was neither as ideologically defensive nor as fleeting as Tennenhouse suggests.[11] Indeed, for all the theatrical display of the monarch in this period, there must have been an increasing awareness, especially among educated men, of the early modern state as an administrative regime in which men dispatch business on behalf of an authority to which they are themselves subject.[12]

The power exerted through delegated authority is nowhere more evident than in the paper trail left by the Elizabethan torturers. But if these plays hold a mirror up to some features of the administrative context within which torture occurred, they also proclaim what no participant in the discourse of torture would acknowledge: that the subject who harbors treasonous secrets is not an avowed enemy of the state but a link within the chain of command. In so doing they provide for a reading of the epistemic crisis of the subject in terms of the various double binds which the administrative state produces: the requirement that men imagine themselves both as equivalent to one another and different, that they remain the loyal subordinates of an authority which relentlessly encourages their ambition. Thus, while both Angelo and Iago are constructed as objects of discovery, harboring secret purposes whose disclosures vindicate the Duke's surveillance of his subjects and Othello's (misdirected) obsession with what lies behind "the door of truth" (3.3.413), their secrecy coexists with a mysterious capacity for intimacy, for knowing or being known by their superiors, that troubles the boundaries of the self which the discovery of the subject so insistently reifies. After all, Iago and Othello are never so close, never thinking so much alike, as when Iago refuses to let Othello know his thoughts. Insofar as discovery posits that truth is autonomous, is in fact autonomy

itself manifested in the stubbornly withheld conscience, then this perception of the a priori knowledge which enmeshes the subordinate's
secret deconstructs the epistemic structure of discovery; we train our eyes
not on a cache of truth but a circuit of power.

Inhering nowhere, state authority realizes itself in these plays through
its conferral onto agents from whom it is then recovered in the discovery
of their secret treachery. In the readings which follow I will be arguing
that marriage, which is to say, the state's attribution of a woman to a
man, can function as a temporary alternative to torture in this process
because a wife (or wife-to-be) serves as a sort of switching mechanism
between loyalty and treachery, sameness and difference. A more circui-
tous and temporarily more successful strategy than torture, marriage
permits the abjection of self-interest, its coding as gender difference
which can then be equated with sexual betrayal. (There is no woman in
either play who is not at some point called whore.) And as long as the
wife is imagined as a potential whore, an attribute not merely of her
husband but of others in the chain of command (Othello extends this to
"the general camp / Pioners and all" [3.3.351–2]), she also holds out the
possibility that there is an act of usurpation men can be caught in
through which they can know one another. In short, the wife furnishes
occasions for framing systemic ambiguities as secrets awaiting discovery.
If the Duke's scheme shows us the power the state accrues this way,
Iago's plot (which is perhaps the Duke's dark dream, Angelo's revenge),
reveals the entropy involved.

"So sound as things that are hollow"

Many readings of *Measure for Measure* turn on whom Angelo is to be
paired with. Is Angelo Isabella's fellow pupil in learning the hard lessons
which thaw out icy virtue? Or is he the confrere of the Duke who, after
all, concludes the play by negotiating the same deal Angelo attempted,
Isabella's body for Claudio's life? To choose the first option is in most
cases to proclaim the Duke's supremacy either because, in humanist
terms, he brings the other characters to "self-knowledge" or because, in
Foucauldian ones, his mind-games reconstruct their subjectivity. To
choose the second is to mobilize the uneasy parallels and reversals that
trouble the Duke's final ascendancy and provide the ground for at least
psychological resistance. Some interesting readings manage to keep both
options in play. In any case, what the deep structure of the criticism
reveals is that the play positions Angelo between the Duke and Isabella
inviting us to identify him *both* with a ruler and with a highly, if
unwillingly, sexualized woman. How, I want to ask, does this double

identification serve to construct Angelo as the secret subject of discovery? What does it do to a subordinate to wonder how much he is like his superior? What does it do to a man to wonder how much he is like a woman? Or to a woman to use her to activate this question?

The issue of Angelo's likeness to the Duke is raised at the beginning of the play in a manner that reveals the ambiguities eddying around the deputy's position. As the Duke makes preparation to leave the government of Vienna in Angelo's hands, he construes the relation between the deputy and his office in terms that suggest two rather different ontologies. Handing Angelo his commission, he admonishes him:

> Angelo:
> There is a kind of character in thy life
> That to th'observer doth thy history
> Fully unfold. Thyself and thy belongings
> Are not thine own so proper as to waste
> Thyself upon thy virtues, they on thee.
>   . . .
> But I do bend my speech
> To one that can my part in him advertise:
> Hold therefore Angelo
> In our remove, be thou at full ourself.   (1.1.26–43)

The Duke will vacate a place and Angelo, in occupying it, is fully to "be" him. The Duke makes clear that this substitution is possible because in a sense Angelo already is him; to possess civic virtue is to replicate authority, as the coin imagery which both the Duke and Angelo invoke to describe the relation between Duke and deputy suggests. If such a situation might make the Duke susceptible to more than just temporary replacement, it also extends his rule well beyond the reach of his personal power, subsuming his subjects into himself. Just before Angelo's entrance here, however, the Duke has claimed that in making Angelo his deputy he has, "Lent him our terror, drest him with our love, / And given his deputation all the organs / Of our own power" (19–21). The power Angelo is to wield is the Duke's "own" and Angelo will assume it as a role. The metaphors of lending and dressing hint at a separate, always hidden, already suspect identity for Angelo. When the Duke explains to Friar Thomas the reason for his scheme – his desire to try the precise Lord Angelo, to "see / If power change purpose, what our seemers be" (1.3.53–4) it is this second ontology he insists on. He is, moreover, at this moment casting *himself* in terms of seeming and being, seeking instruction on how he may "formally in person bear, / Like a true friar" (47–48), thereby calling attention to the "being" he is about to mask.

As the irony of the Duke's own role-playing suggests, however, the ontologies of what may be called replication and hidden authentic identity are, in fact, not really alternatives, but the conditions for producing each other. Thus the Duke's initial accounts of his project of discovery not only oscillate between these possibilities, but wittily collapse them, deploying a lexicon of identity ("belongings," "own," "proper," "virtue") to assert the seamless continuity between Angelo's being and the authority in which the identities of Escalus and the Duke himself are also subsumed. But the Duke's wit also enables an ironic reading of the speech – Angelo's virtues are not his own because he is a hypocrite – that firmly separates Angelo's identity from the authority for which the Duke speaks. Conversely, when the Duke calls Angelo a "seemer" to Friar Thomas, he implies that the truth of the deputy's identity is there from the beginning, waiting to be discovered, but he acknowledges at the same time that if he is to see this truth, power must first change Angelo's "purpose." The discovery of Angelo's true being necessitates altering it, for when he receives the Duke's commission Angelo's purpose replicates the Duke's authority. The secret, transgressive purpose that defines Angelo's proper identity – the "thoughts" that Isabella will argue are "no subjects" – must emerge, paradoxically, from his ability to "be at full" the Duke.

To be sure, Angelo is not the only character in the play who is installed within a regime of substitution that serves to reconstruct his identity at the same time that it fractures a unitary notion of self. Substitution, an Angelo for a Claudio, a Mariana for an Isabella, a Ragozine for a Barnardine, is the play's central trope.[13] This feature of the play lends itself well to Foucauldian readings; the play's substitutions reproduce subjectivity as a condition of self-division, in Jonathan Goldberg's words, a "private theater" in which conscience is displayed to an internalized spectator.[14] This internal theatre results from and comes to embody the slippages between authority and subordination, self and other, that the play's many acts of substitution (especially the central one of deputation) produce. Readings that second each other in their accounts of the self as a site of division and spectatorship, however, differ as to whose self is at issue. Where, for example, the self that Goldberg describes is that of the sovereign, the self that Steven Mullaney describes in quite similar terms is that of the subject. But this apparent contradiction is merely symptomatic; "sovereign" and "subject" are in both cases defined precisely by the fact that they contain within themselves both sovereignty and subjection. Escalus's assertion that "the Duke's in us" (5.1.293) becomes the play's and, by implication, the culture's central truth. This kind of reading resists earlier moralistic readings of the Duke's machinations as a course of spiritual therapy which brings the characters to the truth about themselves.[15] But the Foucauldian reading also shares a problematic feature of the moralistic reading: the formulation of the experience of all the characters, whether Duke, deputy, novice, libertine, unwed mother, or unrepentant criminal, in terms of a single mechanism of subjection. Differences of gender, rank, religious status, and relation to the law are assimilated to the single difference that constructs the self-divided sovereign–subject. But the sovereign–subject's self-division depends, obviously enough, on his assuming, at least in his mind, the mantle of authority, something that several characters, Juliet, Barnardine, Mistress Overdone, for example, are unwilling or unable to do. Isabella can imagine the operation of a self-inspecting gaze but not herself as its subject or object, and her moral dilemma issues not in her secret self-division but in a refusal to be divided, a refusal which, as we shall see, the doubling of the bed trick actually ratifies.[16]

The differential effects which the regime of substitution produces across the play's society arise because there are other forces at work in the play – modes of subjection and codes of representation which interrupt or alter the meanings that duplicating someone or seeing oneself duplicated can produce. For instance, the play insistently circulates discourses about women, what their bodies are like and their functions are, which preclude investing the female characters with the hidden depths that Angelo comes to possess. And the kind of comic delights which low characters such as Pompey and Elbow are meant to deliver makes a painful conscience an unthinkable affliction. Even ideologically inflected matters of decorum, such as who is permitted to be on stage alone (only Angelo, the Duke, and, briefly, Isabella) affect the conviction with which the play can attach certain styles of subjectivity to certain characters. Thus even if we are invited to abstract the initial act of deputation, to read it as a metaphor for installation of a superego in the early modern mind, the action and language of the play returns it to its political specificity, revealing that sovereign–subject selfhood is a function of being the Duke's deputy and, the play hints, of being the deputy's Duke – of being, in other words, a man who shares with other men knowledge of the properties of government.

My point is that the subject formation which the play's substitutions induce in fact is fully realized only among members of a male ruling class. But if the emergence of the self-inspecting subject in the play has to do with the production of a specifically *governing* elite, it is sexual experience as much as the work of state that proves the means to this end. Thus, as the Duke, Angelo, and Escalus leave the stage after Angelo has been invested as deputy, they are replaced by another threesome,

Lucio, and "two other gentlemen." These last remain nameless. Duplicating each other, and Lucio, they have no identity save as participants in the knowing and comradely speculation on one another's sexual adventures, which is the conversation Lucio seeks with every man he encounters:

> LUCIO: Behold, behold, where Madam Mitigation comes!
> I have purchased as many diseases under her roof as
> come to –
> 2 GENT.: To what, I pray?
> LUCIO: Judge.
> 2 GENT. To three thousand doulours a year.
> I GENT.: Ay and more.
> LUCIO: A French crown more.
> I GENT.: Thou art always figuring diseases in me; but thou are full of error; I am sound.
> LUCIO: Nay, not, as one would say, healthy: but so sound as things that are hollow; thy bones are hollow; impiety has made a feast of thee.
>
> (1.2.41–53)

As with the men in the preceding scene, the topic of conversation among these three indistinguishable gentlemen is, reflexively, how much (which in this case means which whores) they have in common. Here, however, the replication of the Duke's authority in his surrogates, which the imagery of "figuring" and coining so aptly expresses, becomes, through the linguistic replication of puns, venereal contagion.

The parody of the deputation scene in the chat of Mistress Overdone's patrons sets in play a conceptual fungibility of governmental and sexual knowledge which provides for the discovery that the perfect deputy is a secret sinner. Exercising one kind of knowledge, in Angelo's case at any rate, seems to lead to the other. At the same time, however, Lucio's joking undermines the moral significance of Angelo's "sin." The comparison this exchange effects between the spread of venereal disease, with the moral corruption it implies, and the replication of the Duke's authority in his deputy, substitutes a mechanical for a moral explanation of corruption's origin, suggesting that "hollowness" spreads simply by one man taking another's place. Thus replication, even of civic virtue – and this is the point of Lucio's pun that makes "sound" into an attribute of hollowness – leads to corruption with the same inexorability that Elbow's attempts to vindicate his wife's honor lead him to cast aspersions on it. Insofar as the "soundness" of the deputy lies in his ability to replicate the Duke, his identity is always split, hollowed out, as it were, by the difference between one man and another that it harbors. Figured as a duplicate, the deputy must prove to be duplicitous, a representative who does not figure his own identity. What Angelo experiences as the painful discovery of a secret self which corrupts the soundness of the chain of command, Lucio and his companions suggest is merely the effect of standing in for someone else.[17]

The play's suggestion that the logic of deputation is the logic of masculine sexual practice is not gratuitous irony but an indication of the conceptual usefulness of sexuality in imagining a paradigmatically bureaucratic elite. Lucio's joking constructs a category, "men," which has no internal markings save the sort that a bout of syphilis can produce. Members of this group, even when they are hierarchically positioned *vis-à-vis* one another, are bound together, not vertically as feudal men are by service and gratitude, but horizontally, as it were, by a sense of common knowledge that also makes the relation between place and occupant a contingent one. That the grounds on which the Duke re-establishes his supremacy (and on which suspicions linger) are those of virtue, rather than, say, hereditary entitlement, indicates how much Lucio is actually a spokesman for the play's political order. So does the fact that the goal of the Duke's plot to try his deputy who "scarce confesses / That his blood flows; or that his appetite / Is more to bread than stone" (1.3.51–3) is the same as Lucio's slanders, to bring another man into carnal confraternity. The play then does not so much ask questions about the right way to deal with sexuality as show what can be done with it, how it can be used to think about and manage relations between men, the structure of which derives from a quite different arena of experience.[18] Such a formulation obviously follows Foucault's insistence that sexuality be understood not as the object of repression but as a means for constructing subjectivity and disposing subjects within a social order. I want to stress, however, the specificity with which this work is carried out in the play, for what is produced are not simply sexualized subjects but a particular organization of state authority, one which positions men and women differently, and genders them by writing its ways of knowing onto their bodies in quite precise ways.

Demanding that Angelo see Claudio in himself (something the plot will force him to do), Isabella invites Angelo also to reimagine his body:

> authority, though it err like others,
> Hath yet a kind of medicine in itself
> That skins the vice o' th' top. Go to your bosom,
> Knock there, and ask your heart what it doth know,
> That's like my brother's fault. If it confess
> A natural guiltiness, such as is his,
> Let it not sound a thought upon your tongue
> Against my brother's life.   (2.2.135–42)

Isabella urges Angelo to think of himself as a "bosom," a cavity within which lies the "vice" which his authority "skins" over – an exhortation that echoes the Duke's defensive response to Friar Thomas's assumption that he is seeking a "secret harbour" for "the aims and ends / Of burning youth" (1.3.4–6): "Father, throw away that thought; / Believe not that the dribbling dart of love / Can pierce a complete bosom" (1–3). In Isabella's formulation the complete bosom becomes corruption's secret harbor, its "hollowness," to use Lucio's term, the resonant interiority from which the heart's "natural guiltiness" confesses itself. Isabella's exhortation makes clear that the confessional body she imputes to Angelo is defined not simply as a corporeal location (a "bosom") and condition ("natural guiltiness"), but also as the site of inter-subjective exchange. Isabella fragments Angelo, representing him to himself as two synecdochic subjects, an inquisitorial, judging tongue and a transgressing, confessing heart. The body that Isabella ascribes to Angelo is thus the "subject" of confession in the double sense that Foucault specifies, functioning both as confession's "speaking subject" and as "the subject [matter] of [its] statement."[19] If Angelo is peculiarly susceptible to these representations, discovering all too soon how much he and Claudio share, it is because he already knows full well his soundness is a "glassy essence," that his very being has been split by assuming the mantle of a higher authority. The hollowness Angelo cannot help but find in himself is thus no more than that difference between one man and another across which confession is made and deputation conferred.

Foucault asserts that confession "unfolds within a power relationship, for one does not confess without the presence (or virtual presence) of a partner who is not simply the interlocutor but the authority who requires the confession, prescribes and appreciates it and intervenes in order to judge, punish, forgive . . ."[20] Just so, that part of Angelo which is like the powerful Duke is to interrogate that part which is like the imprisoned Claudio. But what is striking about the "confession" Isabella envisages is that, predicated on authority's "err[ing] like others," it bears a striking resemblance to other interchanges in the play in which the "partner" is, in fact, "simply the interlocutor." Like Lucio "figuring diseases" in the first gentleman, or speculating to "Friar Lodowick" about the Duke "who had some feeling for the sport," or like Friar Thomas suspecting the "aims and ends of burning youth" harbored in the bosom of the Duke, Angelo is to "go to his bosom" and "ask" his heart about its condition, to engage himself in the speculations about the natural guiltiness of the male body which is the staple conversation between men in the play. The concerns and strategies of confession and those of masculine banter are not easily distinguished. Has Friar Thomas (the only true confessor in the play) spoken as spiritual counselor or as man of the world in his offstage insinuation that the Duke is seeking "secret harbour" for a clandestine tryst? Is Lucio gossiping about the Duke to "Friar Lodowick" or slyly teasing a fellow rake? Or is he even, perhaps, reflecting the Duke's sinful soul back to him? In *Measure for Measure* the confessional subject is formed not so much by the operation of authority on the subject as by the ever-present possibility that, among the men who can claim with Lucio to be "inward" of the Duke, hierarchy will collapse into equality, difference into sameness.

It should not surprise us then that in those exchanges where it is impossible to mistake the confessor for the simple interlocutor, as when the Duke "confesses" Juliet and Mariana and the gender hierarchy reinforces the supposed spiritual one, the "penitent" resists formation as a confessional subject. Confessing Juliet, the Duke explicitly undertakes to do just this:

> I'll teach you how you shall arraign your conscience
> And try your penitence, if it be sound,
> Or hollowly put on.   (2.3.21–3)

But if this scene furnishes a perfect emblem of the proper power relations of confession, the Duke's words bristle with unintended ironies that enmesh his discourse in male intersubjectivity and deflect it from Juliet. Most obviously, there is the reprisal in these lines of Lucio's witty exchanges with his fellow patrons of Mistress Overdone's, an echo that links the hierarchical discourse of confession with the genial equality of the bull session. Moreover we know that whatever the state of Juliet's penitence, it is the confessor's authority that is "hollowly put on," that he furnishes at this moment a peculiarly apt object for Angelo's exclamation about himself, "O place, O form, / How often dost thou with thy case, thy habit, / Wrench awe from fools, and tie the wiser souls / To thy false seeming!" (2.4.12–15) – a recognition that returns us once more to the vexed issue of the relationship between Duke and deputy. But the most telling irony of the Duke's admonition to Juliet, more obvious perhaps in performance, is the ascription of hollowness to the bulging woman, only hours away from childbirth. Her "sin" as the Duke styles the baby she carries, is not an appetite lurking within an apparently complete bosom, a secret that must be carefully brought to light through the confessor's questioning, but an obtrusive presence. (The literal truth of the Duke's assertion, "Then was your sin of a heavier kind than his" (27), affords the actor an obvious bit of stage business.) A hollow vessel full to bursting with "sin," Juliet's incontinent body pre-empts the Duke's attempt to form her as a confessional subject, to sound in her a resonant gap between tongue and heart. It will permit no secrets: "The stealth of our most mutual entertainment," Claudio tells Lucio, "with character too gross is writ on Juliet" (1.2.143–4). Her body is an unerring signifier, a fleshly text revealing inexorably and without the volition of an uttering subject, the truth of the body's stealth. Juliet has, as the Provost says, "blistered her report"; she has produced on her own person the brand that identifies and punishes her as a whore.

If Juliet's body makes her sin transparent to authority, however, this does not mean that she is wholly subjugated. Indeed, as Stephen Greenblatt has argued, it is by no means clear that Juliet is an acquiescent penitent in her scene with the Duke, that her claim "I do repent me as it is an evil / And take the shame with joy" (2.3.35–6) may show a deft equivocation, suggesting that her "sin" is not an evil and that "the shame" she takes with joy is her unborn child.[21] Or it may not; it is not possible to tell, and, as Greenblatt implies, it hardly seems to matter what she intends. But the "tranquillity" that he observes in Juliet's replies, her apparent ability to speak within the Duke's terms without allowing him to speak within her, is evidence not, as he asserts, of the imperviousness of "society at large" to the Duke's techniques for provoking anxiety, but of the gendering of the anxious confessional subject. Moreover, the point remains the same even if what we see is not "tranquillity" but sullenness or even inconsolable grief. If Juliet can seem to introduce double meanings into the Duke's discourse without arousing desires that her real intent be ferreted out, it is because there is no such doubleness located within her. The condition of her body that manifests her difference from her interlocutor and ineluctable subjugation to his law, pre-empting any speculation as to *her* "natural guiltiness," exempts Juliet from the play of replication and difference, of soundness and hollowness that produces Angelo's anxious hypocrisy.

The point here, it must be stressed, is not that Juliet possesses an authentic and undivided self that is somehow prior to the Duke's efforts at moral reconstruction, but that her extravagantly gendered body provides a point of reference within the play's semiotics, one that is echoed in the pregnant bodies of Kate Keepdown, the "punk" to whom Lucio will be forcibly married, and Elbow's wife, in whose craving for stewed prunes the signs of pregnancy and whoredom are conflated. Simultaneously announcing their difference from the bodies of the rulers and their transgressions of the law, the self-exposing pregnant bodies belong to those who will never say "the Duke's in us." Their transparency enables unambiguous establishment of hierarchy. But the expansive cavity of the woman's body is also a terrifying parody of the hollow bosom, a secret enclosure whose contents spill outward, announcing the sexual "will" of the subject, bypassing the speaking will altogether. The woman's body thus holds out to the male onlooker a fantasy of complete transparency and subjugation, something which he can *imagine* happening to him but which can never actually come to pass. Transfixing the male onlooker with this double knowledge the pregnant female body defines his radically secret depths.[22]

This imaginative interdependence of male and female bodies becomes clearer when we consider a more problematic female body in the play. Isabella, too, is represented as a signifying body independent of any volitional subject, and thus with no capacity for deceit. "Hail virgin, if you be –," Lucio greets her, "as those cheek-roses / Proclaim you are no less" (1.4.16–17). Any possible irony regarding the reliability of cheek-roses as signs of virginity fails: Isabella is in the hidden recesses of her body (the location that functions as the soul in this play) precisely what she appears to be on her face. In this respect, Juliet's tranquil acceptance of her "shame" and Isabella's rigid virtue are less opposing psychological or moral conditions than alternate versions of the semiotic integrity, the incapacity for deception and self-division, that the play ascribes to women. Unlike Juliet, however, Isabella is a powerful voice as well as a corporeal signifier. "She hath prosperous art / When she will play with reason and discourse," Claudio remarks of his sister, "and well she can persuade" (1.2.174–6). Yet whatever Isabella's rhetorical skill, her power of persuasion is also mutely corporeal, "a prone and speechless dialect / Such as move men" (172–4). When she speaks it is with her body, a fact, it turns out, that derives from her being as "yet unsworn" (1.4.9) and therefore, whatever her intentions, still sexually available. ("When you have vowed," Francisca tells her, "if you speak you must not show your face; / Or if you show your face, you must not speak" [10–13].) In dividing their speech from the insistent and unerring signification of their bodies, the votarists of St. Clare acquire the capacities for spiritual depth enjoyed by the male hypocrite. It is Isabella's situation at the intersection of two different relations between the body's secrets and signification, not her unconscious disclosure of repressed sexual desire, that gives rise to the double message it is so easy to detect in her pleading.

As Isabella pleads with Angelo they divide these options between them: she prescribes for Angelo a course of spiritual self-examination and cultivation of inwardness predicated on the difference between tongue and heart, a difference which he immediately perceives that she cannot contain. We would thus do well to note that the apparent justice of Angelo's analysis of his encounter with Isabella also entails a gendering of the subject that effectively deprives her of agency:

> The tempter, or the tempted, who sins most, ha?
> Not she; nor doth she tempt; but it is I
> That lying by the violet in the sun
> Do as the carrion does, not as the flower,
> Corrupt with virtuous season.   (2.2.164–8)

Confronted by Isabella's indivisible virtue, Angelo makes *himself* the author of the "prone" dialect that has moved him. For the first time, he proclaims himself to be an originating subject ("It is I") rather than the "metal" on which authority stamps its figures – a status that also makes him the site of corruption. That Isabella might be a subject – the author of discourse, the secret harbor of desire – is denied in the moment Angelo claims this status as his own. Nevertheless, he experiences this transaction as an inversion of their gendered power relations: "This virtuous maid," he claims, "subdues me quite" (185–6). It is not Isabella, however, who gains power over him at this moment, but the man from whom he has just differentiated himself.

Predictably though, Angelo's agonized desire for Isabella manifests itself not in lascivious thoughts so much as in an exploration of the division between tongue and heart that Isabella has demanded that he find in himself:

> When I would pray and think, I think and pray
> To several subjects: Heaven hath my empty words,
> Whilst my invention, hearing not my tongue,
> Anchors on Isabel: Heaven in my mouth
> As if I did but only chew his name,
> And in my heart the strong and swelling evil
> Of my conception. The state whereon I studied
> Is like a good thing being often read,
> Grown sere and tedious; yea my gravity,
> Wherein – let no man hear me – I take pride,
> Could I with boot change places for an idle plume
> Which the air beats for vain. O place, O form,
> How often dost thou with thy case, thy habit,
> Wrench awe from fools, and tie the wiser souls
> To thy false seeming! Blood thou art blood.   (2.4.1–15)

Angelo makes clear here what has been implicit all along: the homology of the confessional subject who discloses the "natural guiltiness" within his bosom and the hypocrite who conceals "strong and swelling evil" under "false seeming." Angelo's self-enclosure tightens even as he confesses to heaven, the audience, and himself the secret of "blood" that hides under false seeming. In the play's final scene Angelo will recognize the spectatorial nature of this scene of apparent secrecy, assimilating the Duke to "heaven":

> O my dread lord,
> I should be guiltier than my guiltiness
> To think I can be undiscernible
> When I perceive your Grace, like power divine,
> Hath looked upon my passes.   (5.1.364–8)

But it would distort the meaning of Angelo's subjection to anticipate this recognition, emphasizing only the irony that attends his "Let no man hear me" and the fundamentally theatrical nature of the interiority displayed in the earlier scene. As he tries and fails to pray, Angelo experiences the contradictory origin of the confessional subject, the superimposition of the hypocrite's terrible privacy on the penitent's sense of his visibility to authority. "Coin[ing] heaven's image in stamps that are forbid" (2.4.45–6), he becomes his own man even as he expands the range of "heaven's" gaze.

In his furtive self-examination before Heaven (following immediately upon the Duke's confession of Juliet) Angelo's self-division issues (so to speak) in a fantasy of feminization; his illicit desire is like Juliet's "sin," "the strong and swelling evil / Of my conception" (2.4.6–7). Angelo anxiously imagines for himself the absolute transparency to authority's gaze and subjection to its (external) constraints that Juliet's pregnancy procures for her. Later in the scene he puts the "conception" in a more functional form. Struggling to make Isabella understand his proposition – she cannot because she has "no tongue but one" (2.4.138) – he entreats her, "Plainly conceive, I love you" (140). Her reply is to the point: "My brother did love Juliet / And you tell me that he shall die for it" (141–2). Isabella can accomplish for Angelo the translation of stealth into gross writing that has associated Claudio not with the adepts of the properties of government, but with women and criminals.

Angelo's demand that Isabella "plainly conceive" explicitly pertains, of course, to interpretation rather than generation. He wants her to grasp his intent, to see the truth that lies behind his speech. To do this she must construe his words – as authority does Juliet's body – as direct and unambiguous signifiers of his sin. "Believe me, on mine honour," he implores, "My words express my purpose" (146–7). Isabella, however, immediately grasps the infinite regress that Angelo's plea sets up: "Ha? Little honour, to be much believ'd, / And most pernicious purpose! Seeming! Seeming!" (148–9). To discern Angelo's purpose is to realize that his words are the most unreliable of signifiers. And Angelo himself gives the screw a last ironic turn, reminding Isabella that it will be impossible for her to expose his "purpose" for precisely the same reason that he has had such difficulty making her "conceive" it; his "unsoil'd name" and his "place i' th'state" do not signify it.

The reversals that attend this exchange bespeak the fundamental difficulty of Angelo's position; the feminization and exposure that the "strong and swelling evil of [his] conception" is to bring about, are unavoidably inscribed within the secret difference that defines the male hypocrite. His words may express a purpose deeper than this Renaissance brother of Hawthorne's Arthur Dimmesdale can comprehend, but his "conception" remains a trick of linguistic duplicity, not a bodily fact. Even if we assume, with the Arden editor, that Angelo is describing a bodily condition, the flocking of humors, as T. Wright puts it, "by certaine secret channels to the heart," it is nevertheless, in contrast to pregnancy, a hidden one.[23] Lying deep in the bosom, the heart takes its meaning from its invisibility. But we do not need to choose between interpretations. The point is that both Angelo's "conception" and the heart that contains it hover ambiguously between bodily fact and figure of speech, promising to expose him and procure his subordination, confirming his secrecy (and with it his power) in the slippage between his purpose and the signifiers he wields. As we shall see, Iago fully grasps the ambiguities of the heart's provision of a corporeal location for a man's "purpose."

In *Measure for Measure*, the confessional subject is a gendered formation, a product of the problems of power and knowledge which haunt relations between men. The play suggests, however, that gender is determined not so much by the possession of essential male or female attributes as, quite the opposite, by the projection of experience across boundaries of sex difference. Gender emerges, we might say, from the mapping of sex, as both bodily difference and desire, onto the highly indeterminate social relations of Vienna. Thus Angelo attains a specifically masculine subjectivity, a subjectivity that depends on a capacity for stealth, in part by casting his hidden desire in terms of the transgressing, stealth-exposing bodies of women. Isabella, in contrast, becomes sexual common ground, a vehicle for men's knowledge of one another, by articulating a subjectivity formed by the doubling motions of male authority. The asymmetry that can be discerned in this formulation – Angelo *introjects* feminine transparency, while Isabella *projects* onto men the self-division she cannot contain – bespeaks the asymmetry of the gendered formations themselves.

"Be that you are, / That is, a woman," Angelo tells Isabella; "if you be more, you're none" (2.4.133–4). "If [Angelo] be less [than an arch-villain]," Isabella warns the Duke, "he's nothing; but he's more / Had I more name for badness" (5.1.61–2). Attempting to fix the essence of the other's being, Angelo and Isabella instead register the possibility that the other, and by implication their echoing selves, are fundamentally unstable entities, more or less than themselves, or even nothing at all. It is through this contingency of the characters' beings that power operates in the play. Thus in the Duke's little drama of discovery Angelo's and Isabella's imaginative cross-gendering is pushed almost to the point of public authorization. Isabella who has had "no tongue but one" (2.4.138), and is "loth" "to speak so indirectly" (4.6.1), at Friar Lodowick's behest finally "put[s] on the destin'd livery" (2.4.137) Angelo had earlier urged upon her, representing herself as a specimen of "ten times frail" (127) womanhood – a representation that, of course, reveals not her essential woman's nature but a masculine ability "to veil full purpose" (4.6.4). The paradox entailed in Isabella's putting on a condition that both she and Angelo assert is intrinsic to women, suggests the degree to which the gendering of roles depends on the alienability of gender signifiers. Not surprisingly, given a performance worthy of Nick Bottom, her representation is immediately recognized as something "put on" and therefore to be seen through, a recognition that momentarily renders Isabella a confessional subject as Escalus goes off "darkly to work with her" (5.1.277). Similarly, when Angelo is discovered as a hypocrite before the people of Vienna, his secrecy is recast as transparency to the Duke's gaze, and he is momentarily released from the duplicity of masculine subjectivity. Like Juliet's "blister'd report," his eager plea, "No longer session hold upon my shame, / But let my trial be mine own confession. / Immediate sentence, then, and sequent death, / Is all the grace I beg" (369–72), seamlessly fuses transgression to discovery and punishment, effacing any resistant interiority. Even his "confession," like Juliet's, is no more than his "shame" itself, since all has been made known without his having uttered a word.

But Isabella's and Angelo's cross-gendering is belied by their bodies' experience. The "secret" that lurks beneath Isabella's representation is no more than her indivisible integrity, the fact that she has never severed her body from her purpose by submitting to sex with Angelo. Nor has she even had a "purpose" of her own in her role-playing. And the bed-trick that maintains Isabella's integrity also preserves Angelo's status as subject, proving that his "conception" has never merged with the verifiable, punishable actions of his flesh. "His act," as Isabella argues,

> did not o'ertake his bad intent
> And must be buried but as an intent
> That perish'd by the way. Thoughts are no subjects;
> Intents, but merely thoughts.   (5.1.449–52)

"Buried," no doubt, "in wards of covert bosom," as the Duke calls the place where he holds *his* knowledge of his deputy's guilty conscience.

If the Duke claims not to heed Isabella's analysis, the denouement he contrives nevertheless enforces his deputy's status as a subject rather than his utter subjugation to sovereign power. This is accomplished not merely by withholding the rites of bodily torment, leaving Angelo to the anxiety of self-scrutiny, but also by the marriages that stand in their stead. The destined marriages are, of course, themselves a means of subjugation, establishing a hierarchy among the men through the range of chastity that Kate Keepdown, Mariana, and Isabella demarcate. But it is also one that permits the Duke at last to take his place *beside* his male subjects, his choice of bride pointedly suggesting how much he and his deputy have in common, his insistence on Isabella's sexual availability confirming Angelo's argument to her that all women are the same. Marriage thus provides a vehicle for the circulation of men's common knowledge, enabling the transfer of office that both produces masculine interiority and makes its secrets always already known. Asked whether he can cut off a man's head, Pompey replies, "If the man be a bachelor sir, I can; but if he be a married man, he's his wife's head; and I can never cut off a woman's head" (4.2.2–4). A married man, in Pompey's joke, is a hybrid creature. Bearing a man's head on a woman's body, he is at once a wielder of patriarchal authority and a feminized subordinate, a secret agent and a knowable body; the witty collapse of a man's head into a maidenhead makes male authority itself the object of male penetration.

And what, we might ask, is a married woman? Isabella's conspicuous silence affords us some indication. But we would do well to refrain from reading this silence as the signifier of the contents of her heart (of her resistance to the Duke or of her self-recognition) or even as an erasure of woman's voice. Instead, I think, it marks Isabella as a rent in the play's coherence, a site of unspeakable confusion in its discourse. There is after all no response to the Duke's proposal that would seem right, that would not discredit either her vows of chastity which make her so desirable or the Duke's entitlement to her. In other words, Isabella cannot speak because she finally embodies the undecidable relation of the Duke and the deputy. Yet, her silence is conspicuous: we hear it underneath the Duke's promise to tell us the official story, "What's yet behind that's meet you all should know" (5.5.535–6). It comes to function almost as a secret, as a residue of the unknowable that escapes the closure of the Duke's plot, and in so doing raises the spectre of a discoverable female subject.

"Noses, ears and lips . . . Confess? – Handkerchief?"

Othello insists on the possibility of the female subject, requiring Desdemona to use her rhetorical art as Isabella cannot to express her own sexual desire, allowing Emilia to announce to husbands that "their wives have sense like them, they see and smell, / And have their palates both for sweet and sour, / As husbands have" (4.3.93–6). Moreover, the implicit concession of Emilia's point by the Venetian Senate, the recognition that Desdemona had eyes and chose Othello, leads the men in the play to impute to her a "mind," a capacity for interiority and secrecy which arouses epistemic anxiety, first in her father and then in her husband. But if *Othello* conjures up the specter of the female subject it just as thoroughly lays it. Othello's wife proves to have been wholly his own; it was Othello's ensign who kept his heart secretly attending on himself. *Othello* validates the epistemic anxiety the subject provokes, an anxiety which from the beginning is linked with misogyny, as in the outburst of thwarted patriarchal authority "trust not your daughters' minds / By what you see them act" (1.1.170–1), but redirects it from women to a subordinate officer.[24] In the process Desdemona is both literally and figuratively emptied of life, rendered as cold and unproblematic as her chastity, while, in what Thomas Rymer pointed out was a highly indecorous end for a tragic villain, Iago is kept alive for questioning.[25] Conversely, Shakespeare's rewriting of the story also involves a diversion of Iago's animus; in Cinthio's tale it is Disdemona, not the Moor, whom the ensign seeks to destroy.

In *Othello*, Shakespeare and his surrogate plotter, Iago, exploit misogyny, its anxious ways of knowing and representing female otherness, in order to reproduce the supervisory gaze which (like power divine in *Measure for Measure*) controls the relations in the chain of command as a site of chronic epistemic lack. Such a strategy is enabled by the fact that misogyny is itself already an expression of the anxiety which circulates through a system of male relations that uses women to establish male identities and make them available to knowledge. Iago might be said to put into play the possibility that all wives are common property on which the Duke's final knowledge of his male subjects depends. He thus makes Othello's access to the minds of his subordinate officers contingent on his wife's infidelity, and, conversely, her absolute chastity finally the sign of the incomprehensible malice and therefore the radical unknowability of his ensign.

Like *Measure for Measure*, *Othello* raises what seem to be essentially philosophical issues – in this case the problem of "other minds," the nature of evidence, the necessity and danger of faith in others – in a manner that at once universalizes them and indicates their specificity to men's positions in a particular order of government. But this order is not exactly the same in both plays; the difference between Angelo's subjugated transparency and Iago's opaque, resilient self-interest is a result not just of a return of the repressed but of a re-imagining of the political world which ensures this return and amplifies its effects. Where Shakespeare's Vienna is an absolutist state centralizing power through skillful harnessing of spiritual and secular techniques of discipline, his Venice is a military enterprise in support of a commercial one, thriving on the circulation of men throughout the Mediterranean world. The styles of empire the two cities represent are obviously both relevant to Shakespeare's England; historically, versions of them occupied the same geographic location, each to some extent the condition for producing the other. What is significant for our purposes, however, is the way in which, at least at the level of the imagination, "Venice" also potentially jeopardizes "Vienna" by revealing it as an atavistic fantasy. Marc Shell has argued provocatively that the world of *Measure for Measure* is fundamentally incestuous, that the play, assisted by its Catholic costuming which makes the Duke a universal father and Isabella a universal sister, is embedded in a Christian notion of the community of believers as family. This idea is given a peculiar literalness in the oft-invoked common "blood" which also denotes the ineluctability of the sexual order, rendering every coupling, to use Isabella's words, "a kind of incest."[26] Shell's formulation usefully points to the pre-emptive quality we have noted in the Duke's knowledge of his subjects, which depends not on method or opportunity but on his being one with them at the level of the body. In the contemporaneous play about miscegenation, the ambiguous zone between one man and another, so narrow and so strictly policed in *Measure for Measure*, is enlarged and marked by cultural and racial heterogeneity. This enlargement means that the issue of evidence, of how to use signs to negotiate this zone (an issue elided in *Measure for Measure* through the divine ubiquity of the Duke's gaze), takes on a deadly urgency in *Othello*.[27] And insofar as *Othello*, as much as *Measure for Measure,* makes that zone women's place, the problem of evidence appears for a time as a problem of how to read a woman.[28]

A good place to begin an account of the relations between men in the play is Iago's notoriously too-prolix motive-hunting, in which he claims that he hates Othello because he has preferred Cassio as his lieutenant, but also because "it is thought abroad, that 'twixt my sheets / He's done my office" (1.3.384–6), or, as he puts it later, because "the lustful Moor / Hath leap'd into my seat" (2.1.290–1), adding this time, "I do love [Desdemona] too" (286), and "I fear Cassio with my nightcap too" (302) – a fellow who, just to keep things reciprocal, he obscurely damns with a fair wife. Iago's enumerations of his grievances, in which the professional slight slides into a fantasy of universal cuckoldry, indicates an alarming slippage in the play between marital and military orders – a condition which the play underscores when Othello, hearing Desdemona speak of "the love I bear to Cassio" (4.1.228), explodes "Fire and brimstone" (229), and Lodovico ascribes his anger to the letter from Venice "deputing Cassio in his government" (232).[29] What makes this slippage between cuckolding and military rotations so alarming is not merely the imaginative threat which military place changing poses to marital exclusivity, but also the way in which marital exclusivity exposes the exchangeability of men on which the military depends as a state of ontological free-fall, a deprivation of fixed status and therefore of identity. Iago's motives represent the consciousness of the career officer: he fears that he is always being replaced by and believes that he can replace the other men in the hierarchy.[30]

It is a fear that the play itself helps to validate. If Iago professes himself a consummate actor, one of those "Who, trimm'd in forms, and visages of duty, / Keep yet their hearts attending on themselves" (1.1.50–1) he in fact does his damage through the ease with which his own state of mind seems to communicate itself to others. It is Iago, after all, who first imagines himself a cuckold and notes "I know not if't be true . . . / Yet I, for mere suspicion in that kind, / Will do, as if for surety" (1.3.386–8), straight away "engender[ing]" the plot that will bring Othello to declare that "to be once in doubt / Is once to be resolv'd" (3.3.183–4).[31] Iago's uncanny success in inducing Othello to replicate his suspicions has to do with the reflexive relation between such replication and the content of the suspicions themselves, which is simply the fear that another man is taking one's place. Thus the point here is not that Iago, rather than Othello, is the origin of these anxieties, but that they are by their very nature without any particular psychic proprietor. Even Cassio, with no prompting from Iago, frets about what will happen, "I being absent, and my place supplied" (3.3.17). Changing places with another may be Iago's technique for subversion, but it is also the condition of service to the Venetian state, as Iago reveals in his representation of his secret difference which simultaneously proclaims his identity with his superior: "in following [Othello] I follow but myself" (1.1.58).

Yet the ability of men in the Venetian army to stand in for one another is obviously complicated by Othello's racial difference, a difference that serves to enforce the discontinuity both between the men in the ranks and their supreme commander and between the commander and the Venetian oligarchy he serves.[32] But the Moor at the head of the Venetian forces is also the most telling sign of the dependence of the professional "gradation" on exchangeability. Although the play signals the fact only obliquely, Othello is, of course, a mercenary, "a knave of common hire"

(1.1.125), like the gondolier who carries Desdemona to him, paid to defend the trade routes of a mercantilist city-state. As both a party to, and a function of Venetian commerce, he is its epitome, as Roderigo's description of him as an "extravagant and wheeling stranger / Of here and everywhere" (1.1.136–7) attests. Othello's generalship reveals that the professional hierarchy he heads is constructed through a system of exchange that makes disparate things equivalent, a fact that differentiates that "gradation" from patriarchy and oligarchy which are maintained naturally (as it were) by blood. This difference underlies Iago's complaints about Cassio's promotion, which oscillate between arguments based on exchange value and nostalgic attempts to assimilate professional advancement to traditional patriarchal transmissions of authority. He tells Roderigo, "I know my price; I am worth no worse a place" (1.1.11), yet laments the "old gradation" in which "each second / Stood heir to the first" (37–8). But if these perceptions seem to contradict each other they are also mutually enabling. It is Iago's racist, misogynist attachment to "natural" order, evident in his ability to reduce "others" to predictable traits as in "these Moors are changeable in their wills" (1.3.347–8), or "She must have change" (352), that permits him the machiavel's perception that the hierarchy in which he operates is artificial and therefore that he need not remain where he has been "placed." Thus "price" is not only a mechanism for making horizontal equivalences (noble Moor = Venetian general, Florentine "arithmetician" = Venetian lieutenant) but also for making vertical ones, such as ensign = lieutenant.

However, it is not only around Iago that we can detect uneasiness about the relation between what might be called trading and tribal relationships. The mercenary foundation of Othello's position remains largely subtextual, hinted at only in Iago's and Roderigo's outbursts of nativist resentment, because it has been mystified through transactions occurring before the play begins. Unlike Shylock, for instance, who tells Bassanio, "I will buy with you, sell with you, talk with you, walk with you, and so following; but I will not eat with you, drink with you nor pray with you" (*Merchant of Venice*, 1.3.30–4), Othello has permitted mercenary exchange to merge into assimilation, first through acceptance of Brabantio's love and invitations and then through marriage with his daughter.[33] The play suggests that there is a cultural imperative at work in this process (Jessica's marriage and Shylock's forced conversion at the end of *The Merchant of Venice* confirm this), that trading relationships must be reconstructed as tribal bonds if the former are to be brought securely under the state's control. Thus when Brabantio protests his daughter's marriage to his "brothers of the state" (1.3.96) the conflict is represented as one, not between patriarchal authority and the state's need for Othello's services (although we must see that this is the issue), but between atavistic and enlightened versions of patriarchal authority, in other words, between constructions of Othello as an "erring barbarian" and as a likely and desirable son-in-law for a Venetian nobleman. (The scene's conflation of state and familial matters which requires that the Duke speak of "Desdemona, as he were her own natural father," puts Rymer, that infallible barometer of ideological strain, beside himself.)[34] In Othello's case, monetary exchange does not so much establish equivalences between things different in kind as beget other transactions that purport to efface difference. Thus Othello's blackness, that apparently unambiguous signifier of otherness, can come and go; Roderigo, whom Iago instructs on the price of men, sees Othello as "the thicklips" (1.1.67), while the Duke, seeking to bind Othello to Venetian interests, finds him "far more fair than black" (1.3.290). In the world of Venice, marriage does not merely mark a realm of private property, opposed but also conceptually vulnerable to military place changing. It also works both to delimit and, at least in Othello's case, promise passage to a tribal "inside," the significance of which is both social and epistemic, a zone of privilege, and more importantly a domain where relationship is achieved without a system of exchange or the anxious reading of signs.[35]

The capacity of Othello's marriage to promise access to this inside zone accounts for a peculiar implication of both the Duke's idealized and Brabantio's enraged accounts of this relationship: that Desdemona is not primarily a body to be advantageously disposed of or controlled, but a "soul" or a "mind" to be known. In the case of the Duke this construction clearly serves his political purpose; the disembodied symmetry of a courtship conducted through "such fair question / As soul to soul affordeth" (1.3.113–14) suppresses the scene of miscegenation that Iago's account of "an old black ram / . . . tupping [a] white ewe" (1.1.88–9) luridly conjures up, effacing the difference that the marriage actually serves to mediate. But the fact that the defeated father follows the Duke in construing the locus of his daughter's revolt as her mind suggests that this essence, which he has discovered to his dismay is not seen, is not so much a metaphor for the social inside of the Venetian oligarchy as a hypostatization of its loss. Desdemona's escape to "the gross clasps of a lascivious Moor" (126), means that what Iago styles "half [Brabantio's] soul" (87) has proved as contingently related to him as his money bags. Having made Desdemona a marker of the inside, patriarchal authority (an interest that includes Othello and the Duke as well as Brabantio) discovers she has taken it with her when she went. Desdemona's mind, as an object of epistemic anxiety, emerges (together with her body as the subject of pornographic representation) when she slips, as she must, from an essential to a contingent relationship to her tribe.

The contradiction between the transactions which construct the Venetian polity and the imaginary intimacy of the inside registers constantly in the language of the play, furnishing the rhetorical resources for Iago's assault against "Othello's occupation." Consider, for example, the way in which, in this world where men have prices and the state is served by hirelings, money is repeatedly invoked as a detachable attribute of self: in Roderigo's purse which he has shared with Iago, in the "bags" (1.1.80) that Iago suggests have been stolen along with Desdemona, in the "purse / Full of crusadoes" (3.4.21–2) that Desdemona says she would rather have lost than her handkerchief, in the purse that is "trash" compared to a good name. In these instances, particularly the last two, the invocation of money is accompanied by disavowal, an assertion of its negative valuation compared to some more precious attribute, such as a daughter, a token from a lover, or a name. Iago's famous sententia makes the point explicitly:

> Good name in man and woman's dear, my lord;
> Is the immediate jewel of our souls:
> Who steals my purse, steals trash, 'tis something, nothing,
> 'Twas mine, 'tis his, and has been slave to thousands:
> But he that filches from me my good name
> Robs me of that which not enriches him
> And makes me poor indeed.   (3.3.159–65)

Iago does more than suggest to Othello that he is being deprived of his name; he uses attributes of the self – a name and a purse – to model different kinds of relationship, and in so doing presses on the contradictions of Othello's position. If one of the suggestions loaded into this burdened utterance is that Desdemona could circulate like a purse of money, it also insists to the "extravagant and wheeling stranger of here and everywhere" that his wife, daughter of the Venetian oligarchy, called "jewel" (1.3.195) by her father as he reluctantly cedes her to her husband, represents the "immediate."

Iago's disquisition on the good name indicates the way in which the epistemic problem he presents to Othello is in fact a problem of social position. In particular it suggests the significance which metonymy and synecdoche, which might be called the tropes of contingent and intrinsic relation, come to bear in a world where so much depends on the difference between mercenary exchange and communion "soul to soul."[36] The language of *Othello* is cluttered with objects and body parts

– the name, Iago's heart, Brabantio's bags, Desdemona's hand and, especially, her handkerchief – which are offered, mostly by Iago but also by others, to stand for people and functions, and for unseen essences such as Desdemona's honor and Iago's thoughts. The capacity of metonymy and synecdoche to do this last trick, to represent in a particularly concrete way the absent or the invisible, makes them figures of evidence as well as relationship. Their structure is that of the clue – of Iago's "imputation and strong circumstances which lead directly to the door of truth" (3.3.412–13). This point is nicely illustrated in the Dell's Case chapbooks discussed in chapter 2, in which the dead boy's green coat identifies him, and the girl's tongueless mouth stands for "that within [which] bids [her] tell truth." What this example also indicates, however, is an implicit hierarchy of tropes; synecdoche, particularly of the body, insofar as it delivers "immediate" access to the thing it represents, seems to promise access to unseen essences – things whose nature is to elude mediation – which metonymy can only gesture at. Hence the centrality of corporeal synecdoche to *Measure for Measure*, in which blood, tongues, hearts, men's heads, and maidenheads stand for men and women, enabling a dispersal and exchange of being itself which reconstructs both bodies and the body politic, knitting them together so that interiors are always already penetrated.

When compared with this powerful trope, metonymy comes to figure the substitution or displacement involved in any act of representation, the discontinuity between an attribute and its possessor rather than the essence of the possessor himself. Such invidious comparison underlies Iago's pronouncements on the difference between a purse and a name, as well as Desdemona's preference for the handkerchief over the purse full of crusadoes. But of course, properly speaking, there are no synecdoches here at all; these examples in fact reveal that the synecdochic status of the handkerchief or the name is constructed through the comparison with the purse. And what is constructed can be deconstructed, as Iago makes clear; the name may be the immediate jewel of our soul, while money, endlessly exchangeable, can hardly be said to belong to us at all, but each is subject to filching. The message is hard to miss; Desdemona may be a part of her husband, but, having married him, she has already started to circulate. Othello's tribal relation to Venice becomes once more a trading one. Not surprisingly then, when Othello finds Desdemona "gone," his racial difference, effaced by communion soul to soul with the daughter of the Venetian oligarchy, reappears in his name. "My name" he laments, "that was as fresh / As Dian's visage, is now begrim'd, and black / As mine own face" (3.3.392–4).

Like Othello in his relation to Venice, the most important representational objects invoked in *Othello* in fact show a propensity to move up and down a continuum of relationships defined by monetary metonymy at one end and corporeal synecdoche at the other – movement produced by continual gestures of comparison. Thus the handkerchief, which in Desdemona's speech is the synecdochic term she opposes to her purse, is, in Iago's fateful suggestion to Othello, the metonymic term he juxtaposes to that most intimate of possessions, "her honour . . . an essence that's not seen" (4.1.16). And when Othello, having realized that the hand-kerchief can circulate, interrogates Desdemona about its whereabouts, he tries desperately to assimilate it to corporeal synecdoche, instructing Desdemona to "make it a darling, like your precious eye" (3.4.64) (an admonition which conflates his fantasy of connection to Desdemona and Venice with his compensatory strategy of vigilant looking) and informing her that "it was dyed in mummy, which the skilful / Conserve of maiden hearts" (72–3). Literally imbued with the body's hidden substances, the handkerchief promises to deliver unseen essences into the possession of an other; it was, after all, the gift of a "charmer" who "could almost read / The thoughts of people" (55–6). But "almost" is, of course, the key word here, signaling an irreducible difference of "thoughts" from the body which can, with skill, be conserved and merged with an object which another can possess.[37] In the handkerchief, corporal synecdoche collapses into metonymy; the body itself proves merely incidental to the psychic interiority it is called upon to signify. The result is epistemic breakdown, a welter of ownerless body parts, dubious circumstantial and confessional "proofs" and metaphysical essences that Othello invokes as he himself goes to pieces: "Pish! Noses, ears and lips. Is't possible? – Confess –Handkerchief? – O devil!" (4.1.42–3).

As Desdemona's innocent participation in producing the handkerch-ief's ambivalence would indicate, the capacity of objects to embody both epistemic hope and futility, to offer and withhold access to a possessor, is the effect not of a particular character's thinking but of the world of the play. But as Peter Stallybrass has noted, it is a feature of *Othello* that Iago is made to function as the origin of meanings which in fact arise from the play's larger discourse.[38] As we see Iago supplementing and organizing tropological instabilities, manipulating them to devastating effect, the contradictions of the Venetian state are reified as his intent. But the point here is not merely that Iago is a scapegoat, a lower-class man made to speak the thoughts about Desdemona that other members of the Venetian polity must disallow, but rather that in using him this way the play makes his intent rather than Desdemona's honor the legitimate object of scrutiny. Thus Iago's construction of Desdemona's honor as a problem of evidence is inextricable from his grafting of her subjecthood to his own, a task he accomplishes by spinning out the metonymic/synecdochic web. When Desdemona's handkerchief, a trifling possession but dyed in conserve of maiden's hearts, comes to occupy the maddening boundary marked by "almost" it joins Iago's heart which he has already situated there, its inaccessibility to all but himself proclaimed in the same moment he imagines that it could be worn on a sleeve like a token or a sign. The epistemic implications of this maneuver, in which the same object is made to furnish hope and frustration, emerge full force when Othello demands "By heaven I'll know thy thought," and Iago replies, "You cannot, if my heart were in your hand, / Nor shall not while 'tis in my custody" (3.3.166–8). The heart, a mere body part, could never yield access to thoughts – and yet it might were it to leave Iago's custody.

In the simultaneous promise and frustration of access to unseen essences that Iago loads onto his heart and Desdemona's handkerchief we seem to encounter once more the impasse marked by the tortured body, in which the attempt to make the body yield the soul's truth only confirms that truth's inaccessibility – the impasse which translates questions of loyalty into fierce encounters with the autonomy of the subject.[39] Desdemona, constructed as a soul to be known and body which circulates, is sacrificed to this dilemma. But Iago goes beyond insinuating that he and Desdemona pose analogous problems for the would-be discoverer, superimposing the slippage between metonymy and synecdoche, or, in other words, between contingent and intimate relation, onto the social categories of wife and subordinate officer. In Iago's insinuations Desdemona stands for an essence that Iago himself will deliver. Woman's honor, Iago insists, is the ultimate object of epistemic desire; behind the door of truth lies Desdemona "topp'd." But he immediately displaces this scene with one that undermines, even as it purports to enforce the feminine location of truth: Iago topp'd, lying with Cassio, who, he reports, would in his sleep "kiss me hard / As if he pluck'd up kisses by the roots" (3.3.428–9). Here Iago is supposed to be a stand-in for Desdemona, the scene "denot[ing] a foregone conclusion" (434) rather than revealing truth's inner sanctum. And yet it also signifies the intimacy of men, Cassio's looseness of soul with his bedfellow representing the looseness that Iago also claims to be guilty of at this moment, as "prick'd to't by foolish honesty and love" (418) he spills the story to Othello. Constructed through a chain of representational displacements, the scene nevertheless proclaims the bond between men in the professional hierarchy as the site of unmediated knowledge, of access to soul. It is this promise which Iago holds out when in the exchange of vows with which this scene concludes, he offers up "his wit, hand, heart" to Othello and declares, "I am your own forever" (486).

Iago's deployment of homoerotic scenes at these crucial moments indicates that his *modus operandi* is not simply the voicing of the crassest ideological and epistemic assumptions of his social world, but the supplanting of the visions those assumptions produce, with the ones they are intended to repress, visions of the work male heterosexual desire and its concomitant misogyny actually perform. Thus if Iago's ostensible message is that Desdemona is sleeping with Cassio, what he pictures for Othello is the effect of that fantasy, the reframing of the chain of command as an unconscious, upwelling chain of confession. Like Lucio's joking, the tableaux of male intimacy Iago offers reframe the professional gradation, in which exchangeability is the first rule of identity, as a *gender* category whose homogeneity affords perfect knowledge, and in whose name Othello murders Desdemona "else she'll betray more men" (5.2.6). This fellowship, formed through the exchange of Desdemona, but also, more importantly, through her subsequent elimination, is not the same as the Venetian oligarchy, an inside always haunted by an implicit outside, but a potentially boundless utopia of masculine immediacy. Nor is it the same as the brotherhood of Mistress Overdone's patrons, Iago's remodeling of homosocial bonds as homoerotic scenes promising an intimacy beyond common knowledge. Thus, once Othello has resolved to kill Desdemona and Iago has made himself his general's "own forever," Othello encounters Desdemona (who represented him so splendidly to the Senate) as a blank, "fair paper made to write 'whore' upon" (4.2.73) but not, apparently, a page on which he can read the word, a surface "whiter . . . than snow, / And smooth as monumental alabaster" (5.2.4–5) which he declines to mark.

The fantasy of male intimacy which Iago promulgates to Othello, a fantasy which I have been suggesting is based on the governmental order within which men operate, is, of course, a deadly delusion. Desdemona will have scarcely been stifled before Iago is revealed to be "a demi-devil" whose reasons for "ensnar[ing Othello's] soul and body" (5.2.302–3) will forever elude ordinary moral natures. But the revelation of Iago's enmity cannot be styled a discovery of the truth in any simple sense, for the perfect knowledge he offers Othello and the utter unintelligibility he finally achieves for himself are alike in promising escape from the epistemic regime in which women make men known to each other, constituting "property" and making it susceptible to transfer. Iago ultimately embodies both a sameness and a difference so absolute that it defeats mediation and can only be imagined as pure metaphysical essence. In fact, the play's final construction of Iago as an impenetrable mystery bears an extraordinary similarity to the process of discovery and enclosure the Jesuit victims underwent in the Elizabethan torture chamber. Like Campion and Cottam, Iago "part confess[es]" (297) before admonishing his captors that from this time forth he never will speak word. His secrets (again, like Campion's) have been opened metonymically in the letters found in Roderigo's pockets, and his unwitting collaborator, Emilia, has informed on him. But this plenitude of evidence, like his overabundant recounting of his motives, only serves to indicate that his mystery will remain forever out of reach. Iago ends as the subject under discovery, sharing with the Elizabethan Jesuits a capacity to defeat the epistemic regime that constructs him.

In the case of *Othello*, however, this regime is not simply the epistemic structure of discovery itself, which posits an oppositional relationship between the discoverer and the secret even when the discoverer fears that the secret may be harbored within something that looks like himself. What produces Iago is normal administrative activity of the kind we see Lodovico engaging in as he commands that the loaded bed be hid, arranges for the succession of "the fortunes of the Moor" to Desdemona's uncle, Gratiano, installs Cassio in Othello's post, exhorting him to torture Iago, and dispatches himself back to Venice to relate the events in Cyprus to the senate. A crisis has occurred but what we see here is maintenance, accomplished through men stepping into each other's places, connecting the margin of the Venetian state to its center, ensuring that its laws are enforced. If Iago is figured at this moment as a pure excess of evil, "more fell than anguish, hunger, or the sea" (363), all he has done is to suggest to Othello that something like this scene would happen, that Othello would lose his occupation and Cassio step into his place. Iago is, we might say, the unconscious of the proto-bureaucratic state, not an ambitious state servant so much as an embodiment of the truth the state and its agents must repress: that its foundation is a radical absence of identity, and, therefore, that the men who operate on its behalf are unknowable.

Southwell's secret and Bellamy's body

I began this chapter by insisting on the relative autonomy of the discourse of discovery as it emerged on the Jacobean stage, and around the resort to torture. Iago may embody the same epistemic impasse as Edmund Campion but the institutional implications of his story are different, in part because the drama was subject to different pressures and had different agendas than martyrological and legal writing. And yet my readings of both *Measure for Measure* and *Othello* presume the connection of these plays to larger ideological, institutional, and epistemic configurations, particularly the burgeoning of an administrative state and a sex/gender system that makes women a means through which men establish relationships with one another. The work the plays do is to place the discovery of the subject in these contexts. What is omitted in the trajectory of my argument are connections between both administrative culture and the sex/gender system, and the situations and discourses that surrounded the Elizabethan resort to torture. This is in part because the discourses of torture do not invite such connections. But I want to conclude by closing the loop with a brief re-viewing of the scenario of torture through the lens provided by Shakespeare's plays, a procedure that brings into relief features of the situation which are hardly noticeable as long as inquiry is framed in terms of the abstract oppositions – secrecy and discovery, truth and treason, body and soul – which torture produces.

Torture was a method of repression visited by the Crown on its perceived enemies, a technique by which "authority" sought to master its "others"; Shakespeare makes that "other" an instrument of authority itself, a deputy or officer of the state.[40] And yet no representatives of the Crown seem to have actually found themselves on the rack. In what way then, might the victims of torture be said to have been insiders of the regime which inflicted their sufferings? In the case of the "Egyptians" (i.e., gypsies) tortured in 1596 the answer would seem to be no way at all. However, the missionary priests, who formed the single largest group of victims and who most fully articulated their resistance, present a more complicated case insofar as their very identity as Catholic priests meant that they had no visible place in the social order at the same time that their education and connections permitted them to pass among the elite. John Bossy has argued that the priests generated class tensions within the English Catholic community because although they were "clerks first and last" (men of non-gentle families educated by the church) their constant disguising as gentlemen led them to pretensions to gentility.[41] Nor was this nervousness around the priests' status confined to Catholic nobility and gentry. So obsessed was Crown counsel with Campion's gentlemanly disguise that Campion was obliged to point out that wearing "a velvet hat and a feather, a buff leather jerkin, [and] velvet venetians" was not in itself an act of treason, nor was he "indicted upon the statute of Apparel," a retort which recognizes the way in which fears about specific concealed identities could fuse with more general anxieties about social place-changing.[42]

The discursive slide here into the ubiquitous Elizabethan concern with maintaining social legibility indicates that the problem posed by the disguised priests was more complicated than is suggested by Bossy's assertion that these men were "clerks first and last," that is, pre-Reformation identities stranded in a post-Reformation society. For one thing, it would appear that in some cases priestly claims to gentility could be based on birth; of the 134 victims of the Elizabethan persecutions listed in Richard Challoner's *Complete Modern British Martyrology* at least a quarter seem to have been "born of a gentleman's family."[43] Robert Parsons was the son of a blacksmith and Edmund Campion the son of a London bookseller, but John Gerard and Thomas Cottam were both sons of gentlemen. Robert Southwell, whose father was the illegitimate son of Sir Richard Southwell who oversaw the dissolution of the monasteries for Henry VIII, was the second cousin of both Francis Bacon and Robert Cecil.[44] More importantly though, no matter what their background, these men, as much as Francis Bacon or for that matter Edmund Spenser, were products of the Elizabethan world with its vastly expanded and secularized educational system intended, in part, to produce men qualified to participate in the royal administration. Edmund Campion, for instance, seems to have been employed before his conversion by the Earl of Leicester.[45] If the priests seemed to trouble class boundaries it was not because they belonged to one category while masquerading as members of another, but because, at the same time that they needed to hide their priestly identities, they belonged, as educated men from lesser gentry, mercantile, or artisanal backgrounds, to a class which itself notoriously destabilized social distinctions in the period, a class whose emergence was tied to the expanding administrative apparatus of early modern England.[46]

To be sure, an education that fitted one for service to the Crown is not the same thing as a career in that line. Clearly these men derived their identity from choosing an oppositional path, offering their allegiance to another authority. Still, some Jesuits seem to have considered themselves councilors in exile. Robert Persons, for example, wrote detailed proposals for legal and administrative reforms of English government, some of which anticipate common law developments.[47] More generally, the propaganda campaign the Jesuits mounted against the government, challenging the legality as well as the morality of its actions, indicates an ability to negotiate discourses of state that testifies to their intellectual membership in an English governing class. But the point to be made here has less to do with whether to situate the priests inside or outside the regime than with the fact that the English state was founded not just on hereditary entitlements and stunning displays of glory and violence, but also on the dissemination of knowledge and skill, and that this fact makes it difficult to draw the line between inside and out. If the priests possessed an authority which threatened the English state such authority was not so much conferred on them by the Roman Church as transferred to it by these men.

What the priests (and possibly other victims of torture) share with characters like Angelo and Iago, then, is a capacity for agency that is a necessary concomitant of the emergence of a administrative state which must rely on the knowledge and abilities of many men in order to extend the range of its control. In making this dangerous agent the state's own employee rather than its avowed opponent, Shakespeare makes available the connection between the subversive autonomy of the subject (which the Elizabethan practice of torture insisted on) and the structure of the state. But if there is a certain deconstructive force in Shakespeare's rendering of the discovery of the subject, locating as it does the state's outside inside, we also need to acknowledge what gets lost in the translation it performs: the possibility that resistance might be ideological as well as epistemic, that a man might use his autonomy to follow not himself, as Iago does, but different principles and institutions.

It is a more difficult matter to make links between the English resort to torture and the sex/gender issues the plays raise. The very connection sketched above between the use of torture and the expansion of educational and administrative systems works to exclude women from the scene. This is not to say, of course, that women did not find themselves in opposition to authorities. But the records of the two episodes in which women were subjected to state torture, while constructing the victims as heroic, do not frame them as harborers of secrets. Robert Southwell's account of Margaret Ward, a woman who had been tortured and executed for having supplied an imprisoned priest with a rope, presents her as a martyr but insists on the anomaly of her situation: "A maiden among a thousand, in whose frail sex shone a courage hard to parallel . . . She had been flogged and hung up by the wrists, the tips of her toes only touching the ground so that she was now crippled and half-paralyzed; but the tortures had only served to strengthen this most shining martyr for her last struggle."[48] The other woman to be tortured was Anne Askew, ardently Protestant associate of Catherine Parr, who was interrogated on the rack about the religious affinities of Catherine and her associates. The record of this event is her own account of her interrogations which were published after she was burnt for heresy in 1546.[49] At issue throughout are doctrine and authority. She is rebuked for violating Paul's prohibition on women preaching. "I answered him," she replies, "that I knew Paul's meaning so well as he . . . and asked him, how many women he had seen, go into the pulpit and preach" (155). Questioned as to "if the host should fall, and beast did eat it, whether the beast did receive God or no" (158), she responds by inviting the bishop to answer his own question. At this point the bishop protests that "it was against the order of schools, that he which asked the question, should answer it" (158). "I told him," she goes on "I was but a woman, & knew not the course of schools" (158). Gender is an explicit concern on both sides, linked to Askew's ability to control and resist her interrogation. But what is interesting about her account for our purposes is the absence of the discourse of secrecy and discovery that is so marked a feature of the Jesuit interrogations. She is racked for information about Protestant courtiers and her torture is prolonged because "she lay still and did not cry" (224), but what she calls attention to is simply her resistance to their force, not a conscience whose privacy she defends.[50]

Witchcraft accusations furnish more numerous instances of women placed under interrogation, sometimes in circumstances that verged on torture.[51] Moreover, witchcraft was construed as an epistemic problem generating debates about what properly constituted evidence of the crime and whether the crime could in fact occur.[52] Nevertheless, the prosecution of witchcraft does not seem to have made the witch *as subject* the focus of epistemic concern. For one thing the witch's body, which supposedly bore a mark which if pricked felt no pain, proffered evidence of her crime that the witch herself had no power to hide, much as Juliet's body "blister[s] her report."[53] For another, the nature of the crime itself, which increasingly was construed as a pact with the devil, meant that the witch was merely a vehicle through which a greater power acts rather than the origin of the evil she does. Even where witchcraft was dealt with as a problem of knowledge, the witch does not seem to have been made the possessor of secret truths. John Cotta, for example, connects the evidentiary problems posed by witchcraft to a true understanding of the crime itself, which he claims is actually a satanically induced delusion – citing the case of a witch who thought she was flying through the air but all the while could be seen to be lying in her bed. If this account locates witchcraft in the mind, its truth is already in the possession of the discoverer.[54]

The way in which the witch's mark differentiates the discovery of witchcraft from that of treason suggests that the secret-harboring subject may have been a deeply rather than accidentally gendered formation in juridical discourse as well as on the stage. The story of Ann Bellamy, the woman who betrayed Southwell to the pursuivants, provides more leverage for a gendered reading of the discovery of the subject. The eldest daughter of a Catholic gentleman, Bellamy was arrested during a crackdown against recusants in the winter of 1592. In prison she was raped by the arch-rackmaster and priest-hunter Richard Topcliffe, and was found after three months' imprisonment, in the words of another Catholic, "in most dishonest disorder," that is, pregnant. Apparently on a promise from Topcliffe that none of her family would be harmed, she agreed to lure Southwell to their house, where he was arrested. Ann was then married off to Topcliffe's loyal servant, Nicholas Jones, according to Southwell's biographer "in church and with the blessing of her parents," thereby providing her husband (a weaver's son) with a country-house.[55] Ann's mother subsequently died in prison. Southwell was tortured relentlessly before his execution. His cousin, Robert Cecil, who was present at some of the interrogations is said in a contemporary Catholic report to have remarked that

> we have a new torture which it is not possible for a man to bear. And yet I have seen Robert Southwell hanging by it, still as a tree-trunk, and no one able to drag one word from his mouth.[56]

The conjunction of Bellamy's fate and Southwell's suggests a complex interdependence between the construction of gender and of the epistemically resistant subject. Like Tamyra on the rack in *Bussy d'Ambois*, Bellamy is placed at a nightmarish intersection of two different realms of discourse and experience: the patriarchal construction of the woman as bride, bearer of children, and vehicle for the transmission of property; and the repression and resistance of the dissenting subject in the early modern state. At the point of her arrest, she is both a marriageable gentlewoman and, as much as Southwell, a potential martyr and guardian of secrets. By the end of the story, however, the layers of her situation have been separated and concretized as two bodies, Bellamy's "in most dishonest disorder" sexualized, violated, but finally the legitimate property of her torturer, and Southwell's brutalized but unmoved, "still as a tree-trunk," sealing the freedom of his conscience. What is striking about this outcome is the alignment it produces between Bellamy's specifically female fate and the spilling of information. Her rape and pregnancy preclude her martyrdom, in part because they defile her, but more importantly because they construct her as a woman, a body which swells and opens without her volition, a means through which boundaries can be breached and things transmitted: land, blood, and, alas, secrets.[57] But Bellamy's openness also helps to produce Southwell's secrecy; she makes his person available to the authorities, only so that they will discover he possesses a truth no woman, and no body, will ever deliver.

Shakespeare may not have been starting from scratch, then, in connecting the epistemic crisis of the subject to marriage plots. But the point I would make is not that Ann Bellamy's story indicates the availability of the connection in recent history – her story is unusual and in it the marriage plot merely crosses the path, as it were, of the discovery of the subject. Rather, it reveals a deep ideological and epistemic current

which propels *Measure for Measure* and *Othello*, the feminine gendering
of representation, of the means for making things known. Specifically,
what all these "texts" reveal is a wholly naturalized connection between
women's inescapable sexual conscription and *plotting*, in the sense of
mapping, locating, manifesting relationship. This connection dictates the
fates of the female characters in the plays. It also suggests why on the
Jacobean stage marriage could substitute for, and in fact surpass, torture
as a means for discovering the subject.

4 Authors and others

I have shotte at many abuses, over shotte myselfe in describing of some;
where truth failed, my invention hath stood my friend.

Greene's Vision, 1592

The subject has occupied mostly a subjugated position in my discussions
of Elizabethan torture and of Shakespeare's plays. The locus of powerful
truth, the subject nevertheless emerges in my account as the object of the
discovering operations of the Elizabethan or Viennese or Venetian states.
What such a formulation tends to leave out, of course, is an account of
the position of the discoverers themselves as subjects, of the way in which
finding and claiming an external truth, as well as withholding or speaking
an internal one, produces an authoritative subject. I have stressed the
epistemic and political oppositions of discoverer and internalized subject
up to this point in order to make clear the way in which discovery
constructs truth as otherness, occluding the discoverer as an original site
of truth, or possible object of knowledge. But we have also seen that the
discovered and the discoverers show sometimes scandalous, sometimes
uncanny affinities with one another. The torturers' secret iniquities
become the object of Jesuitical discoveries; the Duke discloses in himself
the vicious desires he has discovered in Angelo; the impenetrable Iago
understands and controls Othello's and the Venetian state's appetite for
discovery. Thus the discovering subject implicit in my discussion up to
this point is characterized by an objectivity that folds ambiguously into
subjecthood, a primary emptiness that with a shift of perspective
becomes a rich secrecy. Within a fundamentally asymmetrical relationship arise hints of the symmetry of reversal.

In the previous chapter, I argued that this affinity of the discoverer
with the discovered was to some degree a socio-political as well as a moral
reality. Insofar as the discovery of the subject was a practice of a
developing administrative state, it could also be seen as an anxious
response to the dispersal of authority endemic to such a system, hence the
surprising frequency with which the discovered were (or, in the case of the

plays, were imagined to be) relatively elite men rather than members of
clearly subordinated social groups. The development of an administrative
state also helped to define the position of the figure who will be the focus
of this chapter, Thomas Harman, the Kentish gentleman and sometime
Justice of the Peace who in 1566 published the conycatching classic, *A
Caveat for Common Cursitors*. Ostensibly written to assist "Justices and
shrieves . . . constables, bailiffs and borsholders" in the control of
vagrancy, the *Caveat* provides details of vagrant social organization and
sexual practices, a glossary and sample conversations in their language,
and highly particular data like the proper names and identifying char-
acteristics of vagrants that "walk about Essex, Middlesex, Sussex, Surrey
and Kent" (113).[1] In other words, it represents itself as a work of
discovery, a sort of proto-ethnography that is also continuous in some
respects with the investigative procedures specified by the Marian bail
and committal statutes, and later amplified by William Lambarde and
Michael Dalton in their handbooks for Justices of the Peace discussed in
chapter 2. If Harman's work is connected to the administrative extension
of state authority, however, that connection is an ambiguous one.
Harman himself notes that he was at one point "in commission of the
Peace" (93), and is identified by subsequent pamphleteers in this vein as a
"Justice of Peace in Queen Mary's day" (387).[2] But while Harman
assumes a mantle of authority he does not explicitly represent himself
acting in an official capacity.[3] In fact, as we shall see, his position is a
hybrid one, cobbled together from the authority of the Justice, the
responsibilities of a parish gentleman, and, most importantly, the opportunities created by the burgeoning market for printed pamphlets.

Harman's involvement in the print market distinguishes him from the
other figures I have considered so far, giving him an arena in which to
perform the ambiguities of his identity outside of the actual structures
and activities of the administrative state. Specifically, the opportunity to
construct himself as an author which Harman's publication of the
material he has gathered affords him gives new point to the question,
raised insistently by the Shakespeare texts, of whose interest the state's
servants are really pursuing. It is this question, I shall argue, which
produces what is by now one of the *Caveat*'s most famous features: the
readiness with which it discloses the moral fraternity of the assiduous
investigator with the rogues whose secrets he discovers. But Harman's
self-construction as an author also enlarges the significance of this
question, linking it to others about the epistemic status of different kinds
of texts and about writing as a process of self-authorization, which will
be pursued by writers who imitate or steal from Harman, and who work
in contexts wholly outside that of state administration.

By Harman's own account, his method was to counter deception with deception. The vagrants he interrogated were, he claims,

marvellous subtle and crafty in their kind for not one amongst twenty will discover, either declare their scelerous secrets. Yet with fair flattering words, money and good cheer, I have attained to the type by such as the meanest of them have wandered these thirteen years . . . and not without faithful promise made unto them never to discover their names or anything they showed me. (62)

Crowing at his mastery of these deep dissemblers, Harman invites us to see him as the repository of secret intent, and, in the process, to collapse the text's moral polarities. As Stephen Greenblatt has remarked, "such reversals are at the very heart of the rogue literature."[4] Indeed, by the first decade of the seventeenth century, discovering the discoverer became part of the conycatching game when one S. R., in the guise of "Martin Markall, Beadle of Bridewell," discovered Thomas Dekker's plagiarism of Harman in *The Bellman of London* (1608), and Dekker genially responded in his next pamphlet, *Lanthorne and Candlelight* (1608), by discovering several new categories of rogues who made their living through literary filching. But if the Dekker–S. R. exchange seems to have tidily acted out the possibility of reversal raised by Harman's methodological confession, it also suggests why conycatching pamphlets might seem to offer only spurious examples of the discovery of the subject; the discoveries they purvey are frequently obvious literary fabrications, cranked out with little regard for either fact or originality to satisfy consumer demand for printed pamphlets. Even Harman's pamphlet, which in S. R.'s discovery plays the legitimate original to *The Bellman*'s plagiarism, is derived from earlier pamphlets, a redaction of material that goes back through John Awdeley's *Fraternity of Vagabonds* (1561) to the German *Liber Vagatorum* and *Narrenschiff*, returning finally to an original source (or so editorial legend has it) in the records of the trials of vagrants and mendicants at Basle in 1475.[5] Always pretending to discovery, these pamphlets always also depend on literary convention and borrowing.

The apparent contradiction between the epistemic claims of these texts and their mode of production has facilitated the framing of modern discourse about Elizabethan crime-writing in terms of binaries like fact and fiction, history and literature. Harman's text, because of its wealth of specific reference, has occupied an unstable place in this discourse, cited earlier in this century as a moment of empirical observation from which later pamphlets merely borrow, and more recently as one more promulgation of the literary fantasy of an Elizabethan Underworld.[6] In this respect, however, the modern discourse simply follows a course that the pamphlets themselves initiate, replaying S. R.'s "discovery" in finding authenticity in the *Caveat* in contrast to the fraudulence of the later pamphlets, and then displacing it, finding fiction in the *Caveat* (an easy trick) in contrast both to the archives and to the claims to authenticity the pamphlet makes for itself. The point to be made here then is not that these pamphlets are mere literary fabrications (that is, that they belong to one epistemological category and not another) but rather that they seem to invite us to "discover" that their status is not what it is represented to be, an invitation which suggests that what is at issue in these texts is precisely the constitution of epistemological categories and the negotiation of a relationship between them.

The process of discovery these pamphlets invite makes the circumstances of their production the determinant of their meaning. Further, the troping of this process within the texts as the discovery of "subtle and crafty" harborers of "scelerous secrets" suggests that it involves construing the producer as a subject in the double sense that I have used the term, both as the imagined origin of discourse, and as the object of authority's scrutiny. (Thus Harman's admission of his own deep dissembling with the vagrants raises questions not just about his moral authority but also about his text's reliability.) In privileging the moment of the text's production in this fashion, I want to suggest, these pamphlets, together with better-known maneuvers like the publication of Jonson's 1616 Folio, participate in a slow reconfiguration of the early modern discursive field, the emergence of discourse defined by a special relation to its producer, or, to use Foucault's formulation, "discourse containing an author function." Indeed, the coincidence in these pamphlets of the discovery of secrets with concern for the text's origin suggests that the "author," as Foucault defines him, constitutes a special case of the subject whose emergence I have been describing. What these texts reveal is the role that discovery (the establishment of epistemic mastery over the text's dissembling) plays in framing a category of knowledge that we now define as "subjective," that is, as one in which pretension to objective or historical truth is traded for the subject's presence in discourse.

Of course, there is an obvious objection to this line of argument. For, while these texts invite the recognition that what they offer are not discoveries but literary fictions, their origin in the appropriation of previous texts has also facilitated the "recognition" that they are not literature at all, but hack writing.[7] Although framed as a judgment about literary quality, this assessment arises from the fact that these pamphlets seem to traduce the very "subjective" basis of literature, the origin of the text in the author's labor and imagination.[8] Here again, the modern discourse takes its cue from the pamphlets' thematization of plagiarism. But if the Dekker–S. R. exchange serves to expose the degraded origin of these pamphlets in the demands of the print market rather than in authorial genius, its point is not to bracket them as illegitimate but specifically to foreground the issue of writerly work. In fact, I would argue, this exchange offers a discourse about authorship, or, more precisely, its impossibility, an exploration, it might be said, of authorial worst-case scenarios, in which all the grounds on which these writers try to authorize themselves seem to cancel each other out. In fact, what makes the cony-catching pamphlets so scandalous to literature is not the way in which they were actually composed, which in its mixture of copying, imitation, and inspired improvisation is not very different from Shakespeare's writing practice, but precisely their insistence on constructing the text's origin as "subjective," narrativizing it as personal experience. Thrusting the "author" into the text, these pamphlets make his recognition contingent on (sometimes ironic) truth claims that are of necessity belied by actual writerly activity, whether imitation, invention, or plagiarism. The "author" is thus always implicated in the discoverable art of cozenage.

The authorizing gestures in these texts derive their peculiar collapsing quality from the lack of fit between their relentlessly binary structure and the number of different kinds of truth claims that they actually attempt to organize. For what makes Harman's text seem "true" are claims that he discovered, which is to say he neither invented nor borrowed (or at least not without checking his borrowings against his discoveries), while the fraud that S. R. exposes is that Dekker borrowed when he ought to have invented – an activity that he nevertheless codes as discovery.[9] These three options – discovery, invention, and plagiarism – insofar as they define both the epistemic status of the text and the nature of authorial activity, in fact facilitate the construction of two implicit oppositions, between truth and falsehood and between labor and shirking, which seem to function synonymously both in the *Caveat* and in the Dekker–S. R. exchange, but which do not actually line up with each other. Thus, while plagiarism might stand for both falsehood and shirking, and discovery for both labor and truth, invention can stand for both labor and falsehood. To put it another way, claims about labor and claims about truth in these pamphlets signify disruptively in relation to one another. Thus, if the ostensible purpose of these pamphlets is the true discovery of a deceiving, non-laboring class who are undermining the commonwealth ("loitering lusks and lazy lorels," as Harman calls them), what the pamphlets produce instead is a sense of ubiquitous busyness, in which diligent discovery and stratagems to avoid honest work, deep dissembling and writerly invention, all seem disconcertingly hard to distinguish.

The destabilizing effect which foregrounding the author produces in these texts suggests a need to revise somewhat the history implied in Foucault's dictum that "the author is . . . the ideological figure by which one marks the manner in which we fear the proliferation of meaning."[10] Confronted by the textual proliferation of meaning, Foucault seems to say, we posit a subject anterior to the text who serves as an origin and a regulator of meaning – an action in which we are always preceded by the regulating state. But this procedure only produces the policing effects Foucault imagines if the subject position which the author occupies, as originator of meaning and liable owner of discourse, is already articulated and endorsed within the episteme. For, as these pamphlets suggest, the author interrupts any simple transmission of the truths of fact, doctrine, or social custom, indeed of any "truth" not identical with the "author" himself. The modern author confers prestige and stabilizes meaning in his texts because, whatever his texts' specific theme, part of what he transmits is the category of "subjective" discourse itself, with its ideological cargo of possessive, creative individualism. Lest we think Renaissance readers would find such a "truth" wholly reassuring, we should recall the accusation of "secret labors" hurled in the rhetorical struggle between the Elizabethan authorities and the Jesuits, demonizing agency which would alter the body of doctrine or established authority.[11] Indeed, nice evidence for a lingering suspicion of subjective truth can be found in Foucault's own observation of the disappearance of the author function from scientific discourse in the eighteenth century, a disappearance which points to the incompatibility of an "author function," not only with the structure of a knowledge dependent on non-idiosyncratic results, but also with the rise to hegemony of that knowledge. Scientific discourses, in other words, lack a highly developed "author function" both because they do not need one, and because they cannot risk having one. The "author" can perform the work Foucault attributes to him only when certain other truth claims are securely differentiated and hierarchized. If the modern author marks the articulation and subordination of the "subjective" as an epistemological category, the Renaissance author could, in certain circumstances, reveal the epistemic and ideological disruptiveness of the subject – a disruptiveness that could undermine even his own authority.

A poor gentleman

The Caveat for Common Cursitors disrupts and redirects the tradition of which it forms a part because it keeps its "author," the busy Harman, at its center. Harman continually comments on the circumstances of his intervention in the discourse of vagrancy. He tells us that he is expanding and correcting a previous vagabond book (this includes excising categories of vagabonds that in his experience "be not"), that illness forced him to stay at home, thus giving him the opportunity to speak with vagrants, that thieves stole his cauldron but left the pewter dishes soaking in it because they were engraved with his coat of arms, and that he stayed at the Whitefriars when in London to oversee the printing of the first edition of the *Caveat*.[12] Linking the ubiquitous "I" to dates, places, and the business of daily life, including the making of his book, Harman mutually guarantees the text's truthfulness and its author function; what the book tells us really must have happened because it has an author who was there, and it must have an author because its specificity shows its origins in a particular set of experiences. The particularity of Harman's text thus invites us to read the genre's formulae, such as the assertion that the information was obtained from a vagrant through (obviously betrayed) promises of secrecy, as signifiers of the text's double authenticity.[13] By the next "generation" of cony-catching pamphlets, Harman's particularizing moves will have been parodically reframed as conventions, precisely by emptying them of their particularity. Thus, where Harman provides a table of the vagrants' names, Robert Greene slyly assures the reader of *A Notable Discovery of Cozenage* (1591) that "were it not I hope of their amendment, I would in a schedule set down the names of such cozening cony-catchers."[14]

In this respect Harman's text represents an example of the process of appropriation, of "making things one's own" which, according to Robert Weimann, characterizes much Renaissance prose narrative. The *Caveat*, "like *Lazarillo de Tormes*, *Gargantua*, *The Unfortunate Traveller*, and of course *Don Quixote* . . . creates its own condition of reception by breaking up, through referentiality or parody, [here we see Greene's position] long established schemata."[15] This characteristic of Renaissance narrative, Weimann argues, suggests that Foucault's assertion that "discourses [characterized by an author function] are objects of appropriation," must be supplemented with the recognition of the social and economic forces that make the author "an appropriating agency." In other words, the author function in Renaissance narrative must be understood not only in relation to the "recently acquired exchange value of [the author's] works," that is, as something that enhances the value of texts, but also "in terms of the exchange value of *his work*," that is, in relation to the conditions that make the writer construct his discursive activity in terms of labor, property, and self-advancement (469). These conditions emerge in a classical Marxist analysis of the early modern transition to capitalism:

In its earliest, precapitalist form, in which the production and circulation of use value prevailed, *Aneignung* ["appropriation" or "making things one's own"] proceeded under conditions in which the individual was so much a part and parcel of his community that he "relates simply to the objective conditions of labour as being his . . . as the inorganic nature of his subjectivity" [Marx, *Grundrisse*]. In other words, his individual activities were so directly related to the means and modes of social reproduction that the individual's mode of production of his own self was identical with that of his community, which was not felt as anything alien . . . With the rise of capitalism, the emerging to preeminence of exchange value and corresponding patterns of social mobility and individual choice, people begin to live, to produce, to write and read under circumstances which – to a far greater number of individuals – are less "given": conditions are less preordained in the sense that a person's relation to (and his function as a member of) a social conglomerate or community has ceased to be so direct, ineluctable and transparent. (467–8)

Weimann locates the conditions for an emerging author function in the space that opens up between an individual and the means and modes of production, in the "scope for his own choice" that the writer's alienation from the conditions of work allows him (468).

This analysis is of particular relevance to Harman's text, not only because it lets us read the text's insistent particularity of reference as a sign of its maker's historically specific production as an author (rather than naively, as a sign of its authenticity) but also because the loss of a transparent social world furnishes the explicit content of Harman's book. Alienation, in every sense of the term, informs the relationship between Harman and the vagrants whose stratagems he discovers. The disruption of presupposed social and work relations through practices like enclosure (an historical subtext which the *Caveat* never acknowledges) forces the dispossessed rural poor, at least in Harman's representation of them, to resort to "appropriation" – both of guises like those of disabled beggar or respectable citizen, and of other people's property – which in turn enables Harman to engage in ethnographic appropriations of their strange practices and discourses.[16] Alienation and the appropriative relation to another's discourse it enables is even visible on the page, where different typefaces distinguish the words of the "lewd lousy language of these loitering lusks and lazy lorels" from the "plain terms" that unlock their meaning in the glossary and sample dialogue with translation that Harman provides.[17] The point here is not merely that the *Caveat* is founded on and performs the alienation of the vagrants, but, in addition, that the social and economic disruptions that produce the vagrants also increase the "scope for his own choice" that Harman enjoys in relation to his duties as a member of the parish gentry. This scope for choice permits him to reproduce practices like hospitality and charity as strategic encounters between Authority and its subversive Others. On one occasion, as we shall see, such an encounter will even extend to torture. But more importantly, because the changes in the means and modes of production which inform the *Caveat* include the development of the technology and trade of printing, they also permit Harman to become an author: to make his "discoveries" into a book, to go to London to see it through the press, to update subsequent editions, to correspond with readers (activities which he represents in his text), and to become in succeeding decades an acknowledged proprietor of the discourse of vagrancy.

Yet to make alienation the only social mode defining the *Caveat* is to misrepresent Harman's text. For, if the *Caveat* testifies to Harman's appropriations both of the traditions of vagabond literature and of vagrant practices, it also shows us that he does so in the name of, and from a position within, a community that still expects social relations to be, in Weimann's words, "direct, ineluctable, and transparent." Harman delightedly represents himself as an author, and William Lambarde even styles him one of the "Kentish writers."[18] But the position of the heir to the estates of Ellam, Maystreet, and the manor of Mayton, who describes himself as "a poor gentleman [who has] kept a house these twenty years, whereunto poverty daily hath and doth repair, not without some relief" (62), and who was at some point "in commission of the peace," differs significantly from those of later appropriators of this material like Greene and Dekker, whose writing practices were wholly situated in the London market which afforded a subsistence living to men whose literary skill would profit publishers, printers, or players.[19] The difference is not just that Harman was a well-off amateur protected from the degradations of the market but also that the busy author-investigator at the center of the *Caveat* is authorized by his discharge of obligations incumbent on one "placed as a poor gentleman" as well as by his writing. In other words, Harman's appropriations of authority in his acts of discovering, writing, and publishing are backed up by representations and exercises of an authority that is simply a "given".

The givens of Harman's situation emerge, of course, in the position of authority he assumes *vis-à-vis* the vagrants, but they are also evident in an ethic of neighborliness that pervades his book. Harman hopes that his blow against vagrancy will restore a rural culture in which gentlemen "keep hospitality in the country, to the comfort of their neighbours, relief of the poor and amendment of the commonwealth" (63), and he repeatedly connects his discovery of vagrants' tricks to his own ministrations to his poor neighbours. "I have diverse times," he reports, "taken away from them their licences, of both sorts with such money as they have gathered, and have confiscated the same to the poverty nigh adjoining me" (84).[20] This is not merely the rhetoric of *noblesse oblige*, but part of his book's continuous representation of the friendly intercourse of daily life that also includes going to market, gossiping in the street, and drinking in taverns. Where the later conycatching pamphlets construct these interactions uniformly as something that can be simulated or manipulated in the service of cheating and theft, Harman sets the vagrants' exploitation of them against their persistence as reassuringly stable, transparent social commitments and practices in which he participates.[21] Thus a tale of highway robbery begins "I had of late years an old man to my tenant who customably a great time went twice in the week to London, either with fruit or with peascods, when time served therefore . . ." (68). The tenant is set up when he meets a "master ruffler" who, "after salutations had . . . enter[ed] into communication with this simple old man, who riding softly beside them, commoned of many matters" (68). But if the old man's friendly conversation leads to his being robbed, it also becomes the occasion for the affirmation of community and his material solace when he returns home and tells what happened to him, "whereat for the time was great laughing, and this poor man for his losses among his loving neighbours well-considered in the end" (69). In a slightly different vein, there is the robbery of a poor parson, mitigated by the fact that he had only four marks in the house, "for he had lent six pounds to one of his neighbours not four days before" (76). It ends in his telling the story to the local tavern hostess, whose unwitting chit-chat had supplied the robbers with information about their victim. "And sit down here, and I will fill a fresh pot of ale to make you merry again," she soothingly invites the parson, declares the robbers to be "merry knaves" but advises him not to let the story get out lest he be laughed to scorn (77).

In these stories, "loving neighbours" may seem simply to furnish a moral norm against which the dissembling vagrants (and, we might add, the dissembling author) can be judged. But because of Harman's participation in both modes of social relation, this ethic of neighborliness actually functions in the text to disrupt the discursive activity alienation generates. Even at points when the text seems most clearly framed in terms of an opposition of appropriating author and wily vagrant, it also seems to speak for forms of solidarity that cut across the divisions between the vagrants and the more stable rural culture, and to revel in narrative pleasures that are epistemically quite different from discovering the vagrants' secret practices.

Perhaps the richest example of these discontinuities in discursive mode is the story of the "walking mort" in which Harman's attempt to interrogate an unmarried female vagrant becomes an occasion for her to entertain him with a good yarn. Harman, as is his wont, begins the tale by recounting how it came into his possession:

The last summer, *Anno Domini* 1566, being in familiar talk with a walking mort that came to my gate, I learned by her what I could and I thought I had gathered as much for my purposes as I desired. I began to rebuke her for her lewd life and beastly behaviour, declaring to her what punishment was prepared and heaped up for her in the world to come for her filthy living and wretched conversation. "God help!" quoth she, "how should I live? None will take me into service. But I labor in harvest-time honestly." "I think but a while with honesty," quoth I. "Shall I tell you?" quoth she. "The best of us all may be amended. But yet, I thank God, I did one good deed within this twelve months. (100–1)

The mort then exacts the usual promise from Harman, that he will hide what she tells him "and never discover it to any" (101), before launching into her story. The previous summer, being pregnant and craving mussels, she became stuck in some mud by the seaside and was saved by a man only when she consented to have sex with him. She manages to persuade him that it will be pleasanter if she goes to town, cleans up, and hides in his barn where he can come to her in the night, obtaining thereby a respite for which she was glad,

"Because," quoth she, "his wife, my good dame, is my very friend and I am much beholden to her. And she hath done me so much good or this, that I were loath now to harm her any way. (102)

Harman again interrupts, challenging her implicit moral code:

"Why," quoth I, "what and it had been any other man, and not your good dame's husband?" "The matter had been the less," quoth she. "Tell me, I pray thee," quoth I, "who was the father of thy child?" She studied a while, and said that it had a father. "But what was he?" quoth I. "Now by my troth, I know not," quoth she. "You bring me out of my matter, so you do." (102)

"Well say on," shrugs Harman and she continues with her story, recounting how she came to the good dame's house, told her what her husband was up to and was comforted with meat, drink, and a good fire. The woman enlists the aid of her "good neighbours and loving gossips," and with the walking mort they devise a scheme to punish the "naughty, lewd, lecherous husband" (102). Returning home, the husband passes a cheerful evening with his wife and then repairs to the barn where the walking mort exhorts him "untruss yourself and put down your hosen," then loudly chides him "Now, fie, for shame, fie."

At which word, these five furious sturdy, muffled gossips, flings out, and takes
sure hold of this betrayed person, some plucking his hosen down lower, and
binding the same fast about his feet; then binding his hands, and a handkercher
about his eyes, that he should not see. And when they had made him sure and
fast, then they laid him on until they were windless. "Be good," saith this mort,
"unto my master, for the passion of God!" and laid on as fast as the rest, and still
ceased not to cry upon them to be merciful unto him, and yet laid on apace.
(104–5)

Bidding him "from that time forth [to] know his wife from other men's,"
they leave him bloody, and, despite his calls for revenge, so chastened
that now he "loveth his wife well, and useth himself very honestly" (105).
"And was not this a good act, now?" asks the mort and Harman
concedes "It was prettily handled" (105).

Harman is at pains to embed the jest within a specific encounter
between himself and a vagrant, an encounter which he constructs both as a
confrontation between censorious male authority and lower-class, transgressive female sexuality, and as an interrogation by a clever discoverer of
subcultural secrets of a resistant oral informant. *His* aims, he makes
clear, are moral correction and the acquisition of knowledge. Thus he
displaces the telling of the tale with its aim of pleasure (and its obvious
status as a traditional jest) onto the sexually incontinent woman, who, in
turn, marks his interrogations as disruptions of her tale. But it would be
a dim reader indeed who could not to see through this stratagem, and by
the time the gossips are concocting their plan to humiliate the husband,
Harman seems to have forgotten that the mort is supposed to be telling
the story, although he returns to that fiction at the end. Moreover, if
Harman misogynistically insists on seeing only shamelessness when the
mort discloses a code of loyalty and generosity among women, it is hard
not to notice that the values the walking mort's tale promotes – "good
cheer" for the needy, honest marriage, and the reliability of loving
neighbours – seem oddly akin to Harman's. And this observation
suggests a third construction of the encounter between Harman and the
walking mort; "familiar talk" over a gate – the confidential retailing of a
funny story – looks more like gossip than discovery. Thus alienated
social relations fold back into "given" ones. If the voice that tells the
story and articulates principled resistance to Harman's moralizing is that
of a subordinated, female Other – indeed, even if it records the actual
availability to women of moral codes different than the one Harman
propounds – that voice also speaks for Harman.[22]

In the walking mort episode, Harman *stages* the appropriation of
material that seems already to be a given of his situation, constructing a
jest as empirical knowledge and "familiar talk" as investigation, without

sacrificing the satisfactions jests and familiar talk afford. The effect, obviously, is epistemically disruptive, collapsing a subversive "other" into the familiar poor and the secret truth of vagabond life into comic fiction, and even raising the possibility that Harman is ironizing himself. That Harman should produce narrative pleasures he pretends to disown and make strange a story that confirms the social order he defends bespeaks the complex social situation he occupies. At once a subtle and crafty investigator, a charitable country gentleman, a gossiper at his gate, and a writer for the print market, Harman operates from multiple positions, shifting continually between alienated and given relationships to his interlocutors and his discursive modes, creating in the process a self-representation that always differs from itself – and sometimes resembles the vagrants. In other words there is constant, multidirectional slippage in the text between the forms of authority and social order it endorses and the modes of its production.[23] Thus, while the rhetoric of neighborliness that pervades the book may proclaim a genuine ethical engagement, Harman does not act as "a poor gentleman" and "loving neighbour" in writing and publishing the *Caveat*; he appropriates those positions to enhance the authority and the amusement value of his book. If the vagrants seem to speak for Harman it is because he can never, at any given moment, fully speak for himself.

In the walking mort episode the vagrant seems to speak for the charitable poor gentleman while Harman represents the text's appropriating author. In the book's most famous episode, however, the discovery and apprehension of Nicholas Jennings, alias Nicholas Blunt, a "counterfeit crank" or beggar who simulates epilepsy, the *Caveat* suggestively links the peculiar affinity between Harman and the rogues whose secrets he discovers to Harman's position as an author in the print market. Jennings, clothed in "ugly, irksome attire" and spattered with blood and dirt, works the streets of London by day, and returns at night to "a pretty house, well stuffed, with a fair joint-table, and a fair cupboard garnished with pewter, having an old ancient woman to his wife" (90).[24] Concealing a respectable identity beneath a vagrant's costume, the counterfeit crank mirrors Harman's own ability to use the duties of poor gentleman as a cover for his various acts of authorial appropriation that secretly identify him with the vagrants. Thus, if the point of the story is ostensibly the restoration of Jennings/Blunt to a unitary, transparent identity, the character actually reveals both righteous respectability and vagrant desperation to be infinitely exchangeable costumes, a point enforced in the fourth edition by a woodcut of the two versions of Jennings standing side by side, one in rags, and the other in what could be the attire of a poor gentleman.

Harman's telling of the story virtually allegorizes the role he imagines for printing in exposing such duplicity and restoring social transparency.[25] He first encounters Jennings when he is in London to see the first edition of the *Caveat* through the press, and, suspecting that the pitiful beggar is not what he seems to be (he sends to Bethlehem Hospital and receives confirmation that they have never had such an inmate), Harman enlists his printer, who charges two apprentices to follow Jennings.[26] At one point in their pursuit, having no money for boat hire, the apprentices exchange penner and inkhorn, tools of an earlier, less mobile mode of textual reproduction, for transportation. With the printer's aid, Jennings is apprehended and stripped to reveal a fair body beneath his foul surface, but he manages to run away. The episode ends here in the second edition. A few months later, however, the printer again encountered Jennings, first "craftily clothed . . . in mariner's apparel . . . feigning [he] had lost his ship," and (to avoid the printer's suspicion) a few days later in the guise of an out-of-work hat-maker, dressed in "a fair black frieze coat, a new pair of white hose, a fine felt hat on his head, [and] a shirt of Flanders work esteemed to be worth sixteen shillings" (89). Matching Jennings's "deep dissimulation" with "fair allusions," the printer manages to trick him into custody – only to have him again escape (89). But the printer is "lighter of foot" and "with strong hand" once more apprehends Jennings, who is pilloried twice, once in good clothes and once in rags, and set free on the condition that henceforth "he labour truly to get his living" (90).

Harman is at pains elsewhere to insist that print is a tool of social control. He remarks, with naive faith in the law-abiding nature of printers, that printed begging licenses are "of authority" because the "printer will see and understand before the same come to press that the same is lawful," and seems to narrativize that belief when he turns his fleet-footed printer into the agent of Jennings's exposure (81).[27] But if the episode ends in the discovery and punishment of duplicity, it is also possible to find in Harman's account a counter-allegory about printing and social order. The feature of print that the chase foregrounds is its mobility, calling attention to the similarity between vagrancy and print as new forms of circulation (in the case of ballad-sellers this similarity became identity) that the Elizabethan government sought to contain.[28] Moreover, while the expansion of the story through successive editions as the printer repeatedly encounters Jennings enhances the book's truth claims, locating the events it recounts within the circumstances of its material production so that the book seems to be running to keep abreast of its referents, this effect depends on the repeated renewals of the chase as Jennings escapes and re-presents himself under some new guise.[29] The book's credibility and future circulation requires that it fail to produce closure because the logic of Jennings's career is the logic of print, requiring both continual circulation and the repeated "exposures" that justify the continued circulation.[30] In this respect we might wonder what it would mean to "labor truly," as a producer for the print market, and whether Jennings's earlier career might not serve as a prototype.

The walking mort's tale and the Jennings episode present two different versions of the *Caveat*'s production, embedding it both in oral exchange and in the print trade. The vagrants who talk with Harman and who circulate through the countryside symbolically link the two modes of production. Striving to contain the vagrants, the *Caveat* represents itself as moving between these modes, translating conversation over a gate into printed text. Of course, despite Harman's evident fondness for chitchat, such translation is also appropriation and displacement; the dominating drive in the process (and Harman's own stake in it) is evident in the difference between the conclusions of the two episodes, the former in Harman's grudging appreciation of the jest, the latter in Jennings being pilloried and whipped at the cart's tail. This translation of oral discourse into printed text is explicitly figured in the *Caveat*'s *pièce de résistance*, the glossary of thieves' cant with sample vagabond dialogue in English translation in which the opposition between the occult canting tongue and the "plain terms" of respectable people is also one between a supposedly oral language and one we read. When Harman presents for us "the upright man cant[ing] to the rogue," with interlineated translation, oral discourse is rendered sinister and remote, something that we overhear by literally reading between the lines.[31]

But if the *Caveat* transforms conversation into secrets that we can master only through reading, orality nevertheless remains the locus of truth to which the reader desires access, not merely in the form of the secret colloquies of rogues and upright men, but also in the talk between Harman and the vagrants who came to his door.[32] After all, the truth value accorded the *Caveat* in the years to come will derive from its ostensible origin in oral exchange rather than in the reading of previous vagabond books. Such an assertion, it might be objected, conflates the investigator's one-way interrogation of his object of study with the mutuality of conversation, a difference inscribed in the text when Harman pictures himself craftily manipulating the conversations he takes part in. The difference between neighbours and vagrants is precisely whether one "commons" with them or interrogates them. But the peculiar slippage in the walking mort episode between interrogation and "familiar talk," the way in which Harman's "interrogations" rub elbows with other conversations, the "great laughing" and restoration of losses that occurs when the old tenant tells of his being robbed, or the parson's recounting of his ordeal over a pot of ale, suggests that Harman's (purported) investigative methodology arises from habits of small talk. Despite his insistence on the subtlety of the vagrants and his own craftiness, he assumes a primitive connection between talking with others and knowing them. Harman claims to be an empiricist, deriving his findings from actual contact with his object of study rather than from textual authorities. That this contact can look so much like comfortable social practice suggests that the denigration of textuality implied in his, and perhaps all, empiricist claims originates in a nostalgia for transparent social relations – in a longing for the immediate presence of the Other.[33]

Thus, predictably enough, the vagrant who drives Harman to violence is a "dummerer" or fraudulent deaf-mute, a "most subtle" kind of rogue "who will never speak unless [he] have extreme punishment" (91). What Harman wants is, literally, access to the man's tongue. To this end he tells us that he enlisted the aid of a surgeon who

made him gape, and we could see but half a tongue. I required the surgeon to put his finger in his mouth, and to pull out his tongue, and so he did, notwithstanding he held strongly a pretty while. (92)

But producing the tongue yields no speech, until Harman and the surgeon tie the man by the wrists, hoist him over a beam and leave him to hang until "for very pain he required for God's sake to let him down" (92). Like the Privy Council's resort to torture in subsequent years, their methods for procuring the man's speech reveal a desperation to make the body yield access to a withheld enunciating subjectivity. What Harman seeks, however, is not the secrets of the heart but the use of the tongue; he does not desire to penetrate the depths of the Other but refuses to imagine them. In this respect, the story is a proleptic parody of Dell's Case (Harman sarcastically calls the outcome "a merry miracle madly made") in which instead of an absent tongue providing a physiological sign for a radically interior truth, the presence of the tongue restores a flat equivalence between the physical presence of the person and his transparency. The ideological trajectory of the story is profoundly conservative, and its circumstances make clear the forms of social relation that are implicated. Harman first suspects that the man is a fraud when he sees his license, stamped with a seal like one Harman himself had "bought besides Charing Cross"; he closes the matter by dispensing the man's take to "the poor people dwelling there" (92). Beginning in the commodification of authority's signs, the episode ends in charity.

Of course, what this episode actually depicts is not the restoration of orality but a violent displacement of it: the enhancement of Harman's power as he re(pro)duces the vagrant's voice in the laconic report that eventually he cried to be let down. We see that the vagrant's retreat from the circuit of familiar talk actually expands Harman's scope for appropriative activity. It is an unsettling moment in the text, partly, of course, because Harman's casual brutality belies the moral superiority he pretends to as charitable gentleman, but, more importantly, because it undermines the text's means for producing truth effects. As in the walking mort's tale, we sense in this episode a collision of discursive modes, an incongruous construction of the repressive operation of authority as a jest, "a merry miracle madly made." What is particularly disconcerting here, however, is that the violence does not demarcate these modes, as one might hope, but participates in them both at once, conflating state torture with a comic dispensation of justice, hopelessly compromising thereby the epistemic claims of the former and the genial traditionalism of the latter. The effect is discursive crisis, a complete disabling of these modes which separates Harman momentarily from any authorizing discourse. Struggling to regain the vagrant's voice, Harman displaces the scene of conversation/investigation with the spectacle of his unauthorized intervention on the dummerer's body. His "I" exceeds its function as a hinge between the text and the discourses it appropriates, and his labor comes into view as a delegitimating excess that covers and silences the voice it would reproduce.

It is perhaps not surprising, then, that when the canting tongue is produced within the text we find that "Harman" literally goes too far, that the word for the stocks which arrest the circulation of the vagrants is "the harmans." If the implicit claim behind this little joke is that "Harman" is seamlessly identified with the forces of law and order, the appearance of his name, hinting at its allegorical significance, among the secret terms of the vagrants' language also suggests another interpretation: that Harman never conversed with the vagrants, that the text is in fact a literary fiction, a story Harman has made up about himself.[34] Slyly signing his work, the author accomplishes his own "molestation," to use Edward Said's term, his "confinement to a fictive, scriptive realm."[35] But this moment, it should be noted, does not offer the reader any mastery; "harmans" is plausible as a cant term because it conforms to one of cant's lexical formulae ("lightmans" is the day, and "darkmans" the night), and turns up without comment in subsequent canting dictionaries. Thus all we can do is *suspect* the joke, never discover it as a key to the epistemic status of the text.

The effect of this joke is both to raise suspicions about the text's veracity and to name the author as a source of epistemic instability in the text, the site where discovery folds undecidably into fabrication, orality into textuality. Moreover, in locating that name among the shifty terms of the vagrants' language, the joke calls into question the continuity it ostensibly asserts between "Harman" and the penal authority of the Crown. We wonder just which side he is on. The point is not, of course, that he is really on either side, but rather that he cannot be contained within the ideologically describable positions available in the text. Harman may represent himself as the agent both of discovering authority and of traditional forms of neighborliness, but as the maker of his book he bears an opportunistic relation to all the discursive modes he deploys. If Harman's pamphlet, perhaps slyly, perhaps inadvertently, invites us to identify him with the vagrants whose secrets it claims to discover, it is because he shares what Jean-Christophe Agnew calls the rogues' "logic of instrumentalism," manipulating discourses and social roles from a position anterior to any of those he represents.[36] And the scandal, as we have seen, is at once moral and epistemic; the rogues' willingness to make use of, rather than to enter into, the discursive ties that bind one human being to another permits them (as the stratagems of Nicholas Jennings make clear) a marvelous range for invention.

That anterior position, I want to suggest, belongs to the *writer*, by which I mean the *Caveat*'s site of textual origin. If the *Caveat* repeatedly figures its own production – in familiar talk, in crafty interrogation, in the printing of successive editions – it never shows us the scene of writing, the work of composition that cannot be assimilated to any of Harman's public roles, although it marks the elision when the apprentices trade away penner and inkhorn for boat hire.[37] (Indeed, the whole Jennings episode may be read as such an elision, an attempt to join the events the text describes directly to its publication in print.) Typically, however, Harman hides in plain sight what the sometime Justice and loving neighbor would suppress: "Eloquence have I none," he proclaims, "I never was acquainted with the Muses; I never tasted of Helicon . . . I desire no praise for my pain, cost and travail . . . for the profit and benefit of my country have I done it" (66). This ridiculously disingenuous disavowal of literary pretensions suggests that the writer's position represents for Harman an irresistible opportunity for self-aggrandize-ment, and a divorce from both "authority" and traditional forms of social relation.[38] Acquaintance with the muses (or merely with the pleasures of the text) means a withdrawal from the transparent oral world he claims to restore. If, as I argued earlier, the *Caveat* acquires authenticity through extensive representations of its "author" in the text, it also does so by denying its "writer." But the writer, in his opportunism, is the producer of these author effects, and remains a disruptive presence within the text, the unavailable subject who would decide its ambiguities – whether Harman is ironizing himself in the walking mort episode, or whether "harmans" is a joke – and the aggressive agent of our displacement from the scene of truth.

Thieves of wit

The subsequent career of Harman's work entailed a double dislocation of both the "author" and his text from the scene of writing. In the four decades following the publication of the fourth and final edition of the *Caveat*, "Harman" came to signify an authoritative conduit to vagabond culture, and the canting tongue in particular, at the same time that his material was repeatedly appropriated for new conycatching pamphlets. In other words, Harman's name came to stand for the investigative labors that guaranteed the text's authenticity, while his material was reproduced by the print trade for purposes not sanctioned or probably even imaginable by the now-deceased Harman.[39] For example, a good part of the *Caveat* reappears anonymously in 1592 as /*The Groundworke of Conny-catching*, a text coat-tailing, it would appear from the title and title page illustration of rabbits dressed as gentlefolk, on the success of Robert Greene's conycatching pamphlets of the preceding year.[40] ("Cony-catching," it should be noted, is a term Harman never uses.) The title-page promises "the manner of Pedlers-French and the meanes to understand the same, with the cunning slights of the Counterfeit Cranke," and assures the reader that it was "Done by a Justice of the Peace of great authorite who had the examining of divers of them." Tricked out to satisfy a demand for the new literary genre, the text simultaneously amplifies its author's credentials (Harman had identified his status primarily as that of gentleman) so that his ambiguous interventions are now aligned perfectly with the Crown's discovering activities. Having established this alignment, the *Groundworke* names the text's proprietor, admonishing the reader: "I leave you now unto those which by Maister Harman are discovered". In short, this recycling of Harman's text shows that Harman's recognition as an author entails his subsumption on the one hand into the commodifying operations of the print market and on the other into the authority of the Crown – the latter subsumption being in part an attempt to counter the de-authorizing effects of the former.

If Harman's "authorship" seems to elide the work of writing, however, the cultural space his text occupies, that of the commodity pamphlet, had also become, as I suggested earlier, the site of a discourse about literary labor in the print market. Thus, in later pamphlets, writers clinging to the margins of literary respectability and economic viability appropriate

Harman's authority to express (and to mock) their own yearnings for poetic fame and the metaphysical property rights it confers. But the awkward fit between Harman's authority as discovering justice and the literary authorship the pamphleteers would defend also suggests that literary labor is for them a confused and confusing concept, with the capacity to disorganize the distinctions on which Harman's (or indeed anybody's) authorial legitimacy is founded.

When S. R., the author of *Martin Markall, Beadle of Bridewell*, exposes Thomas Dekker's plagiarism of Harman in *The Bellman of London*, he intervenes, with tongue in cheek, in a situation that seems to bear out the implications of the Jennings episode when it links the economy of printing to the mobile counterfeiting of the rogue.[41] "These papers and volumes now spread everywhere," he complains, "so that every jack-boy now can say as well as the proudest of the fraternity: 'Will you wap for a win or trine for a make?' " (386). This textual "spread" has not discovered the truth but made the canting tongue a literary fad. Cant has lost its authenticity; no longer attaching either to sinister otherness or to orality, it has become as current as cheap pamphlets. While Martin speaks in terms of lost authenticity, however, what the passage actually conveys is a shift in the epistemic ground of the genre from the investigative to the textual, so that cant is archly acknowledged to have always been a literary language, implicated in pamphlet production. Thus he begins with a comical appropriation of the convention of betrayal, the "canting caterpillars" in convocation at "Devil's Arse A-Peak" trying to determine who leaked their secrets, which undermines altogether the fiction of a discovered vagrant culture. While some imagine the leak as the sort of oral exchange Harman claimed to have been in on – "daily commercing and discoursing" between members of their fellowship and a spy – others recognize that it must be "some of their own company" who has "been at some free school . . . [and] took pen and ink and wrote" their secrets because the book that exposed them "smelt of a study" (386). But if the point of this joke seems to be the "revelation" that the rogues in question are actually writers, and therefore that their authentic/subversive orality is a literary fiction, writing as a form of inventive labor is only momentarily implicated as the text's roguish origin. For:

At last up starts an old cacodemical academic with his frieze bonnet and gives them all to know that this invective was set forth, made and printed above forty years ago; and being then called *A Caveat for Common Cursitors*, is now newly printed and termed *The Bellman of London*, made at first by one Master Harman, a Justice of Peace in Kent in Queen Mary's days he [the Bellman] being then about ten years of age. (386)

Naming the true author, Martin reveals the study-smelling text to originate precisely in not-writing – that is, in the theft of a previous text. In an allusion to the *locus classicus* of plagiarism, Dekker is disclosed as the Bathyllus to Harman's Virgil: "enough for him to have the praise, other the pains, notwithstanding Harman's ghost continually clogging his conscience with *Hic vos non vobis*" (398).[42]

Upholding Harman as a wronged author, Martin places the gentleman who never tasted of Helicon in distinguished literary company. But when he grants Harman authorial rights to this "invective" comparable to those of Virgil to his poetry, he does not unambiguously vindicate *writing* as the basis of those rights. For he makes clear that Harman's claim lies in his privileged relation to cant; the dictionary is the site where Harman's true authorship is established and the Bellman exposes himself as a fraud. What gives the Bellman away is the fact that "his dictionary (or Master Harman's)" shows only a reading knowledge of cant, "setting down old words, used forty years ago before he was born, for words that are used in these days." He even reproduces a typographical error, giving "chates" for "cheats" (the gallows) "because he so found it printed, not knowing the true original thereof." Copying out old words and typographical errors, the Bellman has revealed himself to be a mere extension of the mechanical means of textual production. There is no enunciating subject behind his text – merely another text. But the nature of this missing subject is difficult to specify; if the invocation of Virgil would indicate that he is a writer in the throes of composition, the location of his absence in the dictionary suggests that he is the Justice of Peace whose authority derives in turn from his transparent mediation of the vagrant's voice. Where in Harman's book the vagrant informant and the writer seemed to be epistemically incompatible origins for the text (though for that very reason Harman, as writer, could be the vagrant's fellow in fraud), here they substitute for each other, as "true originals," their subversive affinity now a positive alliance in opposition to the fraudulence of the Bellman's text.

The alliance that Martin forges between writer and rogue informant as authenticating presences implies that the writer's labor as much as the discovery of the vagrant's voice anchors the text to a subject, and thus imbues it with truth. But if the effect of this alliance should be to disclose the Bellman's text as doubly fraudulent, the discovery seems somewhat lame. For Dekker has not merely plagiarized earlier texts but loudly called attention to this plagiarism, forging the same alliance of writer and rogue in order to expose the work of writing as devoid of truth as a rogue's trick. In other words, the uncertainty about precisely what kind of truth writerly labor produces, evident in the awkward analogy of

Harman and Virgil, is actually Dekker's topic, one that he pursues by relentlessly collapsing the oppositions that would organize a discourse of textual authenticity.

In his conycatching pamphlets Dekker ostentatiously produces himself as a literary author, that is as a writer who makes public proprietary claims on behalf of his labor. Thus he prefaces *Lantern and Candlelight* with an elaborate apparatus: a dedicatory letter to Master Francis Mustian of Peckham, another letter "to my own nation" and several commendatory poems, "to the Author," or "to my industrious friend" (313–17).[43] But this authorizing space Dekker creates is also self-subverting insofar as he uses it to comment on the conditions of "this printing age of ours" that make writing a desperate gambit in which the writer must do whatever it takes to survive (313). In his letter to Mustian, Dekker presents himself confronting a series of binary options ("do[ing] almost nothing contrary to custom" versus being "impudently audacious" in soliciting patrons, writing for glory versus writing for money) in which the authorizing effects that Weimann attributes to early modern conditions of literary production seem unimaginable (313). Because all options entail either egregious self-promotion or utter effacement by the modes of literary production, Dekker would "walk in the midst, so well as [he] can, between both" (313). The desired *via media*, however, proves impossible, so that he is forced to throw his lot in with

they that being free of wit's Merchant Venturers do every new moon (for gain only) make five or six voyages to the press, and every term-time upon booksellers' stalls lay whole litters of blind invention; fellows yet, if they do but walk in the middle aisle, spit nothing but ink, and speak nothing but poem. (313)

And while he would avoid such a condition if he could, Dekker protests that "he is not much to be condemned that having no more acres to live upon than those that lie in his head, is every hour hammering out one piece or other out of this rusty iron age" (313).

Once Dekker has revealed the desperation which drives such relentless and degrading labor it is hard to miss the irony when, embarked as "the Bellman" on his "voyage for discoveries," he encounters among the "savages" whose tricks he brings to light "falconers," and "jacks of the clockhouse" whose racket is plagiarism. Their scams involve "scraping together certain small parings of wit . . . cut[ting] them handsomely in pretty pieces, and . . . patch[ing] up a book," which is then printed up at the falconer's expense, fitted up with an all-purpose dedicatory epistle and palmed off on as many potential patrons as possible (336–7). The Bellman denounces at length these "thieves of wit, cheaters of art, traitors of schools of learning, murderers of scholars," concluding self-righteously "[you] are not worthy to have your names drop out of a deserving pen" (338). When Martin Markall reads Dekker's authorizing maneuvers as a species of roguish dissembling, comparing them to "a horse courser's commendation of a Smithfield jade," he makes a "discovery" that Dekker has done everything he can to assist (385).

Dekker's confession to being one of wit's Merchant Venturers reveals the complicity of his "deserving pen" in the practices of thieves of wit, but it does so not through a direct admission of plagiarism, but through a claim to hyper-inventiveness, to a desperate fertility of mind. If this claim might seem to defend wit's Merchant Venturers against the worst accusation, that they steal other men's work, Dekker's account of their practices – laying "whole litters of blind invention" on the bookseller's stalls – actually collapses invention (that which distinguishes Virgil from Bathyllus) into the mechanical print-driven method of textual production that Martin accuses the Bellman of practicing when he catches him copying a typographical error. In the "madmen of Paul's Churchyard . . . who spit nothing but ink and speak nothing but poem," with whom Dekker has no choice but to cast his lot, writing does not mark the presence of an enunciating subject, but, like plagiarism, displaces him (313).[44]

Recasting as tropes moves that advertise themselves as evidence of authenticity, the game Martin and the Bellman engage in raises the possibility that there is no subject anterior to the objective processes of pamphlet production, even as it points to the author as the guarantor of textual truth. And Martin implicates himself as much as the Bellman in this situation; he styles himself Harman's legitimate successor in discovery, updating the dictionary according to current usage, but he also tells us he made his discoveries in a pamphlet world, on a journey to "Thievingen" on "Knavesborough Plain" where "Don Purloiningo" keeps his court. Locating their discoveries entirely in the papery domain of pamphlet-makers, Martin and the Bellman produce uncertainty about what would constitute a truth worth paying for. Is it the voice of the vagrant? The authority of a Justice of Peace in Queen Mary's day? The "pains" of a writer? A sly confession of what it takes to survive in "this printing age of ours"? Anything it seems might fill the spot because in this age of commodified discourse it is impossible to tell the difference between the labors that guarantee subjective presence and those which traduce it.

Dekker's comment that the dubious labor of pamphlet production is driven by the writer's "having no more acres to live upon than those that lie in his head" links uncertainty about textual authenticity to the dislocation of the writer from any established socio-economic position. If the immediate point of this comment seems to be that these writers are financially desperate, the obvious comparison to Harman's situation which these lines invite also suggests that "acres" provide not only income but supplemental authority which can transform writerly labor into authorial presence. The writer whose situation Dekker describes might be seen as an extreme instance of the subject who is the object of epistemic desire and anxiety in this period. His capital entirely of the intellectual sort, the professional writer is without an easily recognized social identity, but is equipped to appropriate discourse, to promote himself in print. But the wry discoveries of the Bellman and Martin Markall also seem to suggest that the writer's predicament is *too* extreme, that without the kind of authority which Crown and community conferred on Harman, the writer inhabits a field of longing (his own for authority, the reader's for authenticity) but not finally of power. And without power, the writer, as subject, poses no real subversive threat. Recognizing the powerlessness of their position, however, these writers can explore the contradictions which beset their position with a deconstructive playfulness that distinguishes them from all the other "discoverers" we have encountered. These contradictions are embodied in the duality of the rogue as bearer of authenticity and purveyor of fraud. It is Martin Markall's discovery which drives the implications of this duality (and of the writer's position) as far as it can go. Replacing the vagrants' stratagems with the Bellman's thefts, he places the plagiarist in the position occupied by the vagrant informant. Copying "chates" serves finally the same function as speaking "cheats"; it is the trace of an appropriation, a sign that someone was there.

Master poets

The trajectory which the conycatching material follows, from Harman's discoveries to Dekker's plagiarism, would appear to be a deauthorizing one, running counter to the historical narrative implicit in my initial invocation of Foucault's essay, and in accounts of better-known cases of Renaissance authorship such as the self-authorization that Ben Jonson is said to have achieved through the printed book. How, then, are we to understand the relationship between this "worst-case scenario" of Renaissance authorship and the equally print-driven processes that could produce a "Jonson" or "Shakespeare" suitable for appropriation in the eighteenth century as instances of a more ideologically stable, legally encoded "author"? I want, by way of conclusion, briefly to consider this problem by focusing on Jonson's own relation to conycatching literature. The choice of Jonson as representative of the authorizing narrative is determined, in part, by the fact that he *has* an explicit relationship to this material, having drawn on it in *Every Man in his Humour*, *The Alchemist,* and *Bartholmew Fair* as well as in his canting masque *The Gypsies Metamorphosed*. His work thus marks a point of contact between what will eventually be defined as the center and the margins of Renaissance literary activity. But the choice is also motivated by Jonson's service as exemplar in recent accounts of author formation in the Renaissance – accounts which usually situate him in a discursive field defined by poles of "authority" (embodied variously in the King, Classicism, the law, and his own ethical claims) and "subversion" or "transgression" (manifest mostly in his propensity for getting arrested but also in his scatological obsessions and bodily excesses) and describe his authorship as the effect of a complex interplay between them.[45] In other words, Jonson's position seems peculiarly susceptible to characterization in terms similar to those which I have used to describe Harman's position in the *Caveat*. Indeed, I would argue, the plotting of plays such *Every Man in his Humour*, *Volpone*, and *The Alchemist*, in which the scams of clever operators are brought to light, indicates that Jonson as much as Harman used the discovery mode to produce authority within texts whose ideological investments and epistemic stances did not, in fact, perfectly align with the legal and political authorities which they actually represent.

The affinity between Harman's strategies and Jonson's suggests, obviously enough, that the contradictions which defined Jonson's position were not unique to him, and that the cony-catching material does, in fact, figure concerns that were fundamental to problems of authorship in the period. But Jonson's conscious ambition to become a classical poet for this printing age of ours also distinguishes his desires both from Harman's humbler and more fractured intentions and from Dekker's thwarted wish to earn an honest living. In particular, Jonson's Classicism significantly differentiates his position from Dekker's. For if he too had "no more acres to live upon than those that l[ay] in his head," Jonson had, as it were, fertilized his intellectual holdings with a more powerful knowledge than had Dekker. In his rigorous, self-directed study of Classical literature, Jonson had appropriated the knowledge which was most clearly associated with established sites of cultural authority, most notably the grammar schools (including, of course, the Westminster School which he had briefly attended) and the universities, institutions whose function was in part to produce a governing elite. As many writers of Jonson's generation had learned to their disappointment, the connection between Classical learning and access to real political or social authority could be elusive. Nevertheless, the capacity of that knowledge to signify authority meant that Jonson could, if only discursively, graft his own skills and practices to more "given" forms of cultural power. In this respect, his position is perhaps closer to Harman's than to Dekker's. Insofar as these forms are merely literary, however (and the circumscription of the "literary" is part of what the career disappointments of learned men produced) Jonson came to occupy a situation quite different from Harman's. Thus my argument is not that Jonson simply repeated what Harman did with greater subtlety and artistry, but rather that he needed to negotiate a different relation to the contradictions which define the author.

In the Induction to *Bartholmew Fair*, a passage frequently referred to in discussions of Jonson's authorial positioning, the Stagekeeper warns the audience:

When't comes to the Fair once, you were e'en as good go to Virginia for anything there is of Smithfield. He has not hit the humours, he does not know 'em; he has not conversed with the Bartholmew birds as they say; he has ne'er a sword and-buckler man in his Fair, nor a little Davy to take toll of the bawds there, as in my time, nor a Kindheart, if anybody's teeth should chance to ache in his play; nor a juggler with a well-educated ape to come over the chain for the King of England and back again for the Prince, and sit on his arse for the Pope and the King of Spain! None of these fine sights! Nothing! No, and some writer that I know have the penning o'this matter, he would ha' made you such a jig-a-jog in the booths, you should ha' thought an earthquake had been i' the Fair! But these master poets will have their own absurd courses; they will be informed of nothing. (9–26)[46]

The Stagekeeper's identification of the play's author as a "master poet" rests on what are, at least from the standpoint of my reading of Harman, two somewhat disparate accusations: first that the author has "not conversed with the Bartholmew birds," and thus his representation is not accurate, and second that he departs from the popular theatrical traditions that prevailed in "Master Tarlton's time" (33–4) from whence the Stagekeeper derives his authority. Or, to return to Weimann's formulation, the Stagekeeper's complaint is that the Master Poet creates his text's "own condition of reception by breaking up . . . long-established schemata." The Stagekeeper's assumption of the continuity between representation based on conversation with the Bartholmew birds and well-worn gags bespeaks the social nostalgia which I have suggested informs claims to first-hand knowledge in Harman's text, even as those claims mark a rupture with traditional modes of representation through their appropriating function. But the Stagekeeper's conflation of these representational modes is facilitated in this particular case by the fact that the thing represented (the Fair) and the means of representation (the theatre) are continuous with each other as sites of festivity and popular tradition. The threat the Fair/popular theatre seems to pose for the master poet then is not merely the "low" culture against which he defines his "high" art but a set of givens in which occasion, site, and tradition intertwine, threatening to pre-empt his work. Thus, defending against the degradation of the theatre would appear to have epistemic consequences; to know the Fair first-hand, the Induction seems to suggest, is to become implicated in traditional social and representational practices that make no accommodation for the appropriating labors of master poets. So, in an inversion of Harman's violent attempt to regain the dummerer's speech, the master poet kicks the Stagekeeper "three or four times about the tiring house . . . for but offering to put in with [his] experience" (27–9). Here, in the stinking presence of popular sites and traditions, the master poet struggles (in a manner wholly appropriate to Smithfield) to *establish* the alienation which marks Harman's relation to the vagrants.

The alienation he seeks is embodied in the Articles of Agreement between the "hearers at the Hope on the Bankside . . . and the author of Bartholomew Fair," which the Bookholder and Scrivener offer in place of the intimacy of tradition the Stagekeeper so cherishes. This displacement of tradition is framed in terms of a series of substitutions in the representation of the Fair:

Instead of a little Davy to take the toll o' the bawds, the author doth promise a strutting horse courser, with a leer drunkard, two or three to attend him, in as good equipage as you would wish. And then for Kindheart, the tooth-drawer, a fine oily pig woman, with her tapster to bid you welcome, and a consort of roarers for music. A wise Justice of Peace *meditant*, instead of a juggler with an ape. A civil cutpurse *searchant*. A sweet singer of new ballads *allurant*; and as fresh an hypocrite as ever was breached *rampant*. (113–22)

The difference marked by these substitutions, the Articles make clear, is between the past, "the sword-and-buckler age of Smithfield," and "the present." Thus the displacement of the Stagekeeper by Bookholder and Scrivener involves a restructuring of epistemic options. Where to the Stagekeeper traditional stage practice was continuous with the reality of the Fair, here such practice is explicitly recast as nostalgia; realistic representation is now allied with the master poet's innovations. If, however, the master poet appropriates the claim to represent accurately the present Fair, he does not claim first-hand knowledge. He has not conversed with the Bartholmew birds but, as we can infer from his list of offerings, he has read conycatching pamphlets. And indeed, Jonson seems to have gotten the trick of the ballad singer and cutpurse out of Greene's *Third Part of Cony Catching*.[47] The "present" in which he grounds his representation of the Fair is to be found not in the popular traditions that link the theatre to Smithfield, but in the printed pamphlet.

My aim here is not, of course, to play Martin Markall to Jonson's Dekker, discovering previous texts where there ought to have been conversation, but rather to point to the intervention that Jonson makes in the conycatching material: the dissociation he insists upon between conversation and the credibility of his authorship. The conycatching pamphlets, as we have seen, are marked by ambivalence, a claim to offer the presence of an enunciating subject that is countered and even exposed as fraudulent by a textual abstraction which I have linked to the material conditions of these pamphlets' production. What attracts Jonson to the conycatching material, I want to suggest, is precisely its fraudulence, the possibility the pamphlets represent of textual abstraction, of freedom from the pre-emptive occasions of first-hand knowledge that pre-empt writerly inventions. Thus if Jonson's play presents a world akin to that of the conycatching pamphlets, in the failed career of Adam Overdo, wise Justice of Peace, self-styled Columbus of the Fair, whose aim is to hear with his own ears and see with his own eyes, it also satirically dismantles the discovery mode which mediates in the pamphlets between the roguish enunciating subject and the abstraction of the text. In this respect, the collapse of legal authority which the play stages in the humiliation of Adam Overdo and the unauthorized circulation of warrants and licenses constitutes the fulfillment of the conditions of authorship established in the Induction, rather than their defeat by the carnivalesque, subversive world of Smithfield, as is usually argued.

The final collapse of Adam Overdo's enterprise marks the culmination in Jonson's plays of his production of increasingly compromised versions of authority, a process bound up with his abandonment of author surrogates as a strategy for constructing his own authority: in other words, with the disappearance of authorial presence from the scenes he represents. Thus Jonson begins his dramatic career by using moralizing mouthpieces such as the Macilente/Asper diad in *Every Man Out of his Humour*, or Horace in *Poetaster*. In *Volpone,* however, these authorial figures disappear in favor of a dialectical opposition between the agile, self-interested plotters, Volpone and Mosca, and the discovering authority of the Scrutineo. By the time we get to a play like *The Alchemist,* the rogues and gulls are balanced only by Lovewit, a property-owner who knows how to profit from their schemes. As he ceases to represent sites of viable authority within his plays, I would suggest, Jonson constructs his own authorship as a condition of abstraction, an absence marked by the very fullness, indeed incontinence, of his representations. The author is the *primum mobile* of all textual effects, but not a subjective presence within the text who can compensate for its abstraction from first-hand experience. But if *Bartholmew Fair* is the most extreme example of this procedure, it is important to notice that Jonson's authorial retreat depends not only on the uncontained enormities of the Fair, but also on the explicit sacrifice of a character who, in his quotations of Horace, reminds us of Jonson's earlier surrogates, and, in his activities, of the investment of Jonsonian comedy in the discovery of enormities. Jonson marks his detachment from the Fair by defeating the discovering subject; "Columbus" is deflated to "Adam, flesh and blood," and, in a gesture that fulfills Thomas Harman's purported goal to restore a society in which gentlemen "keep hospitality" rather than make discoveries, is reconstructed as a host.

It is by now a critical commonplace that when Jonson left the loathed stage, one place he went was the printed book. The 1616 Folio, *The Workes of Benjamin Jonson,* and its arrangement of texts to evoke a career, constitutes a sustained representation of Jonson's authorial labor. In many recent accounts of his career, Jonson's location of his authorship in the printed book heralds the proprietary author, who is linked, through implication and theoretical filiation, to possessive individualism, modern subjectivity, and bourgeois culture. *Bartholmew Fair,* it is frequently remarked, is excluded from the Folio, presumably because, despite the allegorization in the Induction of the author's removal from stage to book, the play's incontinence offends the classical pretensions the Folio embodies. But speculation on this matter might be also directed another way. In the 1616 Folio and in his earlier forays into print, I would argue, Jonson aggressively colonizes the print medium, forcing the commodity text to signify (and dignify) his authorial labor. In this respect the Folio does consciously and on a grand scale what the *Caveat* does apparently unconsciously. However, as Joseph Loewenstein has remarked (and again, as the *Caveat* demonstrates), such a project depends on a recognition of the abstraction of the printed text, its removal of the author's work (understood as a product) from the occasions of its production.[48] Thus if the Folio purveys an image of Jonson as proprietary author (and, as Loewenstein also notes, embeds him in an "archaic patronage economy"), it does so within a medium that has, as it were, emptied the author's labor out of the text (109). If *Bartholmew Fair* is somehow incompatible with the project of the *Workes* it is because there Jonson does not compensate with authorial claims for the abstraction the printed text produces. Rather, he insists on it, refusing to represent (or in the case of Overdo, Littlewit, and the violent master poet, lampooning) anything that might look like authorial appropriation of the Fair. Even the imagined discoveries by a "state-decipherer or politic picklock of the scene" elicit no Jonsonian assertion of authorial intention – the moralizing "aim" of "this pen" as he calls it in *The Alchemist* – but simply the implication that the meaning of the play is its manifest content, that a pig woman is a pig woman.

The problems of authorship as they emerge in the challenge *Bartholmew Fair* poses to the *Workes* are similar to those foregrounded in the Dekker–S. R. exchange. Jonson, Dekker, and S. R. all offer ironic testimony to their recognition that the signifiers of authorial presence are implicated in the textual abstraction they would resist. In linking this recognition to a fierce pursuit of authorial fame rather than to resignation, the case of Jonson in particular reveals that the "author," at least at this moment in the formation's history, is properly understood not as an enunciating subject *per se* but as an enlarged, beckoning reflection of that subject which can only be seen in the abstract, commodity text. In fact, all the texts considered in this chapter suggest that we should qualify Foucault's assertion that the author is an ideological figuration of our fear of the proliferation of meaning by noting that the author is also a figuration of desire for subjective presence in the text. This desire is a writerly as well as a readerly one, a desire to *be* present as well to find presence. But it is a desire which can't be felt without the phenomenon I have been calling textual abstraction, to which the author ostensibly opposes himself. Textual abstraction is the effect of the multiple alienations which provide the occasions and means for the production and circulation of these texts. As we have seen, these alienations include that of the poor from the land and of neighbors from one another, as well as that of the writer from his work and the reader from everything (s)he reads about. The discovery mode in which the conycatching pamphlets operate is one manifestation of resistance to these alienations, that is, of the desire for presence. Promising to restore a transparent, immediate world, these discoveries instead produce the author and with him uncertainty about what kind of truth, if any, his text could offer. Jonson, in collapsing the discovery mode in *Bartholmew Fair*, embraces textual abstraction as the condition of his authorship. But it is hardly a definitive performance, remaining instead an alternative to the self-assertion embodied in the 1616 Folio. The contradictions which surround the "author" emerge at what seems to be the period of the modern author's inception and are perhaps the effects of novel conditions of literary production and consumption. However, the subsequent dual development of the author, as the legally recognized owner of his labor and as the ineffable genius whose texts seem to transcend their origins in work, suggests that these contradictions are in fact foundational, not so much resolved over time as recuperated in the service of his mystification.

5   Francis Bacon and the discovering subject

> Come forth into the light of things,
> Let Nature be your Teacher.
>
> William Wordsworth, "The Tables Turned"

At the beginning of the *New Atlantis,* Spanish explorers sail from Peru into a "part of the South Sea that was utterly unknown" and discover land (215).[1] What they find there, however, is not the technologically inferior "Indians" who greeted Columbus and who could be made to signify both the emptiness and the otherness of the New World, but a nation of discoverers who already know Columbus and enshrine him in their gallery of "principal inventors" (246). They find, in other words, a nation which has already attained, from its vantage point of secrecy, the epistemic mastery over the "utterly unknown" for which the voyage of discovery is a metaphor. This recursion within the voyage out, the encounter with the discovering subject himself in the position which the discourse of discovery insists belongs to the New World or Nature or the Other, exemplifies with peculiar clarity the phenomenon I have been tracing: the tendency for the discourse of discovery to construct other minds as undiscovered countries whose secrecy is in an equal ratio to the discoverer's will to penetrate the unknown. More explicitly than the secret affinity between Harman and the vagrants, the conflation of discovered world and discovering minds in Francis Bacon's utopian text makes clear that the discourse of discovery, at least in the instances with which we are concerned, is not merely a rehearsal of an alienated, masterful relationship between the discovering subject and his world, a formulation that takes for granted that the structure of discovery is fully achieved, stable, and self-evident. Rather, it is also an attempt to articulate the position of the discovering subject, to make present in discourse a subject who marks a rupture with all previous discourse, and which the logic of discovery makes a primary emptiness: "he that knowest least [and] is [therefore] fittest to ask questions" (221).

Up to this point I have delineated this process by focusing on operations of discovery which readily disclose their own fraudulence and which therefore generate counter-discourses, hostile or ironic, or even simply generic reframings of the scenario of discovery which call attention to the discovering subject as himself an object of discovery. The existence of such a contested discursive field testifies both to the compulsion in this period to construct social relationships in terms of discovery and the ease with which such constructions could be challenged. It indicates, in other words, the as-yet emergent status of the epistemic arrangements which will support the discovering subject's preeminence. I want to conclude by shifting the ground of my discussion to Bacon's attempt in his philosophical writings to provide a rigorous account of the epistemology of discovery and to establish it as a dominant mode of knowing. Doing so will permit me to recapitulate some of the problems of the discovering and discovered subject that I have traced in the more obviously compromised discovery modes operating in torture, in Shakespeare's deputy dramas, and in conycatching pamphlets, and to suggest their connection both to the rise to dominance of a scientific model of knowledge with which Bacon's project has traditionally been associated, and to the ideological endorsement of a recognizably modern idea of the subject in which it has more recently been implicated. My aim in this chapter is thus to join with other recent critics in using political concerns to deconstruct Bacon's epistemology, to reveal the ways in which scientific objectivity constructs and privileges a particular style of subjectivity. But my argument is not that Bacon's scientific program is merely the discovery of the subject writ large, an opening of the secrets of nature analogous to the probing of the conscience during interrogation (although Bacon himself does make this analogy). Rather, I want to argue that the discovery of nature also represents a resolution of the impasse at which the discovery of the subject seems inevitably to arrive, when the hidden truth of the other's soul eludes the discoverer and he is himself revealed as the bearer of the secret, innovative will to power which he attributes to his adversary. For nature, as it emerges in Bacon's writing, does not merely substitute for the discoverable subject but introduces a third term into the diad we have been examining, and so procures a release from its ferocious self-reflexivity.

Bacon's philosophical project (like his legal career) has proved as susceptible to scandal as any of the projects of discovery I have traced so far, although the outbreaks were deferred for several centuries. What might be called the first Baconian scandal, the realization toward the end of the nineteenth century that Bacon was no scientist, that his insistence that the discovering mind must be empty of presuppositions was profoundly naive, that his own proclaimed "discoveries" (such as that of the nature of heat) reiterated commonplaces, points to the discovering subject as the destabilizing element in his project.[2] His subsequent recuperation as the *prophet* of a new science makes his central achievement his vision of the discovering subject's position *vis-à-vis* nature and his fellow men, an achievement that attests to the power of his imagination rather than to the transparency of his own relation to nature. It is this radically utopian nature of Bacon's work, the fact that he imagined a subject position that he did not occupy, even discursively, that has also given rise to the more recent versions of Baconian scandal. Now the will to power that erupts everywhere in Bacon's exhortations to discover nature is adduced to disclose the ideological function of his call for a new knowledge in which "all depends on keeping the eye steadily fixed upon the facts of nature and so receiving their images simply as they are" (*GI* IV:32).[3] The Bacon who announces in presenting the plan of his *Great Instauration*, "I do not propose merely to survey these regions in my mind, like an augur taking auspices, but to enter them like a general who means to take possession" (IV:23), exposes as disingenuous or imaginary the humble passivity he requires of the discoverer when he asserts that "the entrance into the kingdom of man, founded on the sciences, [is] not much other than the entrance into the kingdom of heaven, whereinto none may enter except as a little child" (*GI* IV:69). Claiming a radical innocence for the agent of his method, Bacon nonetheless exposes his implication in a violence that connects the discovery of nature to colonization, patriarchal domination of women, technological elitism, in short, to the emergence of a masterful masculine subject with an instrumental purchase on the world. In other words, Bacon's epistemology can be seen as an (inadequate) cover for the fundamentally political motives of the project. The problem which Bacon's work speaks to but cannot resolve is thus, in Timothy Reiss's words, how "to guide [the enunciating subject] toward its disappearance" so that the authority of the discoverer's discourse will be "the authority of things in themselves," rather than of his own imperious assertion.[4]

But a formulation such as Reiss's collapses two distinct but intertwined problems that give rise to the violence troubling Bacon's writing: the discovering subject's relation to pre-existing discourses and authorities, and his relation to the objects of his investigation. In the passage cited above, "these regions" that Bacon means to conquer refer, in fact, not to nature itself but to sciences of nature that are as yet undeveloped: "For," Bacon asserts, "there are found in the intellectual as well as the terrestrial globe, waste regions as well as cultivated ones" (*GI* IV:23). Bacon makes no attempt to hide the revolutionary violence entailed in his relation to the intellectual globe; his aim is "at once and with one blow [to] set aside all sciences and authors; and that too, without calling in any of the ancients to our aid and support, but relying on our own strength" (*GI* IV:108).[5] But he also denies the "presumption" inherent in such a relation to discursive authority, arguing instead that he has chosen to follow authority of another kind. Previous discourses must be set aside so that "the facts of nature" can speak: "new discoveries must be sought from the light of nature, not fetched back out of the darkness of antiquity" (*GI* IV:109). In short, Bacon must overturn discursive authority so that he can be humble before the truths of nature. Having defined the "truths of nature" in opposition to the discursive "darkness of antiquity," Bacon links the establishment of these truths to repeated assertions of the novelty of the discoverer's position, to demonstrations that he has found truths which have not yet become part of discourse. Thus if Bacon's epistemology is an alibi, what it covers is not, in the first instance, a violence toward nature but the novel, autonomous stance of the discoverer. This is not to say, however, that the opposition between nature and the authority of philosophical predecessors, between Bacon's humble and imperialist stances, is a stable one. Describing his conquest in the domain of discourse, Bacon resorts to his favorite metaphor for the discovery of nature, the exploration of the "terrestrial globe." He thus makes clear that the discovering subject's relation to nature and to discursive authority are the mutually enabling conditions for his empowerment. The freedom from the constraints of authority and tradition permits the discovering subject to encounter the unknown; the encounter with the "unknown" grants him the right to begin discourse anew.

It will be useful at this point to ask *why* the discoverer's will to power should be problematic for Bacon's project, why at points he seems to disavow the conquistadorial ambition that is writ large across his project. Modern readers tend to take as self-evident both the scandalous nature of the violence of Bacon's project and the location of that violence in the relation between the discoverer and nature or its analogs. But the various episodes of discovery that we have traced so far suggest that this might not have been the case for Bacon's contemporaries, that for them, problems of legitimacy might arise just where Bacon acknowledges them, in the "presumption" of his relation to authority that emerges in his claim "to begin anew from the very foundations (*GI* IV:52). What was scandalous about the Elizabethan resort to torture, after all, was not precisely its violence (for it hardly entailed more violence from our point of view than the publicly performed execution of traitors) but the discursive rupture it betokened – the rupture that made it recognizable as violence. Boldly claiming for his position the utter novelty which the Elizabethan authorities, the Catholic missionaries, and Thomas Harman all denied for theirs, Bacon marks a shift in the ideological significance that such a claim could bear.[6] But the nature of this shift must be carefully specified, for while Bacon valorizes novelty, he also seeks to dissociate it from the enunciating subject, asserting again and again his distrust of the mind as an origin of discourse. Although framed as epistemological self-consciousness, this distrust can also be read as a registration of the politically disruptive implications of the subject of Bacon's own discourse who claims to initiate the program which will purge, sweep, and level the floor of the mind.

It has frequently been remarked that, if Bacon himself was a staunch supporter of the King and defender of the royal prerogative, his philosophical project is ideologically as well as epistemically revolutionary, susceptible of appropriation by millenarian Puritans in the service of leveling and of reappropriation by Boyle and the founders of the Royal Society to authorize the privileges and power of an elite aggregate of educated male subjects under a restored but diminished sovereign.[7] I would certainly concur that the knowledge-making system Bacon envisions undermines the position of the sovereign, conferring power instead on those men who possess the secrets of nature's workings. But while Bacon's writing enabled the privileged position which the scientist and his political corollary, the disinterested, rational man, would come to enjoy, his discourse does not simply empower the subject whose position it articulates. Rather, it can also be said to *discipline* him, in the Foucauldian sense of the term, imagining the discovering subject, bringing him under suspicion to precisely the degree that it empowers him, always alerting us to the possibility that the discursive "I" will exceed the "eye" fixed on the facts of nature. Epistemological self-consciousness becomes a tool to contain the discoverer's will to power within institutional agendas, to make its transgressive potential fuel the normal activity of knowledge production.

Examining nature

In Bacon's image of the "eye steadily fixed on the facts of nature," nature is constructed as an object, separate and different from the discoverer who scrutinizes it. Bacon's objectification of nature is, in fact, one of his most celebrated, or notorious achievements, and is arguably implicit in that favorite metaphor for his project, the voyage of discovery. But before we can understand what ends this objectification of nature serves, we also need to acknowledge another, apparently contradictory, tendency of Bacon's writing, that is to construct nature as a subject. This tendency is evident in another of Bacon's favorite metaphors for his project, the discovery of nature as a legal inquisition. Thus in the *Great Instauration* he urges would-be discoverers "not to think the inquisition of nature is in any part interdicted or forbidden" (IV:20) and promises that he will only admit natural facts after "careful and severe examination" (IV:30). And in the *Parasceve* the Lord Chancellor announces:

I mean (according to the practice in civil causes) in this great Plea or Suit granted by the divine favour and providence (whereby the human race seeks to recover its right over nature), to examine nature herself and the arts upon interrogatories. (IV:263)

Critics have adduced such passages to reveal the drive to dominate nature which fuels Bacon's project, often equating such domination with objectification. And yet, such a critique speaks its ethical horror at Bacon's project by affirming what his metaphor actually suggests: that nature is not in fact an object and is therefore capable of being brutalized in the same way that (we assume) a person could be de-humanized in the course of inquisition. As John Michael Archer notes after citing a string of such moments in Bacon's writing, "the sciences of nature impl[y] the unwritten methodology of the sciences of human control within the modern state," a comment which should remind us that if the discovery of nature is linked to the coercive techniques of the early modern English state, then it involves the anthropomorphism of nature as well as its objectification.[8]

However, it is worth pausing over just what the "science of human control" which is implied in the term "inquisition" consists of. For if "inquisition" conjures up to modern readers the most extreme forms of testimonial coercion, in Bacon's time it also signified more generally the method of inquiry practiced in the English civil courts and in Roman-canon law. In the passage from the *Parasceve*, for instance, Bacon is specifically invoking the procedures for interrogating witnesses in Chancery, where mere property, rather than state or religious matters (and hence the secrets of the soul) are at issue. And yet, as we saw in earlier chapters, inquisitorial procedure generally was the object of common lawyers' suspicion particularly insofar as it was associated with Star Chamber, *ex officio* oaths, and interrogatory torture. Moreover, Bacon's self-construction as a careful and severe examiner is unnervingly juxtaposed to his assertion that, contrary to Aristotelian precept that natural history concerns only the ordinary course of nature, his project will be "a history not only of nature free and at large . . . but much more of nature under constraint and vexed; that is to say, when by art and the hand of man she is forced out of her natural state, and squeezed and moulded" (*GI* IV:20). Thus the metaphor of inquisition is not innocent; it was associated in the minds of Bacon and his contemporaries with problematic techniques of "human control" and was haunted by torture. But it also suggests a range of more complex relations between the discoverer and nature than simple domination. In an essay tracing Bacon's use of the metaphor in the philosophical works, Kenneth Cardwell has argued that when he describes the investigation of nature as inquisition, the distinguishing features of the various civil court procedures and the differentiated positions of defendant, plaintiff, witness, and judge tend to disappear. In the philosophical work inquisition stands for the diadic encounter at the heart of Roman-canon legal procedure, the inquisitor's careful examination of another's heart and mind.[9] Moreover, as Cardwell points out, in Roman-canon judicial science the primary technique of inquisition is not the use of force but empathic identification of the inquisitor with the examinee, so that the inquisitor, with only minimal discursive intervention, can bring the examinee to confess himself. Thus the metaphor actually makes subjectivity the common ground between nature and the discoverer. Imagined as an inquisition, the discovery of nature is an intersubjective process in which the truths one "mind" harbors can be reproduced as the knowledge of another. And yet in the passage from the *Parasceve* Bacon has also cast nature as an estate to be litigated over. In fact the metaphor comes unmoored from the civil procedure it invokes (and slides toward the more sinister procedures of Star Chamber) because, according to Cardwell, Bacon seeks to make nature a witness in a case in which she herself is also the issue (282). For Bacon nature *is* an object properly under man's control, but to gain that control he must come to know her as a subject like himself.

Bacon habitually styles the workings of nature as "secrets," suggesting that they are hard to get at, both because of the limitations of the mind and the dissembling surface of nature herself. He wants to "reach the remoter and more hidden parts of nature," to penetrate the "deceitful resemblances" which make the universe "like a labyrinth" (*GI* IV:18), to make "the secrets of nature reveal themselves" (*GI* IV:95). But while this emphasis on secrecy would seem to proclaim the otherness of nature, Bacon also makes clear that it is precisely the secrecy of nature which links it to human subjectivity in his mind:

For even as in the business of life a man's disposition and the secret workings of his mind and affections are better discovered when he is in trouble than at other times; do likewise the secrets of nature reveal themselves more readily under the vexations of art than when they go their own way. (*GI* IV:95)

Nor in Bacon's thinking is secrecy merely the attribute of *otherness* whether human or natural, constituting instead the chief characteristic of the discovering subject himself. This emerges powerfully in the *New Atlantis*, where the purpose of Salomon's House, the island's research institute, is the discovery of "Causes and the secret motions of things" (239) and the Fathers of that institute "take all an oath of secrecy for concealing of those [discoveries] which we think fit to keep secret" (246). Thus when a Father of the House comes to the city where the travelers are staying they are told "we have seen none of them this dozen years. His coming is in state, but the cause of his coming is secret" (237). Moreover, the whole island of Bensalem maintains a policy of secrecy in its relations with the rest of the world, reposing as it does in "a secret conclave of a such a vast sea . . . hidden and unseen to others [and yet having] others open and as in a light to them," a situation which it carefully maintains by bribing any accidental discoverers to stay with them forever, and sending its own discoverers forth into the world incognito (224–5). Bacon's obsession with secrecy testifies to the instrumentality of the discoverer's relation to the world; it makes clear the dimension of power in knowledge relations that is elided in the account of discovery as the eye steadily fixed on the facts of nature.[10] What's more, in styling the truth of nature's causes as secret, something enclosed and guarded, whether by nature herself, or by her discoverers, Bacon constructs that truth as a *possession* from its very inception. Although we may have to assume an objective stance *vis-à-vis* nature in order to glean her secrets they are also only imaginable, even in their undiscovered state, as the property of a subject.

And yet, if the secrecy of nature's causes means that they always have a (not necessarily permanent) owner and address, Bacon's promiscuous assignment of secrecy in his philosophical writings, to the natural as well as the human, the discoverer as well as the discovered, also gives it a disorienting ubiquity. It becomes a kind of floating property, suggesting not epistemic barriers to be overcome (the darkness and enclosure which the discoverer penetrates) but, paradoxically, a chain of furtive, but unstanchable communication. That Bacon understands intersubjective, if not scientific discovery, in these terms is suggested in the essay, "Of Simulation and Dissimulation." "Secrecy," Bacon writes,

is indeed the virtue of a confessor. And assuredly the secret man heareth many confessions. For who will open himself to a blab or babbler? But if a man be thought secret, it inviteth discovery; as the more close air sucketh in the more open; and as in confession the revealing is not for worldly use, but for the ease of a man's heart, so secret men come to the knowledge of many things in that kind; while men rather discharge their minds than impart their minds. In few words, mysteries are due to secrecy. (VI:388)

A familiar scene of discovery is being modeled for us, and yet it is hard to see exactly what is going on because of the surprising and unstable locations of agency in the passage. Secrecy here is the attribute of the gleaner of knowledge, the figure I have called the discovering subject. A form of not-doing, it nevertheless "inviteth" others to open their hearts. Discovery, on the other hand, is performed by the one initially possessed of secrets.[11] An action ("discharging"), it is nevertheless nearly involuntary, in contrast to the more judicious "imparting" and to the passive yet strategic "com[ing] to knowledge" of the "secret man [who] heareth many confessions." But if it seems that there is simply an inversion of agency here, the impassive, secret man emerging as the purposive, methodical discoverer, the analogy with the circulation of air undermines such an interpretation, insisting on the non-volitional character of the process of discovery. The analogy suggests, in fact, that once the "confessor" is fully possessed of the other's confession he must himself "discharge" what he knows, although presumably to another "confessor" as close and secret as he has been. Hence in the final ambiguous sentence, a statement of entitlement (mysteries are rightfully delivered up to secrecy) competes semantically with a tautology that effaces agency altogether: mysteries are caused by secrecy.

In the *New Atlantis* a program of strategic secrecy is similarly undermined by what seems to be non-volitional principle of information circulation. Thus when the governor of the House of Strangers has summed up the strategic relation of the Island of Bensalem to the rest of the world – "we know well most part of the habitable world and are ourselves unknown" – he immediately departs from this economy of simple secretive accumulation of knowledge: "Therefore," he tells the strangers, "because he that knowest least is fittest to ask questions, it is more reason for the entertainment of the time that ye ask me questions than that I ask you" (221). Moreover, if Bensalem's scientific and technological mastery is inextricably bound up with asserting and maintaining the secrecy of truth, the *telos* of the work is toward the Island's complete discovery of itself to the narrator. Thus the text concludes (or breaks off) with the Father of the House of Salomon's blessing following his relation to the narrator of the experiments and achievements of the establishment, "'I give thee leave to publish [this relation] for the good of other nations, for we here are in God's bosom, a land unknown'" (247). Although Bensalem's reasons for its secrecy are explained (life on the island is so felicitous that contact with the outside world would lead only to degeneration) there is no reason given for the apparent reversal of policy indicated by the Father's narrative.

In these accounts of discovery as an intersubjective process, the strategic seems to slide into the automatic; what begins as the effect of a policy of secrecy in aid of discovery becomes a movement of secrets from one subject to another that is unaccountable, or accountable only by analogy to a natural law, a "discharge" or reflex action that Bacon distinguishes from the more circumspect and therefore subjective activity of "imparting."[12] At the same time, the one-way trajectory of discovery from secrecy to disclosure seems to dissolve into a kind of oscillation between the reproduction of secrecy and "publication" as possible outcomes of discovery. This ambivalence in these scenarios of discovery suggests that the discovering subject for Bacon is defined not so much by his position or his activity (that is, by secrecy, objectivity, or domination of nature) as by his liminality, his continual movement between secrecy and openness, even between being a subject and a kind of object. More generally, the slippages in Bacon's discourse between the discoverer and the discovered, strategy and natural process, even between publication and secrecy reveal the tensions that structure the disciplinary regime that I have suggested is incipient in Bacon's project and suggests the means by which that regime not merely recapitulates, but also departs from the infinite regress of mirroring subjectivities produced by interrogatory torture.

The liminality of the discovering subject in Bacon's discourse is produced in relation to variations in his characterization of nature. Troped as the possessor of secrets, nature can be mapped as a kind of crafty interiorized adversary whose secrets must be "searched out and brought to light" by a similarly crafty, secretive discoverer (*GI* IV:58). But, in his epistemological self-consciousness, Bacon also insists that nature is a form of outwardness, that which lies beyond the idol-beset enclosure of the human mind.[13] Nature is altogether different from subjectivity, a collectivity of analyzable, usable principles. "Matter," he writes sternly,

rather than forms should be the object of our attention, its configurations and changes of configuration, and simple action and law of action or motion for forms are figments of the human mind, unless you will call those laws of action forms. (*GI* IV:58)

And so, striving to discern matter's laws of action, the discovering subject must himself become an "eye" from which subjective contents – "infusion from the will and affection" (*GI* IV:58) – have been eliminated, or, still more drastically, a kind of mechanism. The strength of his method, Bacon argues, is that "the mind itself [is] from the very outset not left to take its own course, but guided at every step; and the business . . . done as if by machinery" (*GI* IV:40). In Bacon's writing these two conceptions of discovery, as the secretive appropriation of secrets, and as the mechanistic acquisition of information about predictable laws of action, emerge simultaneously, interrupting and troubling each other. Thus, for example, in "Of Simulation" the intimate confession of a secret is also a kind of "discharge," a predictable motion of nature like "the close air [which] sucketh in the more open." The result is an instability in Bacon's account of discovery that is simultaneously ethical and epistemic. For, if the inquisition of a secretive nature casts the discovering subject as the hero who recovers for the human race its right over nature, the one in whom knowledge and power meet, the mechanistic analysis of laws of action means that the same discoverer must be regarded with constant suspicion, as the source of self-aggrandizement and delusion.

The ethical ambiguity that attends the discovering subject in Bacon's discourse becomes especially noticeable around the problem of labor. Nor should this surprise us, given the suspicion of secret laborers we have noticed in previous discovery scenarios. Describing the myriad ways in which the mind is cut off from attaining true knowledge of nature by its own propensities, Bacon impugns not particular faculties (such as the imagination) but mental labor itself. The pre-Socratics (whom Bacon generally admires) went astray because they "made everything turn upon hard thinking and perpetual working and exercise of the mind" (*GI* IV:39). The problem with such an approach is not merely that it does not yield knowledge of the true workings of nature, but that it makes the thinking subject a self-enclosed, self-promoting entity. In the *Advancement of Learning* Bacon makes plain the morally suspect nature of such hard thinking:

Upon these intellectualists Heraclitus gave a just censure, saying "Men sought truth in their own little worlds and not in the great and common world"; for they disdain to spell, and so by degrees to read the volume of God's works; and contrariwise by continual meditation and agitation of wit do urge and as it were invoke their own spirits to divine and give oracles unto them, whereby they are deservedly deluded. (*AL* 34)[14]

Less willfully treacherous perhaps than other secret laborers we have encountered, these intellectualists are nevertheless like them, presumptuous, self-interested meddlers displacing truth with their representation of their own invention. Bacon responds with a rather conservative rhetorical maneuver, resorting to classical authority to frame his project as a restoration of these intellectual laborers to community with each other and God. But if the passage exhibits affinities with the conservative claims of other discoverers we have encountered, it also adumbrates the possibilities for new social order that the discovery of nature makes available.

Nature defines a common world; the discovery of it brings men out of the caves of their minds into the light of truth. But the point is not, it should be made clear, that the discovery of nature enables an intersubjective knowledge, the entry into the secrets of other men's souls which the discoverers we have encountered so far were seeking. The common world that nature defines is outside the subject; if he is to join it, his mind must be controlled, and even made redundant by an externalized, non-idiosyncratic set of procedures. Bacon is quite explicit that the virtue of his system is that it makes men interchangeable, not because *they* are alike but because their agency has been separated from the problematic mind and made the extension of a pre-established set of procedures:

For my way of discovering sciences goes far to level men's wit and leaves but little to individual excellence, because it performs everything by the surest rules and demonstrations. (*GI* IV:109)

In the *New Atlantis* this depersonalizing of discovery is represented through the carefully detailed division of labor at Salomon's House. There, research is executed by numerically determined teams named only for their function:

"We have three that collect the experiments which are in all books. These we call Depredators.
"We have three that collect the experiments of all mechanical arts; and also of the liberal sciences, and also of practices which are not brought into arts. These we call Mystery-men.
"We have three that try new experiments, such as themselves think good. These we call Pioneers or Miners . . ." (245)

And so forth. And while the principle of heroic individual discovery is celebrated in the "very long galler[y] . . . where [they] place statua's of all principal inventors," of these inventors only Columbus is named, the others disappearing into a formulaic catalogue: "the inventor of works in metal: the inventor of glass: the inventor of silk of the worm . . ." (246). Indeed, given the wholly anonymous and collaborative research practices of Salomon's house, it is difficult to see how such "inventors" are ever identified.

The depersonalized, mechanized process of discovery embodied in Salomon's House limits what any individual man may do. But the disciplinary effect of this fantasy, I would argue, is not directed at other less intellectually reliable men but rather at the mind that created it. The mechanization of discovery is the defense adduced to answer the charge of "presumption" that Bacon concedes must arise in response to his own claims of novelty:

And as for the presumption implied in [Bacon's rejection of all previous authorities], certainly if a man undertakes by steadiness of hand and power of eye to describe a straighter line or more perfect circle than anyone else, he challenges a comparison of abilities; but if he only says that he with the help of a rule or a pair of compasses can draw a straighter line or a more perfect circle than anyone else can by eye and hand alone, he makes no great boast, and this remark, be it observed applies not merely to this first and inceptive attempt of mine, but to all that shall take the work in hand hereafter. (*GI* IV:109)

Bacon does what he can to divorce the novelty of his discourse from its thinking, working, enunciating subject, "Francis of Verulam [who] reasoned thus with himself" to initiate it (*GI* IV:7). His revolutionary program has come to him through "luck"; it is "a birth of time rather than of wit," proleptically, an effect of the new mechanistic methodology that it offers to the world (*GI* IV:109). If, as I suggested at the outset, the logic of discovery offers Bacon an alibi, new discoveries requiring "a totally new" way of thinking, what stands in as the legitimating origin of scientific discourse is not so much the facts of nature as the routine of discovery and the division of labor it requires. The subject of Bacon's philosophical writing proclaims himself a solitary explorer, "a pioneer, following in no man's track nor sharing these counsels with anyone," but he is nevertheless anxious to install his solitary activity within a collectivity, and his "inceptive attempt" within repetition.

Larceny from the King

In the *Novum Organum* Bacon declares: "I plainly confess that a collection of history natural and experimental, such as I conceive it and as it ought to be, is a great, I may say a royal work, and of much labor and expense" (IV:101). Appearing as it does in a work addressed to the King, this "confession" is clearly a bid for funding, a hint to James to establish the kind of institution which Bacon believes can accomplish the discovery of nature's secrets, and which he models in Salomon's House. It reprises a more direct suggestion that Bacon had made in *The Advancement of Learning*, another work addressed to James, when he noted the need for allowances for the expenses involved in experiments. "And therefore," Bacon concluded, "as secretaries and spials of princes and states bring in bills for intelligence, so you must allow the spials and intelligencers of nature to bring in their bills; or else you shall be ill advertised" (64). In his insistence on reliable payment for royal service, Bacon is perhaps pushing the King toward a utopian future in which civil servants can reject gratuities because, like those in the *New Atlantis*, they have "salary sufficent of the state for [their] service" (41). But if Bacon hints at reform here, he can only do so because the new institution he imagines is constructed on analogy with present practice: the systematic discovery of nature can be extrapolated from the existing royal administrative systems. Indeed, as Julian Martin has exhaustively demonstrated, Bacon's vision of a systematic discovery of nature can be seen in many respects as an extension of the thinking about state administration he developed under the tutelage of Elizabeth's Privy Councilors.[15] Not only is the examination of nature imagined on analogy to the practices of Chancery or Star Chamber or the intelligence networks developed by Walsingham, Essex, and Robert Cecil, but the collaborative, institutional research program envisioned in *The New Atlantis* is indebted to structures for disseminating royal authority, such as the rationalized court system which employed so many lawyers (and in an early phase gave Thomas Harman his official function). Bacon is a pioneer of bureaucracy as much as of science.[16] His writing forges positive ideological links between the state, knowledge production, and the control of information. Of course such links had been hostilely noted before, as in the Catholics' struggle with Elizabeth's government when William Allen asserted that the state's control of the media gave it the means to promulgate lies.[17] But for Bacon the control of information signifies something much larger than the means to win particular political battles. The institution Bacon envisions is one in which the secrets of nature will be met by administrative order and turned into data that can be used to promote the good of the commonwealth and to consolidate the power of the state which, at least in the *Advancement*, he explicitly identifies as the Crown.

The bid Bacon makes in *The Advancement* is in many respects a normalizing one: the work of discovering nature, though "totally new" (*GI* IV:11) cannot only be routinized, but also in a manner that is simply an extension of existing institutional practices which support the monarchy. While Bacon's resort to analogy smoothes the connection between present practice and the totally new, however, what is striking about this passage (written, it will be recalled, on the eve of the Gunpowder Plot) is the awkwardness of the analogy, the difficulty it presents to the reader of lining up nature with subversion, the apparently gratuitous and indeterminate element of threat it carries. What does it mean for the King to be "ill-advertised?" Would ill-advertisement arise from incompetence or a resentful hoarding of information? And are the consequences dangerous to the monarch in the way that poor intelligence about foreign enemies and domestic subversives would be? The very administrative niche to which Bacon compares the discovery of nature (espionage) arises from the ambiguous limits of the monarch's power over the hearts and minds of his subjects, and even threatens to expand, through ill-advertisement, the subjective territory beyond the King's knowledge. Bacon seeks to contain the revolutionary subject of his discourse within intellectual and institutional routine, but he also manages to suggest that such routine is founded on, and even perpetuates, the power of the subject. It can thus become a staging ground for the revolutionary work of imagining a new institution with the potential to eclipse any existing site of authority, whether church, parliament, university, or even monarch. In the *New Atlantis*, after all, where the Fathers of the House of Salomon control the dissemination of intelligence, ill-advertisement of the (never-named) monarch has become standard operating procedure. Thus the Father concludes his recital to the travelers:

And this we do also: we have consultations, which of the inventions and experiences which we have discovered shall be published, and which not, and take all an oath of secrecy, for the concealing of those which we think fit to keep secret: though some of those we do reveal sometimes to the state, and some not. (246)

"The glory of God is to conceal a thing and the glory of the King is to find it out" (40). Thus Bacon elsewhere in the *Advancement* cites Solomon, James's prototype, adding, "as if according to the innocent play of children, the Divine Majesty took delight to hide his works, to the end to have them found out" (41). But this representation of discovery as an absolutist pastime that produces a transparent world is qualified by the reminder to the King of how he actually gets his intelligence, of his dependence on secretaries and spials whose services require compensation. Bacon's program occupies and enlarges the space between the King and the secrets of the world, turning his innocent play into the protracted "royal work" which will engage many subjects, each one of whom Bacon encourages to think of himself as analogous to the King, striving "to win the kingdom of nature [and] govern it" (*GI* IV:108). More particularly though, in bringing up the matter of payment, Bacon signals the private interests of those who gather knowledge on behalf of the King, suggesting that each man involved has the capacity to act for himself, to have desires or commitments beyond his loyalty to the monarch and, therefore, to become, like other state servants we have encountered, the harborer of secrets of his own. There is, in fact, a persistent conjunction in Bacon's writing of pecuniary self-interest, potential subversiveness, and the work of thinking the "totally new."[18] This conjunction underlies the rhetorical gesture with which Bacon begins the dedicatory epistle to the *Great Instauration*: "Your Majesty may perhaps accuse me of larceny, having stolen from your affairs so much time as was required for this work" (IV:11). Such an admission is, of course, disingenuous, and Bacon continues by reminding the King

that "what has been abstracted from your business may perhaps go to
the memory of your name and the honor of your age" (IV:11). In
framing the *Great Instauration* as the fruit of larceny from the King,
however, Bacon indicates, despite his disavowal, the Promethean character of his project. His "kindling of this new light" (IV:11) for the good
of mankind has involved abstracting from the King not just time, but
also power and authority, which he locates firmly in the facts of nature
and in the procedures for discovering them.[19] But the disgrace that was
to befall the Lord Chancellor within the year in his conviction for bribery
also adds a bitter irony to this rhetorical gesture, serving as a reminder of
the self-interest of which secretaries and spials are capable.[20] In taking
bribes Bacon was not, of course, stealing from the King. But the
customary defense of Bacon, that he was disgraced for a practice
everyone engaged in, only goes to underscore the point that self-interest
and the appropriation of power and resources are systemic possibilities
of royal service. The resonances of Bacon's "larceny" suggest that the
Promethean bringer of new light is also a civil servant in pursuit of his
own interests. The heroic (and problematic) subject of Bacon's discourse
who wants "at once and with one blow to set aside all sciences and all
authors" (*GI* IV:108) proclaims a rupture between past and future
knowledge, but he also already has an institutional history, one that
portends a rather different kind of institutional future in which the King
has been superseded in favor of the institutions of knowledge manage-
ment themselves.

In linking Bacon's roles as intellectual revolutionary and state servant,
then, I am ultimately making quite a different argument from one such
as Julian Martin's, which stresses the continuity between Bacon's political career and his natural philosophy, with the implication that each of
these represents a stable system of practice and thought. As we have
seen, service to the early modern state entailed not only the development
of administrative apparatuses and appropriate knowledges but entry into
a complex relational field in which neither power nor allegiance could
stay in their officially assigned locations. And this instability arose
precisely because the monarchy's foundation was not God nor theatrical
display but, as Bacon understood, the institutions for the production and
control of knowledge it had spawned. The Promethean subject of
Bacon's philosophical writing is the imaginative product of the
institutional contradictions of the Renaissance state which empowered a
class of educated male subjects in order to make them servants of the
Crown and thereby generated the obsession with the discovery of the
subject I have been examining. Thus, at points the effect of Bacon's will
to power is simply to make plain the subversive identifications that can

so easily be read out of other crises in Renaissance authority, as in the *Advancement* for example, when he writes that knowledge is to be desired above all things:

> For there is no power on earth which setteth up a throne or chair of estate in the spirits and souls of men, and in their cogitations, imaginations, opinions, and beliefs, but knowledge and learning. And therefore we see the detestable and extreme pleasure that arch-heretics, and false prophets, and imposters are transported with, when they once find in themselves that they have a superiority in the faith and conscience of men; so great as if they have once tasted of it, it is seldom seen that any torture or persecution can make them relinquish or abandon it. (57)

Aligning his wholly valorized internal "throne" of knowledge with the (to him) dangerous, deluded resistance of the torture victim Bacon reveals (like the hapless Thomas Harman) the subversive kinship of the subject whose power he seeks to enlarge. But Bacon's project does not merely perpetuate the processes of subjection that characterize the Renaissance state. While Bacon rhetorically gives the King his due, his discourse also resolutely shifts power from the sovereign to nature, with the implication that from thence it can be appropriated for human use by all men who can stay "the legitimate, chaste and severe course of inquiry" (*GI* IV:32).

What is achieved in the discovery of nature is not simply a new relation between men and nature but the occulting of power relations between men. The forms of domination and subjection which are so painfully evident in the various scenarios of discovery we have been examining, and so scandalous to the discoverer's knowledge claims, have no place in Bacon's philosophical writing save as metaphors for the discovery of nature. In the *New Atlantis* (in striking contrast to More's *Utopia*) there is no account of penal methods, or, indeed, of social regulation of any kind save that which impinges on the circulation of knowledge. There is, however, a detailed relation of a ceremony, the Feast of the Family, which celebrates any man who has produced thirty offspring: "For they say the king is debtor to no man, but for propagation of his subjects" (233). The Feast of the Family, which takes place with the monarch's blessing but in his absence, emblematizes the displacement of the power relations of the Renaissance state by a new relation between the autonomous male subject and nature. The man who has made the King his debtor is set upon a platform decorated with materials both beautiful and symbolic and beholds his ceremonially clad offspring arranged before him. Thus one significance of this ceremony, obviously enough, is the appropriation for the male subject of the trappings proper to the monarch. But a striking feature also differentiates it from traditional display of the monarch:

and if there be a mother from whose body the whole lineage is descended there is a traverse placed in a loft above on the right hand of the chair with a privy door, and a carved window of glass leaded with gold and blue where she sitteth, but is not seen. (232)

Although the valence of the Feast is obviously rigorously patriarchal, it also departs from the representational schema of gender ideology. The mother is neither repressed nor displayed as a subordinate, but is instead at once ostentatiously hidden, elevated, and afforded a privileged view of the proceedings.[21] Almost certainly an allegorical figure for nature, the mother literally backs the father whose potency is displayed in the ceremony; hers is the latent power which he makes manifest. As in Shakespeare's deputy dramas, heterosexual relations figure forth the larger relational field which defines the male subject. In those plays, however, men's connection to women, always manifested as desire, makes them the harborers of secrets and thus objects of discovery. Women and the desire they provoke thus define for men an incipiently private domain which is then exposed or threatened through the logic of the play's political relations, making visible the male subject's subordination to a more powerful man. The Feast of the Family voids sexual relations of desire, and makes them ostentatiously public. Secrecy is stripped of subversive significance and attributed to a force which both authorizes and serves the male subject. And sovereignty, the power divine which exposed Angelo's transgressive desire in *Measure for Measure,* concedes its indebtedness and its ceremonial forms to the single, potent, and fruitful male subject displayed on the dais.

This tableau of the triumphant, solitary patriarch, however, is not the only model of the subject's position and privileges within Bacon's brave new world. The singularity of the male subject the Feast celebrates is a function of the backward-looking negotiation which the Feast, with its recognizably Renaissance ceremonial aesthetic, effects between monarchical sovereignty and the subject who will command the new knowledge. This ceremonial model is supplemented in the *New Atlantis* by the wholly unallegorical account of the dynamic, quotidian, collaborative work of Salomon's House.[22] Here we do see relations between men, but they are conspicuously not defined in terms of power. The Fathers scrutinize each other's work ("we have three that bend themselves, looking into the experiments of their fellows" [246]) but not each other. Men divide the labor of experimentation, compare notes, make inductions; power flows from nature to men. The sphere of scientific discovery, as Bacon represents it, will be self-regulating and self-limiting. In the work of discovery, subjection will be reformulated as self-discipline. "Severe laws and overruling authority" may be brought to bear on the discovering subject, but he devises and administers them himself, under the rubric of obedience to nature (*GI* IV:57). Objectivity rather than loyalty thus becomes the optimum condition of subjection. The result is a circuit of empowerment, for, as Bacon tirelessly reminds us, "we cannot command nature except by obeying her" (*GI* IV:114). The collaborative work of Salomon's House is not inconsistent with the model of the solitary, possessive patriarchal subject honored in the Feast of the Family, since it is precisely through the routinized labors of discovering nature that the subject can supersede sovereign power. But Bacon's double modeling of subjecthood, the fact that neither the Feast of the Family nor the House of Salomon quite furnishes the definitive account, suggests that a certain restlessness always attends the subject in Bacon's imagination. The subject does not occupy a position but embodies a process whereby individual desire and power is recognized, legitimized, and controlled through the discipline of research.[23]

The domain that nature defines in Bacon's project is not precisely a public one – Bacon is explicit that the enterprise of discovery is both secret and elitist – but it is nevertheless a sphere in which privileged male subjects collectively enforce the method that will permit them to control nature. Here the kind of epistemic crisis which wracked the administration of the early modern state, the repeated encounter with the subject's opacity, will become business as usual. For Bacon's insistence that the mind itself will keep the discoverer from nature's power means that every manifestation of the subject's desire, or will, or capacity to initiate discourse potentially violates "the legitimate, chaste and severe course of inquiry" (*GI* IV:32) necessary for the discovery of nature. The effect, paradoxically, is reassuring. The subject's inevitable transgression (no longer treason but merely premature theorizing) is a sign that there is simply more work to be done, confirmation that "severe laws and overruling authority" are required to eliminate the "feign[ing] and suppos[ing]" to which the mind is given (*GI* IV:56–7). This capacity to imagine (if not to enact) the institutionalization of the epistemic crisis which the discovering subject produces makes Bacon's discourse discernibly more modern than that of the Elizabethan torturers (who, of course, included Bacon, the state servant) or the Catholics, or Harman. Sharing their anxiety about the autonomous subject their own discovering relation to the world calls into being, evincing an excitement at the power it accrues that Harman might have understood, Bacon nevertheless eschews their untenable assertions of continuity with past discourses and authorities – with English law, with a Catholic Church, with the customs of the country – in favor of the ongoing discovery of the facts of nature, a process which will permit the novelty and power of the discovering subject to be produced and regulated again and again. Thus the sort of impasse which the resort to torture seemed to result in, in which every effort to know and control the subject only produced evidence that the discoverer had not succeeded, becomes for Bacon a source of reassurance that the process of discovery must continue: "of knowledge," he writes, "there is no satiety, but satisfaction and appetite are perpetually inter-changable" (*AL* 58).

Coda: the future of science

It is difficult not to read Bacon as a prophet. In modern science, knowledge and power have indeed met as one. As Bacon predicted, it has been a great work, unfolding over the last 350 years, and of much labor and expense, the latter borne in the twentieth century largely, but not exclusively, by the state. Moreover, in our century, the production of scientific knowledge has been an institutional endeavor, conducted in universities, corporations, and state agencies such as the National Institutes of Health or Los Alamos. Both the ubiquity of these institu-tions and their heterogeneity, the fact that they serve multiple, if tightly imbricated interests, suggest that the scientific knowledge we now have is not so much the tool of the state as itself our latent sovereign. So too, the complex regulatory and intellectual property arrangements which allo-cate corporate profit, "liberal and honourable reward" for discoverers, and state control indicate, like the reservation of some secrets from the state by the Fathers of the House of Salomon, that while science supports the state, its powers and rewards do not wholly belong to the state. Meanwhile, the sort of spectacular sovereignty represented by Elizabeth or James I has long since disappeared, and with it the forms of bodily domination and resistance which supported it. But to read Bacon prophetically is also to read him tautologically, to fail to acknowledge either that we encounter Bacon through the lens of a particular scientific and political culture or that Bacon was an important ideological resource in the self-representation of that culture. In other words, to read Bacon as foretelling scientific modernity is to lose the distinction between discourse and practice, something which is easily done when making sweeping generalizations, as I have just done, about a construct like modern scientific culture.

In the preceding chapters I have argued that a particular obsession, the discovery of the hidden truth of others' hearts, is evident in various kinds of Renaissance writing, and that this obsession arises because of the collision in this period of burgeoning state administrative apparatus, older forms of authority, and certain legal and religious traditions, most notably the Augustinian concept of spiritual inwardness. The various episodes of discovery I have explored suggest that discourse and practice, or for that matter, discourse and discourse, seldom fit seamlessly with one another, that the participants were appropriating discursive resources for new situations and in the process changing what those resources could mean. Bacon, we have seen, appropriates the discovery of the subject itself, troping its techniques (inquisition), its institutions (courts and spy networks), and its epistemic concerns (hidden, inward truth) in order to imagine the discovery of the facts of nature. The Baconian discovery of nature recapitulates some features of the other discovery scenarios, especially the anxiety that attends the novel position of the discovering subject himself; in this respect both kinds of discovery are responses to the problematic redistribution of power and knowledge effected by the early modern state. But the discourse of the discovery of nature offers an escape from the infinite regress the specular struggle to discover the subject produces insofar as it locates authority in systematic, institutionalized procedures, rather than in the person of the sovereign, and truth in the non-subjective facts of nature. The discovery of nature is thus a more stable project than the discovery of the subject, partly because the truths it seeks are more concrete and therefore less susceptible to hysterical reification, but, more importantly, because it places authority in a structure akin to the one where power and knowledge are already beginning to be produced and controlled. In other words, I am suggesting that the discovery of the subject is a transitional phenomenon because it manages an historically specific contradiction between discourse and practice, while the discovery of nature has a future ahead of it because it more closely aligns them.

Of course such a statement requires immediate qualification. After all, royal administration, the structure from within which Bacon wrote, did not, in fact, support scientific research, while the bureaucratization of science is a rather late development in modern scientific practice. The scientific discovery of nature has historically been conducted in a wide array of institutional settings and political contexts. The gentlemen of the Royal Society had different sources of financial support, resources for personal identity, institutional responsibilities, and expectations for the knowledge they produced than do researchers at, say, a modern chemical company. And yet the Baconian idea of the subject and his relation to the world have been remarkably persistent in the rhetoric and the epistemic goals of scientists from the Royal Society onwards, as well as becoming increasingly pervasive in the more general discourse of the societies which support them. It might be more accurate, then, to say that in imagining the discovery of nature Bacon articulated a discourse of subjectivity which could be appropriated by differently situated practitioners in order to manage local contradictions or opportunities. And as with all such discursive appropriations these invocations and even implementations of Baconian ideas are partial, their precise form contingent on the circumstances under which they occur. Bacon imagined a totalizing regime, but he did not, indeed could not, inaugurate one.

The experimental activity of Robert Boyle and other early members of the Royal Society, as described by Steven Shapin and Simon Schaffer, furnishes a suggestive example of such partial, contingent appropriation of Baconian discourse.[24] Shapin and Schaffer argue that Boyle's experiments with the air-pump, a device designed to test the effects of air pressure on matter, served, among other ends, to model the production of knowledge as a collective, semi-public task. Air-pump trials were deliberately conducted in the ordinary assembly rooms of the Royal Society. Thus, "the space where these machines worked – the nascent laboratory – was to be a public space, but a restricted public space . . . If one wanted to produce authenticated experimental knowledge, matters of fact – one had to come to that space and see them with others" (39). In the laboratory, Thomas Sprat noted, it was the assembly of virtuosi who "resolved upon the matter of fact . . . [making] the whole process pass under its own eyes" and signing a register to verify what they had seen.[25] Shapin and Schaffer make clear that the ends which the laboratory served were at once epistemic and social. The artificial trial of nature and the collective witnessing it enabled eliminated the issue of the reliability testimony, of the subjective mediation of information which arises when nature is investigated in its ordinary courses, outside the laboratory. Individual testimony was problematic, not merely because it might be unreliable but because, like all authored discourses, it placed the subject himself in question and this could lead to violent, unproductive dispute. And the precedents for such dispute were not merely scientific controversy but the recent Civil War, in which claims of conscience or inspiration, of private access to truth, had produced bloody political upheaval. Boyle thus resisted any introduction of the personal into controversy, proclaiming "I love to speak of persons with civility, though of things with freedom," a stance in which he was assisted by the very nature of laboratory experiment, in which objects could furnish an alibi for possible problems of subjectivity.[26] "[I] question not his Ratiocination," he wrote of one disputant, "but only the stanchness of his pump."[27]

The self-representation and, to some extent, the practice of Boyle and his fellows seems to be continuous with Bacon's project in several respects. First, there is the stress laid on collective production of knowledge, with the political ramifications this emphasis carries. Despite the loyalty of the Royal Society's members to the restored king, meaningful authority resides with the assembled virtuosi as they reach consensus in their public rooms about experimental outcomes, much as it does with the Fathers of the House of Salomon. Second, there is the function of the properties of matter (whether they are manifest in a tool or the phenomenon which it tests) in distracting the discoverers from direct scrutiny of one another. Finally, in Boyle's insistence that persons are *not* in issue, there is the indication that the experimental discovery of nature is in part a defense against the kinds of epistemic and social crises the subject had provoked over the previous hundred years. At the same time, however, Boyle's discourse and practice reveal strategies for handling concerns about subjectivity which depart in crucial ways from Baconian models. Boyle, after all, was engaged in actual experimentation whereas Bacon was for the most part merely imagining it. Thus, while Bacon indicates that the discovery of nature is for those who can stay "the legitimate, chaste and severe course of inquiry," Boyle must decide who actually possesses this quality and therefore can join the semi-public community of knowers described above. In other words, Boyle's activity is embedded in a social milieu which offers its own specific resources and impediments to scientific work.

In his more recent work on Boyle and the social construction of credibility in Restoration science, Shapin argues that the investigations of Boyle and his fellows were supported by recourse to arguments, promulgated in philosophical treatises and conduct books alike, linking credibility to social class.[28] Truthfulness, Shapin argues, was seen as requiring freedom from dependency. If a man's livelihood or position made him dependent on others, then he was not always at liberty to pursue and speak the truth as he saw it. Rigorous intellectual honesty was thus the prerogative of gentlemen, particularly gentlemen such as Boyle, the younger son of a wealthy if parvenu Anglo-Irish aristocrat. Shapin makes a convincing case that the distinction between gentlemen on the one hand, and servants, professionals, or merchants on the other, proved stable and epistemically productive for Boyle and his fellows. The members of the Royal Society were gentlemen of independent means; as such they recognized one another's claims to objectivity and credibility. Although non-gentlemen (and some women) were extensively involved in experimental work as servants and technicians, their contribution was rarely acknowledged because their agency was supposed to be subsumed by that of their employers. And yet, in Shapin's account of experimental discourse and practice, servants do not function merely as dependents, doubling instead as interferers who carelessly or willfully deviate from instructions, thereby contaminating results. They crush substances they should have left whole, move tubes that should have stayed put, and shake volatile chemicals causing explosions. "Technicians' free will," Shapin notes, "was apt to erupt at any moment, turning laboratory good order into carnival" (390). Moreover, while the gentlemen scientist cultivated the open exchange of ideas and disavowed intellectual proprietorship (for example Boyle invited "all true lovers of Vertue & Mankind, to a free and generous Communication of their Secrets and Receits in Physick") the servant was construed as a repository of intellectual secrets.[29] Boyle even drafted an oath to be administered to technicians swearing them "to keep secret and not impart" experimental processes and results without their master's consent.[30] They are the master's secrets, to be sure, but what is striking here is that it is through the relationship with the servant, possessed of his own disturbingly ambiguous agency, that the master's own secretiveness, banished from the free and generous exchanges of the virtuosi, can surface. In Shapin's account servants serve as the vehicle for the expression of disciplinary concerns about subjectivity which are conspicuously directed away from the virtuosi. The virtuosi are free, rigorous, and open with one another; servants are potentially willful, heedless, and loquacious. That openness and loquacity might appear to overlap only underscores the function of servants in permitting the gentlemen scientists to disavow anxieties about competence, trustworthiness, and proprietorship among themselves.

I have argued that the Baconian discovery of nature subsumes and transforms the discovery of the subject. In scientific work the inherent self-reflexiveness of the discovery of the subject, the fact that the educated man who produces and manages knowledge is himself the one who subverts traditional authority, can be acknowledged and recuperated as epistemological self-consciousness. Particularly in the doctrine of the Idols we see Bacon normalizing the Renaissance sense of the subversiveness of subjectivity, redirecting and thereby controlling a cultural anxiety. But this is not to say that Bacon thereby dissipates this anxiety; rather, it suffuses and energizes his philosophical writings. In contrast to Bacon, however, Boyle and his fellows seem rather relaxed about their own position. However much the gentlemen of the Royal Society acknowledge the perils of the Idols and even guard against them in their experimental protocol, they do not link their epistemological concerns to the policing of one another's subjectivity. Boyle declines to question his adversary's ratiocination, only interrogating the "stanchness of his pump." Boyle can assume this stance because he does not have to rely exclusively on scientific practice itself to identify and authorize its legitimate participants, but can supplement it with a discourse of social distinction. Although Bacon was himself a gentleman, such tactics would have been of little use in his situation. Shapin notes that in the discourse of gentlemanly credibility it was not only men of humbler rank who were compromised by their position; places of power such as the Court were recognized as hives of dissimulation. In this regard he quotes Bacon's essay "Of Great Place" to the effect that "men in great offices are servants, having no freedom compared to private men."[31] Bacon, who also writes in the same essay that "the rising unto place is laborious," knew whereof he spoke, having spent many frustrating years under Elizabeth waiting for preferment. Shapin cites this passage in order to suggest the consistency with which social independence (as opposed to mere rank) was made a criterion of credibility. However, it should also remind us that Bacon imagined the experimental discovery of nature from within a very different regime of subjection from that in which Boyle practiced it. Boyle was a wealthy gentleman who established his identity through scientific experimenting. Bacon was a servant of the Crown, the lifelong inhabitant of a system which encouraged ambition and therefore made being above suspicion a structural impossibility. Knowing too well how unstable is the distinction between master and servant, Bacon prescribed a new system in which the distinction would hardly signify because all would be policed by the facts of nature. Trusting in this distinction, which meant a great deal in his Pall Mall laboratories, Boyle was able to follow (some of) Bacon's prescriptions.

If Boyle manages the problem of subjectivity without making himself and his peers the object of epistemic suspicion, such is not the case with the late-nineteenth- and early-twentieth-century scientific atlas-makers whose activities Lorraine Daston and Peter Galison describe.[32] Daston and Galison demonstrate that scientists during this period approached the problem of the pictorial representation of the facts of nature with increasing anxiety about their own agency in the production of images. In undertaking to represent natural phenomena such as human bones, organs, or tissues, or different kinds of plants and animals, or fossils, atlas-makers have always had to make decisions about what exactly constitutes a fact of nature. Should the atlas-maker faithfully depict a single example of rhododendron flower with all of its idiosyncrasies, make a composite which shows what rhododendrons typically look like, or select a single, actual rhododendron which he judges to be as close to typical as possible? According to Daston and Galison, scientific concerns about the subjectivity of these judgments begin to emerge in the nineteenth century and are initially framed in terms of a necessity that scientists monitor artists lest, as the anatomist Ludwig Choulant feared, "purely individual and arbitrary representation . . . result" (91).[33] Prone to "subjective alterations" or "Zolaesque superfluous realism," the atlas-maker's artist served a function similar to that of the technician in Boyle's laboratory, as the bearer of a potentially subversive willfulness against which the scientists' authority could be produced.[34] Thus the introduction of mechanical means of image production such as photography and radiography initially provided a new means for policing artists. However, these techniques held out a powerful fantasy of objectivity, and so provoked more generally "a relentless search to replace individual volition and discretion in depiction by the invariable routines of mechanical reproduction" which soon led scientists themselves into a discourse of "self-surveillance" (98): "Scientific authors came to see mechanical registration as a means of hemming in their own temptation to impose systems, aesthetic norms, hypotheses, language, even anthropomorphic elements on pictorial representation" (103). Thus, if in the mid-nineteenth-century Choulant feared his artists' subjectivity, by the 1920s Erwin Christeller, author of *Atlas der Histotopographie gesunder under erkrantur Organe,* could instruct his fellow scientists to resist the temptations to produce drawings themselves, but instead to entrust the task to technicians because this way the procedure would be "fully mechanical and as far as possible, forcibly guided by this direct reproduction procedure of the art department" (113).[35]

Daston and Galison argue that this relocation of potentially subversive subjectivity from artists or technicians to scientists was in the service of an emerging *moral* discourse whereby scientists authorized themselves "as worthy to perform priestly functions in an ever more secularized society" (122). Possessed of wayward desires like everybody else, scientists distinguished themselves by their extraordinary demonstrations of self-government. Thus, for example, the late-nineteenth-century British physicist Michael Faraday proclaimed that: "The world little knows how many of the thoughts and theories which have passed through the mind of a scientific investigator have been crushed in silence and secrecy by his own severe criticism and adverse examination: that in the most successful instances not a tenth of the suggestions, the hopes, the wishes, the preliminary conclusions have been realized" (118).[36] Although they observe that there are very old religious traditions behind such language, Daston and Galison treat this concern with self-examination and self-discipline, and the form it took in the case of the atlas-makers, as symptomatic of the machine-age. They note that at the same time that the machine promised to fulfill the "standardizing mission of the atlas" through its capacity for mass-production, it also modeled for the scientist a new kind of indefatigable, incorruptible agency (119). The machine showed the scientist a way of being to which he could aspire, from which he must inevitably fall short. And yet in reading the passage from Faraday it is hard not to be struck by how specifically Baconian its rhetoric is, how, with its image of the examination of the secret, transgressive inner life of the scientist, it returns us to the discovery of the subject, and Bacon's rescripting of that scenario in terms of epistemological self-consciousness.

In fact, as we have seen, the conjunction of an anxious, moral self-surveillance with the pursuit of objectivity has been part of scientific discourse from at least the seventeenth century onward. The hegemonic drive which gives Bacon's writing its prophetic quality derives in part from the promise he imparts to natural philosophy to remake the men who pursue it, to subdue their erring minds to procedures that function "as if by machinery." But as both Shapin and Schaffer's and Daston and Galison's work reveals, the kind of self-surveillance at the heart of Bacon's vision is also only intermittently salient in the disciplinary regimes which scientists either imagine or put into practice. Much of the time scientists authorize themselves by means of quite different resources, such as class distinction or institutional traditions – which, of course, may complement as well as preclude a discourse of self-discipline. What Daston and Galison's account of the connection between self-surveillance and machine-age dreams does suggest, however, is that modernity has been marked from its early days by repeated (but not constant) objectifications of power in the very systems that knowledge spawns, be they royal administration, or mass-producing machines. The dream of moralized, epistemological self-discipline emerges, I would argue, as educated men confront power in the alienated forms that their own knowledge has produced and strive to re-enter it, to claim it as subjects. But to reclaim such objectified power, men must identify with it, acquire its properties, become themselves objectified – a paradox that Bacon captures in his famous dictum that "Nature to be commanded must be obeyed" (IV:47). Such a predicament may be distinctively "modern" but this does not mean that it ever recurs in quite the same way twice, in part, of course, because the subject's response to it exerts its own formative pressure on the world. Nor is its occurrence confined to the realm of science. Nor is this predicament as purely masculine as it once was. Like the Augustinian discourse of spiritual inwardness which it transmutes, the Baconian discourse of the chaste, severe discovery of nature is a conceptual resource, a way of orienting the self to the world which has proved usable in a succession of circumstances.

The legacy of the discoveries this volume has traced is not a disciplinary regime under which we all now live. Rather, it is an ongoing dialectical encounter between the subject and the external world, whether the latter be understood as the law, other people, media of communication or nature. Both the author and the scientist are imaginary heroes of that encounter. In practice, of course, their avatars share much, most notably a concern for intellectual property and claims to mediate truths greater than themselves, and differ in vastly complex and unpredictable ways. Conceptually though they demarcate for us a difference – between a made truth and a found one. If this difference seems simple, perhaps too obvious to be meaningful, we should pause to register its uneasiness, the difficulty and the necessity it confronts us with of embracing truth as a duality. The Renaissance discoveries confront us with this uneasiness, marking it as constitutive of subjectivity. Showing us the genealogy of our ways of knowing they offer us this uneasiness as itself a truth, and as a means for locating ourselves in the world.

Notes

I   INTRODUCTION

1 All citations to *Hamlet* are from the Arden edition, ed. Harold Jenkins (London, 1982).

2 Richard Simpson, *Edmund Campion: A Biography* (London, 1896), 391.

3 See Leonard W. Levy, *Origins of the Fifth Amendment* (New York, 1968), 1–300. I discuss these issues in greater detail in chapter 2 but it may be useful to note here that English common-law procedure in which the fact-finder was a jury differed considerably from Roman-canon legal procedure, also called "inquisitorial," in which an accused would be interrogated by the judge who was also fact-finder. Other English courts, such as High Commission, Admiralty, Chancery and, later, Star Chamber, used procedures that were closer to the Continental model, although they never seem to have attained the ferocity, evident in features like the use of judicial torture, that could characterize their Continental analogs. Over the course of the sixteenth century, however, these courts resorted more and more frequently to the practice of securing an accused's conscience on oath before questioning him, often before indictment, a practice which common lawyers found extremely objectionable.

4 Robert Persons, *A Treatise Tending To Mitigation Toward Catholick Subjects* (St. Omer, 1607).

5 Howard Felperin's "Cultural Poetics vs. Cultural Materialism," in *Uses of the Canon* (Oxford, 1990), 142–69, offers a useful account of the synchronic focus of New Historicist analysis. Francis Barker also offers a trenchant critique of the problems with New Historicists' approach to cultures as synchronic systems in *The Culture of Violence: Tragedy and History* (Manchester, 1993), 151–65.

6 See Stephen Greenblatt, *Shakespearean Negotiations* (Berkeley, 1988), 64, and Steven Mullaney, *The Place of the Stage* (Chicago, 1988), 94, for the classic formulations of this argument. More recently, scholars have begun to acknowledge the proto-bureaucratic nature of the early modern English state and its consequences for subject formation. See, for instance Mary Thomas Crane, *Framing Authority* (Princeton, 1993), esp. 116–35, and Richard Rambuss, *Spenser's Secret Career* (Cambridge, 1993), 29–48. Recent historical work on intelligence-gathering in this period also suggests that the English state power was enforced as much through "paper work" as through theatrical displays of power. See Alan Haynes, *Invisible Power: The Elizabethan Secret Services 1570–1603* (Stroud, Gloucestershire, 1992), and Alison

Plowden, *The Elizabethan Secret Service* (Hampstead, Hertfordshire, and New York, 1991).

7 Catherine Belsey, *The Subject of Tragedy* (London, 1985); Francis Barker, *The Tremulous Private Body* (London, 1983).

8 David Aers, "A Whisper in the Ear of Early Modernists," in *Culture and History 1350–1600*, ed. David Aers (London, 1992), 177–202.

9 Jacob Burckhardt, *The Civilization of the Renaissance in Italy*, trans. S. G. C. Middlemore (2 vols., New York, 1958), I:143.

10 Katherine Eisaman Maus, *Inwardness and Theater in the English Renaissance* (Chicago, 1995), also offers an important critique of the cultural materialist narrative, demonstrating that claims (such as Hamlet's) to an epistemically problematic inwardness are not anachronistic anomalies, as Barker argues, but commonplaces. Obviously enough, I share with Maus the sense that inwardness was in fact a cultural obsession in this period, manifesting itself in problems of legal evidence, the discursive construction of gendered bodies, the self-reflexiveness of theatrical representation, et cetera. I would stress, however, that the very ubiquitousness of the anxiety about inwardness which Maus so compellingly reveals actually supports the cultural materialist narrative of emergence, insofar as it suggests the seismic effects of claims of inwardness on prevailing institutions and ideologies.

11 In addition to the essays in Aers, *Culture and History*, see *Bodies and Disciplines: Intersections of Literature and History in Fifteenth-Century England*, ed. Barbara Hanawalt and David Wallace (Minneapolis, 1996).

12 Michel Foucault, *Discipline and Punish*, trans. Alan Sheridan (New York, 1979).

13 Clearly Barker's chronology arises from his English focus insofar as he aligns the shift he is positing with the Civil War. While this timing also keeps the cultural change in England in synchronization with Descartes's writing, it seems worth commenting on that in both England and France the spectacular modes of punishment which characterize the Renaissance, and which Foucault persuasively links to the style of sovereignty which Barker associates with the earlier dispensation, continue unabated into the eighteenth century.

14 *The Order of Things* (New York, 1970), 208.

15 I derive these examples from Rita Copeland, "William Thorpe and his Lollard Community: Intellectual Labor and the Representation of Dissent," and Seth Lerer, "'Representyd now in yower syght': The Culture of Spectatorship in Late Fifteenth-Century England," both in Hanawalt and Wallace, *Bodies and Disciplines*.

16 For the history of the jury see Thomas Green, *Verdict According to Conscience: Perspectives on the English Trial Jury, 1200–1800* (Chicago, 1985).

17 See Thomas N. Tentler, *Sin and Confession of the Eve of the Reformation* (Princeton, 1977).

18 John Bossy, "The Social History of Confession in the Age of the Reformation," *Transactions of the Royal Historical Society*, 5th ser., 25 (1975): 22.

19 On the abolition of the ordeal and the legal repercussions of the Fourth Lateran Council see Levy, *Origins of the Fifth Amendment*, 3–42, and Robert Bartlett, *Trial by Fire and Water* (Oxford, 1986), 70–102, 127–52.

20 Bossy, "Social History of Confession," 22.

21 DuBois, *Torture and Truth* (New York and London, 1991).

22 For similar observations see Maus, *Inwardness and Theater*, 29, and Alan Sinfield, *Faultlines: Cultural Materialism and the Politics of Dissident Reading* (Oxford, 1992), 60–1.

23 Carolyn Merchant, *The Death of Nature: Women, Ecology and the Scientific Revolution,* (San Francisco, 1980), exemplifies this tendency.

24 I should make clear that the problem I describe here arises in duBois's framing argument; her explication of how torture functioned in Athens is exemplary in its situatedness.

25 Aers, "A Whisper in the Ear of Early Modernists," 183, cites Charles Taylor's *Sources of the Self: The Making of the Modern Identity* (Cambridge, 1989), for the proposition that St. Augustine "introduced the inwardness of radical reflexivity and bequeathed it to the Western tradition." I share Aers's admiration for Taylor's work and his sense that Taylor is essential reading for anyone interested in the history of the subject. It should be noted, however, that Taylor clearly distinguishes Augustinian inwardness from the subjectivity which Descartes articulates: "For Augustine God is behind the eye as well as the One whose Ideas the eye strives to discern clearly before it" (136). For Descartes, in contrast, the mind can only ever construct representations of the world, because it is profoundly different from the objective domain it struggles to know. Taylor connects Cartesian dualism to a drastic shift in Western consciousness which he calls "the loss of ontic logos" (187), the disappearance of a sense that the truths of the soul, language, and world are one, which sounds very like the departure toward modernity that Foucault posits at the beginning of the Classical age.

26 William Scott, *An Essay of Drapery* (London, 1635), ed. Sylvia Thrupp (Cambridge, Mass., 1953).

27 Scott, ibid., mentions the exception of the lie to save a friend from a persecutor twice, first in retailing the story of Athanasius' escape from the Arrian persecutor Lucius (19 in Thrupp's edition) and again in a quotation from Augustine that Thrupp omits. See first edition (London, 1635), 34. There is no reason why Scott's thinking here need link him to the Jesuits, for an interest in casuistry was widespread among Protestants as well. Milton, for example, also makes much the same argument: "we are undoubtedly commanded to speak the truth; but to whom? not to an enemy, not to a madman, not to an oppressor, not to an assassin, but to 'our neighbour,' to one with whom we are connected by bonds of peace and social fellowship" (*Christian Doctrine* in *The Works of John Milton*, gen. ed. Frank Allen Patterson, 18 vols. [New York, 1931–8], XVII:305). On Protestant casuistry generally see Camille Slights, *The Casuistical Tradition* (Princeton, 1981), and Lowell Gallagher, *Medusa's Gaze: Casuistry and Conscience in the Renaissance* (Stanford, 1991).

28 Thrupp's introduction (Scott, *Essay on Drapery*) offers insightful remarks both on Scott's stoicism and on the ways in which his economic vision differs from that of full-blown capitalism.

29 Hamlet, after all, is under scrutiny not simply because he has "that within which passes show" but because that which is within is (rightly) thought to be a plot to kill the King.

30 The appropriation from conduct literature is quite direct. Scott's subtitle, "the Compleat Citizen," is indebted to Henry Peacham's *The Compleat Gentleman* (1622).

31 In view of Scott's interest in Stoic philosophy it is interesting to note that Taylor links an interest in neo-stoicism both to the emergence of the administrative state and to a "growing ideal of a human agent who is able to remake himself by methodical and disciplined action" (*Sources of the Self*, 136). See also Gerhard Oestreich, *Neostoicism and the Early Modern State*, ed. Brigitta Oestreich and H. G. Koenigsberger, trans. David McLintock (Cambridge, 1982).

2   TORTURE AND TRUTH

1 The inscription is located on the wall in the Beauchamp Tower, Tower of London.

2 Ibid., 111; Edward Coke, *The Third Part of the Institutes of the Laws of England* (London, 1797), 34–5.

3 The warrants are reproduced in James Heath, *Torture and English Law* (Westport, Conn., 1983), 201–29.

4 Foucault usefully distinguishes between the "unrestrained torture of modern interrogations" and judicial torture, which he calls "a torture of the truth" (*Discipline and Punish*, 40). DuBois, *Torture and Truth*, and Edward Peters, *Torture* (New York, 1985), 41–4, similarly treat judicial torture as what it claimed to be, a method for obtaining truth. These writers take the claims of judicial torture to produce truth seriously because they can demonstrate that torture was dictated by the epistemic assumptions of Roman-canon or Athenian law. My argument will similarly be that English torture arose because it met certain epistemic needs, although these needs were generated not by a stable legal system, but by a transitional moment in English legal institutions.

5 The *OED* offers as one sample of sixteenth-century usage of "try": "the boulter tryeth out the branne." Myagh's account of his torture supports Foucault's interpretation of judicial torture as a kind of "duel," in which the victim's (exculpating) ability to endure pain is pitted against the torturer's (inculpating) ability to inflict it. Insofar as torture can be seen as a contest, it marks the survival of elements of the ordeal which the Roman-canon investigative procedure had officially superseded (*Discipline and Punish*, 41). The relationship between English torturers and their victims that I will delineate clearly involves elements of the contest Foucault describes. However, while the contest of Roman-canon torture depends on mutual consent as to the operative epistemic assumptions, what fueled the contest of English torture was the challenge both torturer and victim posed to each other's epistemological claims.

6 Timothy Reiss, *The Discourse of Modernism* (Ithaca, 1982), offers a sweeping account of the emergence of a discourse of objectivity and demonstrates the precariousness of truth claims within it. See also Merchant, *Death of Nature*, who notices Bacon's affinity for torture. For older discussions of this epistemic shift see Herschel Baker, *The Wars of Truth* (Cambridge, Mass.,

1952), and Hiram Haydn, *The Counter Renaissance* (New York, 1950). Reiss designates the telescope and the voyage of discovery as the principal "metaphors" for the emerging discourse. For discussions of the epistemology of the anatomy lesson see Devon Hodges, *Renaissance Fictions of Anatomy* (Amherst, 1985); Luke Wilson, "William Harvey's Prelectiones: The Performance of the Body in the Renaissance Theater of Anatomy," *Representations* 17 (1987): 62–95.

7 Francis Bacon, *The Great Instauration* in *The Works of Francis Bacon*, ed. James Spedding, Robert Ellis, and Douglas Heath, 7 vols. (London, 1878–92), IV:20; Bacon, *Preparative Towards a Natural and Experimental History* in *Works*, IV:263. The metaphor Bacon is using here is not explicitly that of torture, but of the legal procedures he was familiar with in Chancery and Star Chamber (see chapter 5 below). The connection between torture and inquisitorial legal procedure particularly in the mind of common lawyers is dealt with later in the current chapter.

8 William Allen, *A True, Sincere and Modest Defence of English Catholics* (Rheims, 1583), ed. Robert M. Kingdon (Ithaca, 1965), 75.

9 Robert Southwell, *An Humble Supplication to Her Majestie* (1600), ed. R. C. Bald (Cambridge, 1953), 18–25. There is considerable historical evidence for Walsingham's having facilitated the Babington plot from the beginning, if not precisely instigating it. See Alan Haynes, *Invisible Power*, 54–71, and Plowden, *Elizabethan Secret Service*, 95–103. The currency of the idea that the government was stage-managing the perpetration and discovery of treasons is demonstrated by Curtis Breight in " 'Treason Doth Never Prosper': *The Tempest* and the Discourse of Treason," *Shakespeare Quarterly* 41 (1990): 1–28. In a similar vein, William Allen argued that all government representations of the truth were suspect because the government controlled the media: "having the name of authority the shadow of laws, the pens and tongues of infinite at their commandment. They may print and publish what they like, suppress what they list" (*Defence*, 59).

10 It is interesting to compare the Catholic accusations regarding the fraudulence of torture with Elaine Scarry's discussion of torture based on evidence of twentieth-century practice in *The Body in Pain* (New York and London, 1985). Scarry asserts that all claims that the purpose of torture is discovery are fraudulent, that torture is itself a form of fraud. She argues that torture tends to be employed "on behalf of a cultural artifact or symbolic fragment or made thing (a sentence) that is without any other basis in material reality" (127). Torture, in Scarry's argument, is a strategy for conferring "truth" upon statements that are felt by the torturers themselves not to be inherently true by juxtaposing such statements to a demonstration of the torturers' power to produce the incontestable reality of pain. If Scarry and Cardinal Allen concur in their perception of the fraudulence of investigation by torture, however, they differ in their understanding of the truth that opposes fraudulence. Scarry's critique of torture bespeaks a modern epistemology that opposes power to knowledge, suggesting that true knowledge possesses a "basis in material reality" and, therefore, does not need the demonstration of power torture provides to make it seem true. Allen's critique protests this materialist, objectivist notion of truth but in terms that already signal its new persuasive-

ness. Scarry's analysis is in fact extremely helpful in accounting for what happened in the Elizabethan torture chamber, but what required verification through its juxtaposition to the incontestable reality of pain was, precisely, a way of knowing that asserts that truth is that which possesses "a basis in material reality."

11 Many of the English victims were trained as Jesuits, and their responses to torture reflect the role that physical pain seems to have played in the development of Loyolan spirituality. As Loyola tells it, his conversion from courtier to the founder of the new order occurred after the agonizing experience of having an improperly healed broken leg freshly broken and stretched. Throughout the rest of his life, he seems to have carefully calibrated his penance so that he could remain in a state of perpetual pain without actually risking death. See generally: *The Autobiography of St. Ignatius*, ed. J. F. X. O'Conor (New York, 1900). John Gerard admiringly alludes in his autobiography to another priest who performed devotions of such intensity that he vomited great quantities of blood: in *Autobiography of an Elizabethan*, trans. Philip Caraman (London, 1951), 45. Anthony Munday's account of the English college at Rome contains several prurient descriptions of penitents inflicting pain on themselves (*The English-Romayne Life* [1582], ed. G. B. Harrison [London, 1925], 33–6). This is not to say that the victims did not suffer intensely: Southwell is reported to have claimed that he had been tortured ten times, "each one worse than death" (Christopher Devlin, *The Life of Robert Southwell* [London, 1967], 286). The point is that the meaning of even an experience so basic as extreme pain is culturally constituted.

12 John Langbein, *Torture and the Law of Proof* (Chicago, 1976), 5–10, 75–8; Peters, *Torture*, 40–54.

13 See Langbein, *Torture and the Law of Proof*, and Heath, *Torture and English Law*, for the legal historical context of the use of torture in England. The common law was not, of course, the only legal system used in England. The procedure of the ecclesiastical courts, the Court of Admiralty, and some of the prerogative courts was based on Roman-canon law rather than the common law, but even in these courts torture does not seem to have been used. A famous early case which suggests the conformity of the ecclesiastical courts to English rather than Continental procedures with regard to torture is the prosecution of the Knights Templar in 1309–11. Initially Edward II refused to allow the Continental Inquisitors to torture the Templars on the grounds that it was contrary to English custom, although it appears that he eventually gave in on this score. The Archbishop of York recommended that the Inquisitors send to the Continent for assistance because no torturers were to be found in England (Heath, *Torture and English Law*, 36–48). That torture was not used in the Admiralty courts is suggested by a statute from the reign of Henry VIII providing for the trial at common law of piracy, an offense proper to Admiralty jurisdictions. The reason offered for the transfer of jurisdiction was the impossibility of securing convictions without resort to torture if the Roman-canon standard of proof, two witnesses or a confession, had to be met, since pirates tended to kill all potential witnesses. Rather than use torture, Henry's government elected to jettison the standard of proof (Heath, *Torture and English Law*, 70).

14 Thomas Smith, *De Republica Anglorum,* ed. Mary Dewar (Cambridge, 1982), 117. The *locus classicus* for this proposition is Sir John Fortescue's *De Laudibus Legum Angliae,* ed. and trans. S. B. Chrimes (Cambridge, 1942), 46–7, written from exile in France in the 1470s and favorably comparing the English jury system with the horrible and unreliable French practice of judicial torture.

15 Coke, *Third Institute,* 34–5.

16 The phrase "any prescription lately brought in" is puzzling as it suggests that Coke is arguing against a body of legal opinion that gave torture a place in English prosecutions. As I demonstrate below, such a body of opinion did not exist in England. Possibly Coke is alluding to the conciliar warrants with their tacit assertion of torture's legitimacy. Or he may be glancing at his rival, Bacon, and his assertion, discussed in the text below, that torture may be used for "discovery."

17 Langbein, *Torture and the Law of Proof,* 94–123, provides a list of conciliar warrants for torture from 1540 to 1640. Langbein bases his analysis solely on the pattern suggested by the conciliar warrants. It is clear, however, that if we consider other evidence such as letters, personal testimony, or diaries there were many more incidents of torture than the warrants indicate. Also, insofar as conciliar warrants only began to be issued in 1540, their absence in the early Tudor period tells us nothing about the use of torture during that time.

18 Langbein's *Torture and the Law of Proof* is the most sustained and credible attempt to account for torture's appearance in England during this period. Langbein analyzes this juridical aberration in the context of the history of English criminal prosecutions and concludes by rejecting the sufficiency of every explanatory theory. The summary of the problem I offer here is based on his work; see particularly 129–39. Where I part company with him, however, is his assumption that the self-evident seriousness of the Catholic threat can be taken as a cause for the resort to torture without our needing to specify why that particular threat was so much more serious than other ones or why torture was an appropriate response to it. The other recent study of English torture, Heath's *Torture and English Law,* is remarkable for its lack of any thesis at all regarding the peculiar appearance and disappearance of torture in England.

19 Officially sanctioned torture was conducted only by order of the Privy Council, and then only in the Tower or Bridewell. The only exception to this tight monarchical control concerns the Council of the Welsh Marches which enjoyed a considerable amount of delegated royal authority, including the right to torture. See Langbein, *Torture and the Law of Proof,* 81–4, 134.

20 Frederick Pollock, ed., *Table Talk of John Selden* (London, 1927), 133. A similar remark is attributed to Ralegh: "The rack is used nowhere as in England; they take a man and rack him I know not why or when." Quoted in Paul Johnson, *Elizabeth I* (London, 1974), 350 (no note provided).

21 John Strype, *Life and Acts of John Whitgift,* 3 vols. (Oxford, 1822), I:401–2.

22 Francis Bacon, *Letters and Life of Francis Bacon,* ed. James Spedding, Robert Ellis, and Douglas Heath, 7 vols. (London, 1868–90), III:114.

23 The terseness of English commentary on torture is in striking contrast to the

"thousands of pages of discourse on the jurisprudence of torture between the thirteenth and eighteenth centuries" generated on the Continent. See Peters, *Torture*, 58. The very ambiguity of torture, its recognized ability to produce untrue confessions, generated a discursive scaffolding of rules and theories governing its use. See also Foucault, *Discipline and Punish,* 40.

24 This gap is exemplified by the later case of Samuel Peacock who was charged with "practising or pretending to have infatuated the King's judgment with sorcery." In 1619, Bacon wrote to the King that "if it may not be done otherwise, it is fit Peacock be put to torture. He deserveth it as well as Peacham [an earlier accused in whose torture Bacon had been instrumental] did." The same letter also suggests that Coke will be involved in the examination. Spedding notes that here we see Bacon actually instigating torture, rather than simply following orders, and states that "we must . . . conclude that both Bacon and Coke at that time held [torture] to be legal. Nor indeed could they well have held it to be otherwise, if legality was to be presumed where custom had been long and uniform and unchallenged." It is at about this time that Coke was composing the *Third Institute* in which he categorically states that torture in England is illegal. Spedding's reasoning replicates what he finds in Bacon's letter. The availability of torture as a method of interrogation is assumed, but the grounds of this assumption are merely that the practice is available. Insofar as there is legal doctrine against which to read Bacon's letter, however, it contradicts the assumption on which the practice proceeds (Spedding, *Letters and Life*, VII:77–9).

25 *A Declaration of the Favorable Dealing of Her Majesty's Commissioners . . .* (1583), in Allen, *Defence.* This pamphlet is apparently by Burghley. The justification of torture, however, seems to be based on a letter to Walsingham by Thomas Norton, a Puritan who was commissioned to torture Campion and his companion, Alexander Briant. The letter is printed in William Durrant Cooper, "Further Particulars of Thomas Norton, and of State Proceedings in Matters of Religion, in the Years 1581 and 1582," *Archaeologia* 36 (1855): 105–19.

26 For incremental notions of proof in Roman-canon law and their relation to the regulated use of torture see Foucault, *Discipline and Punish*, 36–9, and Peters, *Torture*, 56–7.

27 Thomas H. Clancy, *Papist Pamphleteers: The Allen–Persons Party and the Political Thought of the Counter-Reformation in England, 1572–1615* (Chicago, 1964), 128. The pictures were principally of canonized saints, but nine of them concerned more recent martyrs, including More and Fisher and contemporary Elizabethan victims. Clancy also states that pictures of English cruelties to Catholics were set up in the cemetery of St. Severin in Paris, where "English and French priests were on hand to give illustrated lectures on the subject" as a warning of what could be expected if Protestants ever gained control in France. In general, the illustrated martyrologies seem to have been circulated more on the Continent than in England.

28 Robert Southwell, *An Epistle of Comfort to the Reverend Priests* (1583; St. Omer, 1616), 387.

29 It should be noted that it is only with regard to torture, rather than to the larger issue of the nature of the priests' activities, that Elizabeth's government

appears reticent. It was quite prolific in its production of pamphlets against the missionary priests and their activities.

30 William Allen, as head of the English College at Rheims from which many of the most famous Jesuit missionaries came, was dispatching priests to England on religious missions at the same time that he was extensively involved from the mid-1570s until the defeat of the Armada in a variety of plots with Spain, the Vatican, and the Dukes of Guise to establish a Catholic government in England (Allen, *Defence*, xxxiii–xxxv). As a matter of policy, however, Allen kept these activities strictly separate.

31 Allen, *Defence*, 78.

32 Gerard, *Autobiography*, 113.

33 Smith, *De Republica Anglorum*, 112.

34 Ibid. Smith is probably correct with regard to London and the larger towns. Assize records suggest, however, that much Elizabethan crime continued to arise from disputes within small communities, where all parties would be known to one another. See J. A. Sharpe, *Crime in Early Modern England, 1550–1750* (London and New York, 1984), and Louis A. Knafla, "John at Love Killed Her: The Assizes and Criminal Law in Early Modern England," *University of Toronto Law Review*, 35 (1985): 305–20.

35 Thomas Green, *Verdict According to Conscience*, 77–8.

36 1 & 2 Philip and Mary, c. 13 (1554–5) and 2 & 3 Philip and Mary, c. 10 (1555). For a thorough account of the development of the investigation see Langbein, *Prosecuting Crime in the Renaissance* (Cambridge, Mass., 1974).

37 Michael Dalton, *The Countrey Justice* (London, 1618), 265.

38 Peter Westen, "The Compulsory Process Clause," *Michigan Law Review* 73 (1974): 83–5.

39 William Lambarde, *Eirenarchia* (London, 1588), 216. This volume went through many editions. I have relied on the 1588 edition, which includes Lambarde's revisions. Dalton's book is basically a revision of Lambarde's.

40 Lambarde, *Eirenarchia*, 213, and Dalton, *Countrey Justice*, 264. See also Levy, *Origins of the Fifth Amendment*, 107. In Dell's Case, discussed below, however, the accused making a deposition on oath is an important part of the story, and never seems to be questioned as irregular.

41 Lambarde, *Eirenarchia*, 220.

42 It should be stressed that the legislation and literature prescribing investigative methodology are better understood as attempts to re-imagine the truth at issue in criminal proceedings than as signs of an accomplished reorganization of practice. Assize records indicate that until well into the seventeenth century actual prosecution procedures were far more disorganized than the statutes and handbooks would indicate (J. S. Cockburn, "Trial by the Book: Fact and Theory in the Criminal Process, 1558–1625," *Legal Records and the Historian*, ed. J. H. Baker [London, 1978], 70). Cockburn notes that much of the time Justices of the Peace took little care to produce an accurate account of the crime; even the names, places of domicile, and occupations of accused given in indictments were frequently made up, as the nature of Elizabethan crime meant that the accused often had none of them in lawful form (66). Juries, too, continued to produce verdicts that showed a lack of concern for historical truth, sometimes exonerating the accused by pinning the crime on such

dubious personages as "John at Death," "John at Love," or "John in the Wind." See Knafla, " 'John at Love Killed Her,' " 314–17. While much of this disorganization was due to an insufficiently developed state apparatus, the juries' behaviour in particular also suggests the persistence of older notions of the truth of the crime, and thus the fact that the investigation had yet to establish its hegemony.

43 Spedding, *Letters and Life*, III:114.

44 A statute of 1401 (2 Hen. IV, c. 15) which gave jurisdiction to the church to punish heretics (Lollards, in this case) permitted *ex officio* procedures. In 1533, however, a new law (25 Hen. VIII, c. 14) required that before an accused be sworn he had to be "presented or indicted" or "duly accused of two lawful witnesses." Under Edward VI the jurisdiction over heresy was abolished. Under Mary the statute of 1401 was revived. In 1558, Elizabeth placed the church's powers under her own control with the Court of High Commission. It was apparently not until Whitgift's appointment that the *ex officio* procedure again became current. See John Henry Wigmore, *Evidence in Trials at Common Law*, rev. John T. McNaughton, 11 vols. (Boston, 1961) VIII:2250, and Levy, *Origins of the Fifth Amendment*, esp. 43–82, 109–72.

45 For a history of this issue see Wigmore, *Evidence*, 266–92. Wigmore makes clear that objections to the oath itself arise from concerns about the limits of ecclesiastical jurisdiction which go back to the twelfth century. Common lawyers' jurisdictional concerns thus fused with repugnance at the practice's violation of the privilege against self-incrimination.

46 Wigmore, *Evidence*, VIII:285–6.

47 35 Eliz. I, c. 2, s. 11.

48 Wigmore, *Evidence*, VIII:289, n. 102.

49 Strype, *Life and Acts*, I:401–2. See also Levy, *Origins of the Fifth Amendment*, 139–41.

50 Wigmore notes that "the last recorded instances of torture, and the first instances of the established privilege coincide within about a decade" (*Evidence*, VIII:287, n. 89).

51 Catholic accounts of the interrogatories put to priests during torture suggest that a distinction between questions pertaining to the accused's actions and those of others was neither observed by the interrogators nor considered important by the victims. William Allen, for example, asserts that Alexander Briant was tortured "because he would not confess where F. Parsons was, where the print was, & what bookes he had sould," information that would have been of value in suppressing Catholic activities generally. The next question he recounts, "whether the Queen were supreme head of the Church of England or not," is clearly intended to make Briant incriminate himself (*A Briefe Historie of the Glorious Martyrdom of the xii Reverend Priests* [Rheims, 1582], ed. J. H. Pollen [London, 1908], 49).

52 [Burghley], *The Execution of Justice in England* (1583), in Allen, *Defence*, 38.

53 *The Horrible Murther of a Young Boy* . . . (London, 1606); *The Most Cruell and Bloody Murther* . . . (London, 1606). In *Prosecuting Crime*, Langbein adduces *The Horrible Murther* as "a faithful typification" of the Justice of the Peace at work (48–9). His study brought this case to my attention. The indictment and conviction of George Dell, baker, and Agnes Dell, widow, of

Hatfield, for the murder of Anthony James is recorded in J. S. Cockburn, ed., *Calendar of Assize Records: Hertfordshire Indictments, James I* (London, 1975), 163.

54 The assize records give the date as July 4, 1602.

55 Simpson, *Edmund Campion*, 455.

56 The story of how Judge Alliffe's hand was instantly bloodied when the jury returned the verdict against Campion is attributed to Persons and recounted by Simpson, *Edmund Campion*, 433. Many such stories are to be found in *Publications of the Catholic Record Society*, vol. V, ed. J. H. Pollen (London, 1908); the tale of the stinking bowels of Thomas Pilchard is found in a martyrology identified as being in John Gerard's hand, reproduced at 288–9. The felicitously named Pilchard is also reported to have appeared following his execution, to another imprisoned priest, as "a thing like a fishe. . . from which light proceeded" (289).

57 Southwell, *An Epistle of the Comfort to the Reverend Priests*, 357.

58 It is interesting to compare Southwell's anxiety about the ambiguity of martyrdom with Foucault's description of the essential ambiguity of the victim's suffering on the scaffold, which "may signify equally well the truth of the crime or the error of the judges, the goodness or the evil of the criminal, the coincidence or the divergence between the judgment of men and that of God" (*Discipline and Punish*, 46). Southwell makes clear that the church has a right to execute heretics, as does the state to execute criminals. It is perhaps his investment in the suffering body both as a vindication of the truth of the victim and of the executioner that provokes his anxiety on this score.

59 Allen's book was compiled from reports sent to him from England. He carefully preserves the reportorial nature of the accounts, including the reporters' use of the first person, although he makes no attempt to distinguish these reports from the parts of the text he wrote himself. See Pollen's introduction, Allen, *Glorious Martyrdom*, viii.

60 Cooper, "Further Particulars," 116.

61 Of course, the Jesuit torture victims' insistence on the interiority of their truth depended heavily on Loyolan conceptions of spiritual inwardness, the development of which preceded their encounter with the Elizabethan authorities. My point is not that torture caused a sense of inwardness, but that it participated in the ongoing articulation of an inward spirituality.

62 In *Cobbett's Complete Collection of State Trials*, ed. T. B. Howell, 34 vols. (London, 1811), I:1060.

63 *A Treatise Made in Defense of the Lawful Power and Authoritie of Priesthood to Remitte Sinnes* (Louvain, 1567), 73–4.

64 Bossy notes that at the Council of Trent in 1551 the analogy with juridical confession was adduced in arguments that the sacrament was reconciliation of the individual soul to God rather than to the Christian community ("The Social History of Confession in the Age of the Reformation," 23).

65 *Acta ecclesiae mediolanensis . . . Federici Card. Borromei* (Milan, 1843–6), quoted in Bossy, "Social History of Confession," 30. See Tentler, *Sin and Confession on the Eve of the Reformation,* 83, for the public performance of confession.

66 Allen, *Defence*, 72. Allen also tells this story in passing, in *Glorious*

Martyrdom, 88, again to make the point that the Elizabethan authorities were religious persecutors, not investigators of treason.

67 In a sense the structure of these confessions heightens the division that equivocation produces so that what is spoken becomes in Persons's terms "a grosse lye" while what remains in the mind is "hidden truth" (*Treatise Tending to Mitigation*, 322).

68 [Burghley], *The Execution of Justice in England*, 8–9.

69 Persons, *An Epistle*, 87.

3   BROTHERS OF THE STATE

1 On the apparent taboo against representing torture and execution on the Renaissance stage see James Shapiro, " 'Tragedies naturally performed': Kyd's Representation of Violence," in *Staging the Renaissance*, ed. David Scott Kastan and Peter Stallybrass (London and New York, 1991), 99–113. For an account of tortures inflicted on stage see Alexander Leggatt, *Jacobean Public Stage* (London and New York, 1992), 61–2. None of Leggatt's examples involve state torture of the kind I'm concerned with, instead representing torture as a practice of the Spanish or the Turks committed in the course of war or revenge, although they do suggest an interest in torture devices, as does the scene from *Bussy d'Ambois*. The fascination exerted by the boundary between state violence and theatrical representation is suggested by other Jacobean tragedies (Webster's *The White Devil* [1612], Tourneur's *The Atheist's Tragedy* [1611]) which conclude by gesturing toward state violence that is not going to happen on stage. *The Atheist's Tragedy* is a particularly interesting example, putting ironic pressure on the taboo by bringing the scene of execution on stage at its conclusion, only grotesquely to pre-empt it by having the executioner dash out his own brains by mistake.

2 There is evidence of only two women, Anne Askew and Margaret Ward, having been subjected to interrogatory torture in Renaissance England. Their experiences are discussed below. At the same time, as Sara Eaton reminds us, wife-beating in the home rather than the calculated and spectacular violence of the early modern state was the more usual husbandly response to adultery ("Defacing the Feminine in Renaissance Tragedy," in *The Matter of Difference*, ed. Valerie Wayne ([Ithaca, 1991], 181–98).

3 To be sure, most of the cases of torture I have examined were plotted to the extent that torturer and victim were representatives of the Crown and the Church of Rome. However, the point of their encounter was not to institutionalize their relationship but to annihilate each other, hence their tendency to define themselves in abstract moral and metaphysical rather than social terms.

4 All citations to *Measure for Measure* are to the Arden edition, ed. J. W. Lever (London, 1965).

5 With the exception of Escalus's attempt to rack the Duke, the threats of torments at the end of both plays could refer either to interrogatory torture or to punishment, a distinction that has been important to my argument because of the peculiar status of interrogatory torture in English law. But whatever practices are meant in the concluding threats of these plays, the contexts make

clear that it is the (un)knowability of the victim (the obsession of the Elizabethan torturers) which obviates or induces state violence.

6 The arguments I will make about the role sexual rivalry plays in the construction of a male ruling class are indebted to Eve Kosofsky Sedgwick, *Between Men: English Literature and Male Homosocial Desire* (New York, 1985).

7 All citations to *Othello* are to the Arden edition, ed. M. R. Ridley (London, 1958).

8 Katherine Eisaman Maus ("Horns of a Dilemma: Jealousy, Gender and Spectatorship in English Drama," *ELH* 54 [1987]: 561–83) provides a valuable discussion of the relation between theatrical decorum, sex scenes, and the epistemic construction of the audience. Michael Neill ("Improper Beds: Race, Adultery and Hideous in *Othello*," *Shakespeare Quarterly* 40 [1989]: 383–412) offers a nuanced account of the indecorousness of the final scene and its relation to the off-stage sex scenes Iago conjures up.

9 Leonard Tennenhouse, "Representing Power: *Measure for Measure* in its Time," in *The Power of Forms in the English Renaissance*, ed. Stephen Greenblatt (Norman, Oklahoma, 1982), 141. On the engineering of James's succession see Paul Johnson, *Elizabeth: A Study in Power and Intellect* (London, 1964), 438–9.

10 Of course, the governing orders in *Othello* and *Measure for Measure* are quite different: Othello and Iago are soldiers while Angelo is a sort of legal administrator. In fact, however, the Venetian forces on Cyprus seem to function more as a civil administration than as an army; the need for war dissipates and Othello's tasks become entirely disciplinary and governmental ones. Julia Genster links *Othello* in this respect to new military regulations in the period which "attempt[ed] to constitute, as it were, a civil government structure within the army" ("Lieutenancy, Standing In, and *Othello*," *ELH* 57 [1990]: 790).

11 Leah Marcus's "topical reading" of *Measure for Measure* offers a useful corrective on this point, suggesting how much the various moral conflicts and ambiguities in the play are connected to an imperial politics of "bureaucratic centralization and its imperative for legal reform" (*Puzzling Shakespeare: Local Reading and Its Discontents* [Berkeley, 1988], 186).

12 On the historical overlap between theatrical sovereignty and the proto-bureaucratic work of intelligence-gathering see John Michael Archer, *Sovereignty and Intelligence: Spying and Court Culture in the English Renaissance* (Stanford, 1993), 1–16. Archer's concern is with spying, the most overtly disciplinary mode of bureaucratic work. My concern is with administrative activity generally which (unlike espionage) is not wholly driven by suspicion, but produces and manages suspicion in the course of attending to the more general work of the state.

13 A few of the numerous treatments of this trope are: Nancy Leonard, "Substitution in Shakespeare's Problem Comedies," *English Literary Renaissance* 9 (1979): 281–301; Meredith Skura, "New Interpretations for Interpretation in *Measure for Measure*," *boundary 2* 7, no. 2 (1979): 39–58; and Alexander Leggatt, "Substitution in *Measure for Measure*," *Shakespeare Quarterly* 39 (1988): 342–59.

14 Jonathan Goldberg, *James I and the Politics of Literature* (Baltimore, 1983), 151; Mullaney, *The Place of the Stage*, 26–59. Greenblatt's reading in *Shakespearean Negotiations*, 129–164, tends in a similar direction. For a version of the argument that deals with Shakespeare's political drama generally, see Christopher Pye, *Regal Phantasm: Shakespeare and the Politics of Spectacle* (London and New York, 1990).

15 See, for example, Leonard, "Substitution."

16 See Maus, *Inwardness and Theater*, 172–81, for an argument that the interpretive work the play demands of its audience is precisely the discernment and reflection on the different meanings of the various acts of substitution. The differences with which Maus is concerned are, however, primarily moral ones, rather than those of power with which I am concerned.

17 On the relation between the Duke and Lucio, particularly the way in which the numismatic imagery links Lucio parodically (or "piratically") to the Duke, see Jacques Lezra, "Pirating Reading: The Appearance of History in *Measure for Measure*," *ELH* 56 (1989): 255–92, esp. 263–5.

18 This is not to suggest, however, that the issue of the right way to deal with the situation Claudio and Juliet find themselves in would not have been of interest to members of Shakespeare's audience. Martin Ingram has demonstrated an increase in prosecutions for bridal pregnancy in many areas of England after 1600 which "fitted into a broader pattern of the strengthening of public control over marriage entry and of the hardening of attitudes toward sexual immorality" (*Church Courts, Sex and Marriage in England, 1570–1640* [Cambridge, 1987], 237). Nevertheless, Ingram's account suggests that no easy correlation is possible between this phenomenon and the scenario presented in the play. Increased prosecutions were a feature of cloth-producing districts, and were, not surprisingly, class-based, intended to regulate the numbers of poor people within a parish. They were conducted by the church courts, and punishment usually consisted of confessing the offense, often just to the minister and churchwardens, and paying a fine. The level of state terror Juliet's pregnancy calls up and the ethical abstraction with which it is presented, not to mention her social status, suggest that Shakespeare is forging rather than reiterating discursive connections between the regulation of sexuality and the production of an early modern ruling class.

19 Michel Foucault, *The History of Sexuality: Volume 1, An Introduction*, trans. Robert M. Hurley (New York, 1978), 61. It should be noted that the confession Foucault has in mind here is specifically that of the Counter-Reformation, with its technologies for self-enclosure and its obsessions with the secrets of the body, rather than the earlier more public practice. In England in 1604 there had been no public dimension to confession for almost half a century, while, as I argue in chapter 2, the persecution of Catholics had powerfully reinforced the Counter-Reformation ideology of confession that the Jesuit missionaries promoted and brought it, ironically, into public discourse, making this version of confession the one which would have been imaginatively available to Shakespeare's audience.

20 Foucault, *History of Sexuality*, 61.

21 Greenblatt, *Shakespearean Negotiations*, 140.

22 See Maus, *Inwardness and Theatre,* 182–209, for an excellent discussion of the

complex and contradictory relationship between masculine imaginings of inwardness and the female body in this period.

23 In his note to 2.4.6–7, Lever cites T. Wright, *The Passions of the Mind* (1630 edition), 45, for a description of the physiology of love. See also Donald Beecher, "The Lover's Body: The Somatogenesis of Love in Renaissance Medical Treatises," *Renaissance and Reformation* 24 (n.s. 12) (1988): 1–12.

24 This fact, that the plot of *Othello* evacuates the anxiety about the secrecy of women which its characters express, seems to have made remarkably little impression on critics. For instance, Patricia Parker charts the conjunction in *Othello* of the discourse of discovery of secrets as it emerged in contexts such as espionage and torture, and the discourse of secrecy that marks anatomical literature about the female genitals ("*Othello* and *Hamlet*: Dilation, Spying and the 'Secret Place' of Woman," *Representations* 44 [1993]: 60–95). This argument interestingly enforces the connection I want to make here, between the constructions of Desdemona's sexuality and of the secrets the Elizabethan state sought to extract through torture. Our readings diverge, however, insofar as Parker's analysis presupposes a more or less stable feminine gendering of the object of epistemic anxiety in *Othello*. Such a presupposition takes Iago at his word, making his voice and the anxieties it speaks for identical to the discourse of the play, ignoring the fact that the play also demonizes this voice and, in the process, unloads the feminine gendering of the secret.

25 Thomas Rymer, *A Short View of Tragedy* (1693; reprint, Menston, Yorkshire, 1970), 144.

26 Marc Shell, *The End of Kinship: "Measure for Measure," Incest and the Ideal of Universal Siblinghood* (Stanford, 1988).

27 That evidence is important to the political and marital order of Venice in a way that it is not to Vienna is illustrated in the senators' deliberations at the beginning of 1.3 over how to interpret the conflicting dispatches about Turkish movements. Insofar as the problem of evidence they grapple with is predicated on the senators' absence from the object of their deliberations it is one that the entire plot of *Measure for Measure* defends against by insisting on the Duke's omnipresence. At the same time, the scene draws attention to the comparative complexity of the Venetian state, which comprises far-flung trading routes, an oligarchy which proceeds deliberatively, and an army which executes its orders. For a valuable discussion of the relation between juridical problems of evidence, including some of those dealt with in the preceding chapter, and Iago's torment of Othello, see Maus, *Inwardness and Theater*, 104–27.

28 I concur here with Lena Cowen Orlin's important observations that, contrary to the modern semantic associations of "domestic," Renaissance domestic tragedy is "man-centered, that is concerned with men's issues" and that in the case of *Othello* these "men's issues" include the emergence of a notion of professional identity which destabilizes the binary oppositions which structure Renaissance generic categories (*Private Matters and Public Culture in Post-Reformation England* [Ithaca and London, 1994], 252, 243).

29 On the slippage between marital and military orders see Genster, "Lieutenancy, Standing In, and *Othello*."

30 For a rather different reading of Iago, which stresses his position as servant, see Frances Dolan, *Dangerous Familiars: Representations of Domestic Crime in England 1550–1700* (Ithaca and London, 1994), 112–13.

31 William Empson makes the point that "Iago is dragging Othello into his state of mind" in *The Structure of Complex Words* (London: 1951), 246.

32 Lewis Lewkenor, whom Shakespeare possibly read, asserts that "the Captaine Generall of [the Venetian] Armie . . . is always a straunger" in order to prevent political ambitions arising in the military (*Commonwealth and Government of Venice* [1599], sig. S2v, cited in David C. McPherson, *Shakespeare, Jonson and the Myth of Venice* [Newark, 1990], 73).

33 Citation is to the Arden edition, ed. John Russell Brown (London, 1955).

34 Rymer's complaint interestingly then shifts ground. He asserts that if such a marriage were to meet with acceptance in the House of Lords, "the black-amoor must have changed his skin." Removing the racial issue apparently makes it easier for him to imagine the state dealing in family matters (*Short View of Tragedy*, 103).

35 On Othello's status as an outsider permitted to enter a social "inside," see Peter Stallybrass, "Patriarchal Territories: The Body Enclosed," in *Rewriting the Renaissance: Discourses of Sexual Difference in Early Modern Europe*, ed. Margaret W. Ferguson, Maureen Quilligan, and Nancy J. Vickers (Chicago, 1986), 123–44.

36 *Othello* has furnished rich material for critics seeking to connect rhetorical tropes to social and epistemic issues. See Patricia Parker, "Shakespeare and Rhetoric: Dilation and Delation in *Othello*," in *Shakespeare and the Question of Theory*, ed. Patricia Parker and Geoffrey Hartman (New York and London, 1985), 54–74; and Joel B. Altman, "Preposterous Conclusions: Eros, *Enargeia*, and the Composition of *Othello*," *Representations* 18 (1987): 129–57.

37 Desdemona's wondering response to Othello's account of the handkerchief's exotic origins ("Is't possible?" [3.4.66], "I'faith, is't true?" [3.4.73]) suggests that what we see here is a reprise of their courtship, that exchange which so fits the model of "request and such fair question as soul to soul affordeth" (1.3.113–14), that Othello can placidly claim, "This only is the witchcraft I have us'd" (1.3.169). But the magical powers Othello attributes to the handkerchief to "subdue" another to one's love also serve to confirm Brabantio's association of witchcraft with his foreign son-in-law. The idea-lized version of Othello's relationship to Desdemona thus becomes the ground on which his difference, and hence the impossibility of his communion soul to soul with a "super-subtle Venetian," appears.

38 Stallybrass, "Patriarchal Territories," 139.

39 This point is true at the tropological as well as the conceptual level. Cardinal Allen, for instance, describing the torture of Edmund Campion, declared that "if they had torn him in ten thousand pieces or stilled him to the quintessence, in that holy breast they should never have found any piece of those fained treasons" (*Glorious Martyrdome,* 13). If Allen's ostensible point is that Campion was not guilty, his words also suggest a fantasy of making the body yield the soul's truth ("still[ing] him to the quintessence") which must collapse

into the discovery that such truth cannot be found in the flesh. The remark Catholics attributed to one of Campion's torturers that one "might sooner pluck his heart out of his bosom than rack a word out of his mouth that he made conscience of uttering" (Simpson, *Edmund Campion,* 391), which I quoted at the beginning of this book, similarly seems to harbor a version of Iago's taunt about knowing his thoughts, "You cannot if my heart were in your hand" (3.3.167).

40 Alan Bray, *Homosexuality in Renaissance England* (London, 1982), 19, 52.

41 John Bossy, "The Character of Elizabethan Catholicism," *Past and Present* 21 (1962): 45.

42 *Cobbett's Complete Collection of State Trials,* ed. T. B. Howell (London, 1811), I:1060.

43 Richard Challoner, *Complete Modern British Martyrology* (London, 1836). Of course, only a fraction of this group were interrogated under torture; however, social status appears to have had no part to play in determining that outcome. Priests who were important enough to be sent to London to be interrogated were tortured; otherwise they were simply executed. While in theory gentlemen were not subject to interrogation by torture, there were many bases for a claim to be a gentleman, and it is evident that at least some of them, such as having a degree from one of the universities or having a gentleman for a father, did not bar torture.

44 Devlin, *Life,* 5.

45 Haynes, *Invisible Power,* 15; Plowden, *Elizabethan Secret Service,* 67.

46 On the social instability connected with the Tudor expansions of education and bureaucracy, see Lawrence Stone and Jeanne C. Fawtier Stone, *An Open Elite?* (Oxford, 1984), 397–405; Mark H. Curtis, "The Alienated Intellectuals of Early Stuart England," *Past and Present* 23 (1962): 25–43; and Roger Chartier, "Time to Understand," in *Cultural History: Between Practices and Representations,* trans. Lydia G. Cochrane (Ithaca, 1988), 127–50. For the relation between the Jesuits and the class of men whose capital was their education, see Plowden, *Elizabethan Secret Service,* 62–5.

47 *The Jesuits Memorial for the Intended Reformation of England under their first Popish Prince* (London, 1690). (The title is the work of the Protestant publishers.)

48 Quoted in Devlin, *Life,* 175. See also Richard Challoner, *Complete Modern British Martyrology* (London, 1836), 113. Another Catholic martyr of the period, Margaret Clithero, was pressed to death at York, March 25, 1586, when she refused to enter a plea to charges pertaining to harboring priests. Pressing to death was not an investigative technique but a method for forcing people to participate in judicial process. People who were pressed to death were not convicted of an offense, and in this way an accused could avoid the forfeiture of his property to the Crown. Nevertheless such a practice could clearly bring notions of a resistant interiority into play.

49 *The Examination of Anne Askew* (1546), and *The Lattre Examination of Anne Askew* (1547), transcribed and ed. by John Bale in the Parker Society's *Select Works of John Bale,* ed. Henry Christmas (Oxford, 1849). *The Examinations* are also reproduced in John Foxe, *Actes and Monuments of the Latter and Perilous Days* (1563), ed. George Townsend, vol. V (1838; rpt. 1965).

50 Askew replies to questions about fellow heretics equivocally. Presented with a list of names she answers "if I should pronounce any thing against them, that I were not able to prove it" (220). As soon she is released from the rack, and having fallen to the floor, she resumes theological debate with the Lord Chancellor. At one point in her earlier questioning she is urged "boldly . . . to utter the secrets of [her] heart" (163) but her response is not that they have no right to ask these things (the Jesuit response to the "bloody question") but that they already know her opinions. The absence of the secrecy/discovery issue from Askew's account may have had more to do with her historical circumstances than with her gender. She was tried for heresy and not treason, and as a Protestant rather than a Catholic, so that neither the distinction between matters of state and matters of conscience nor the one between juridical and religious confession which worked so powerfully to define the Jesuits' interiority plays a part in her situation.

51 The cases involving forms of physical coercion (specifically practices such as sleep deprivation rather than direct infliction of acute pain) are mostly connected with Matthew Hopkins's campaign in 1645–7. See Keith Thomas, *Religion and the Decline of Magic* (Harmondsworth, 1971). My remarks here are extremely speculative, based on secondary reading and on some evidentiary treatises. A detailed examination of archival and pamphlet material would undoubtedly complicate my argument.

52 See Barbara Shapiro, *Probability and Certainty in Seventeenth-Century England* (Princeton, 1983), 194–226, for an excellent discussion of the epistemic construction of witchcraft in the context of changes in religious, legal, and scientific notions of proof and truth in the period.

53 For an account of the various ways in which the witch was constructed as a legible body see Karen Newman, "Discovering Witches; Sorciographics," *Fashioning Femininity and Renaissance Drama* (Chicago, 1991), 51–70. For the ways in which witches were constructed in terms of continuity between subjectivity and their object-world generally see Dolan, *Dangerous Familiars*, 182–7.

54 John Cotta, *The Trial of Witchcraft* (London, 1616), 20.

55 My source for this story is Devlin, *Life*, 256, 274–90. Devlin's sources are mostly reports of news obtained by Catholic informants and dispatched in letters by Henry Garnet and Richard Verstegan to Jesuit authorities. Devlin offers no account either of Ann's motives in betraying Southwell or of her parents' in consenting to her marriage, implying that both seemed to follow inevitably from her rape and pregnancy.

56 Apparently from a letter from Garnet, May 1, 1595. Cited in Devlin, *Life*, 288.

57 Everything about this story seems overdetermined. Bellamy not only lured Southwell to her family's house, but also told Topcliffe the plan of the house and where Southwell's hiding place was (Devlin, *Life*, 280).

4   AUTHORS AND OTHERS

1 All quotations from the *Caveat* are from A. V. Judges, ed., *The Elizabethan Underworld* (London, 1930).

2 S. R., *Martin Markall, Beadle of Bridewell* (1610). All quotations are from Judges, *The Elizabethan Underworld.*

3 Harman was evidently not a Justice at the time he wrote and published the *Caveat*; the *Calendar of Assize Records, Elizabeth I, Kent Indictments*, J. S. Cockburn, ed. (London, 1975) does not list Harman among the Justices acting during Elizabeth's reign.

4 Greenblatt, *Shakespearean Negotiations*, 51.

5 The *Liber Vagatorum* as edited by Martin Luther was translated by John Camden Hotten as *The Book of Vagabonds and Beggars: With a Vocabulary of their Language* (1528; London, 1860), xiii.

6 In 1913 Frank Aydelotte could assert that "the earlier pamphlets [especially Harman's] have the interest that belongs to honest and real descriptions of a little known phase of sixteenth-century life," while "the later ones are mostly borrowed from the earlier," and make discoveries of his own, like the fact that a number of the vagrants' proper names that Harman appends to his text are also found in the certificates of watches and searches of 1571–2 in the Southern and Midland counties (*Elizabethan Rogues and Vagabonds*, vol. I [Oxford, 1913], 114, 123). A more recent example of such a reading is Gamini Salgado, *The Elizabethan Underworld* (London and Totowa, 1977). Most recent historians of Elizabethan vagrancy and crime, however, have re-placed these pamphlets in the same unreliable "literary" category as the later ones, prefacing their findings with phrases like "Contrary to the literary sources . . . " (A. L. Beier, *Masterless Men: The Vagrancy Problem in Early Modern England* [London, 1985], 144) or "Turning from statutes and rogue literature to court archives . . ." (Sharpe, *Crime*, 100).

7 For example, in one of the two treatments I have encountered of the Dekker–S. R. exchange in the context of Renaissance notions of authorship, Edwin Havilland Miller announces, "The rules of serious literature did not apply to hack work" (*The Professional Writer in Elizabethan England* [Cambridge, 1959], 148). See also H. O. White, *Plagiarism and Imitation During the English Renaissance* (New York, 1965), 146–8. The "rules of serious literature" Miller refers to have to do with the vital Renaissance practice of imitation, which in the hands of modern scholars is recuperable as a form of authorial labor, despite the fact that it can look like plagiarism by the standards of subsequent generations. See Stephen Orgel, "The Renaissance Artist as Plagiarist," *ELH* 48 (1981): 476–95.

8 Indeed, for two of the earliest English rogue books, Robert Copland's *Highway to the Spital-House* (1535–6) and Awdeley's *Fraternity of Vagabonds*, printers serve as "authors." The un-authored nature of this literature has also facilitated its use in New Historicist and cultural materialist analysis, permitting it to serve as an unmediated symptom of "the culture." Stephen Greenblatt, for example, uses the conycatching literature as an example of Elizabethan authority producing and containing its own subversion. But he also does not miss the opportunity for making literary distinctions, noting that Harman's version of this dynamic is "so much cruder than Shakespeare['s]" (*Shakespearean Negotiations*, 52). Jean-Christophe Agnew, in an account more attentive to the material context within which these pamphlets

were produced but no less homogenizing, sees them as "a reminder of the social and psychic distance to be travelled within the interior of England's new exchange relations" (*Worlds Apart: The Market and the Theater in Anglo-American Thought, 1550–1750* [Cambridge, 1986], 68). For a valuable account of the fate of authorial labor in the print market, see Alexandra Halasz, *The Marketplace of Print: Pamphlets, Printing and the Early Modern Public Sphere* (Cambridge, 1997).

9 It should be noted that I am using the terms "discover" and "invent" in their modern sense, rather than in their sense as terms of art in Renaissance rhetoric, where they could be synonyms for the activity of finding arguments. When Francis Bacon criticizes this rhetorical understanding of discovery in favor of a discovery of nature, he uses the terms interchangeably. That invention could nevertheless mean literary fabrication as opposed to a revelation of historical truth is indicated by its use in the epigram to this chapter.

10 "What is an Author?" in *Textual Strategies*, ed. Josue V. Harari (Ithaca, 1979), 148.

11 On this point see also Crane, *Framing Authority*, 6–7.

12 The previous book is probably Awdeley's *Fraternity of Vagabonds* (1561).

13 For example, *The Fraternity of Vagabonds* (which is simply a catalogue of stratagems and a taxonomy of rogues) is prefaced with a verse describing its origin in a vagabond who was brought before "justices and men of lands" and "who promised if they would him spare / And keep his name from knowledge then / He would as strange a thing declare . . . as ever they knew . . ." (Judges, *Elizabethan Underworld*, 52). In contrast, on several occasions Harman turns this scenario into a narrative studded with homely details. Similarly, where the *Liber Vagatorum* (which also has no narrator) baldly states, "Item, there are some of the afore-mentioned who neither ask before a house nor at the door, but step right in the house" (Hotten, *Liber Vagatorum*, 43), Harman tells us that this particular outrage has been perpetrated on two particular families, one at a place "between Deptford and Rotherhithe, called the King's Barn, the other [at] Ketbroke standing by Blackheath" (109).

14 Judges, *Elizabethan Underworld*, 122–3.

15 Robert Weimann, "'Appropriation' and Modern History in Renaissance Prose Narrative," *New Literary History*, 14 (1983): 480, 469.

16 On the post-feudal character of the rogue literature generally, see Jonathan Haynes, *The Social Relations of Jonson's Theater* (Cambridge, 1992), 107.

17 In the second and third editions the difference is simply one of size; in the fourth edition the cant words are in black letter and the definitions are set in Roman type. If, as Keith Thomas has argued, more readers were fluent in reading black letter type than in reading Roman, the difference in typeface would serve to emphasize the reader's sense of being able to master and move among multiple languages ("Literacy in Early Modern England," in *The Written Word: Literacy in Transition*, ed. Gerd Baumann, [Oxford, 1986], 97–132).

18 *Perambulation of Kent* (1826 ed.), 66, cited in *Rogues and Vagabonds of Shakespeare's Youth*, ed. Edward Viles and Frederick James Furnivall, Early English Text Society Extra Series, vol. 9 (London, 1869), xxvii.

19 Viles and Furnivall, *Rogues and Vagabonds,* i–xxx, provides some bio-graphical data, principally from Hasted's *History of Kent.*
20 As with so many other particularities of Harman's text, his accounts of his acts of local charity following his discovery of vagrant tricks narrativize one of the genre's formulae that first appears in the *Liber Vagatorum.* As I go on to suggest, charity for Harman seems to signify a rural way of life to which his text is ambivalently related. That this ambivalence is culturally overdeter-mined is suggested by a confusion about the identity of the dedicatee, whom Harman is addressing at this point. The *Caveat* is dedicated to Elizabeth, Countess of Shrewsbury, a figure whom Judges identifies as the famous Bess of Hardwick, a rising courtier, who married George Talbot, Earl of Shrews-bury, in 1567. Viles and Furnivall, on the other hand, identify her as the second wife of George, Earl of Shrewsbury (Judges, *Elizabethan Underworld,* 496; Viles and Furnivall, *Rogues and Vagabonds,* xxvi–xxvii). The Earl had died in 1542 and the dowager Countess lived in the parish of Erith, which adjoined Harman's parish of Crayford, and is buried there. The confusion arises because the dowager Countess died in 1567, the same year that Bess of Hardwick married George Talbot, and the first edition of the *Caveat* (1566) which, if it carried the dedication, would decide the issue in favor of the Dowager Countess, is lost. The difference these women figure, the one a rising courtier, the other an elderly local noblewoman, is one between ambition and local commitments. The dedication itself suggests that the person in question is likely to have been the dowager Countess. Harman praises her for "not only in the parish where your honour most happily doth dwell, but also in other environing or nigh adjoining to the same; as also abundantly pouring out daily your ardent and bountiful charity upon all such as cometh for relief unto your lucky gates . . ." (61).
21 Cf. the stories in Greene's *Notable Discovery of Cozenage* (1591). In Greene's account of "the art of crossbiting," for example, married men are lured into sexual indiscretions; then "the party, afraid to have his credit cracked with the worshipful of the City and the rest of his neighbours, and grieving highly lest his wife should hear of it, straight takes composition with this cozener for some twenty marks" (Judges, *Elizabethan Underworld,* 140). The trick works because it is so easy to make a member of the community into someone with a secret to hide. The crossbiters are countered not by the victim's restoration to a transparent relation with wife and neighbours, but with a power play, when one victim proclaims, "I serve a nobleman, and for my credit with him, I refer me to the penalty he will impose on you" (142). The victim's victory depends on an allegiance based on "credit," but one that also makes wives and neighbours irrelevant.
22 Readings of this episode tend to emphasize Harman's prurience and his deafness to the misery and oppression to which the woman's story testifies. See, for instance, William C. Carroll, *Fat King, Lean Beggar: Representations of Poverty in the Age of Shakespeare* (Ithaca and London, 1996), 89–94; and Jodi Mikalachki, "Popular Fictions, Court Records and Female Vagrants in Late Sixteenth and Early Seventeenth-Century England," paper delivered to the Seminar on Women and Early Modern Culture, Center for Literary and Cultural Studies, Harvard University, September 30, 1992. My point is that

while Harman's voice and the story diverge considerably in their construction of the woman's experience, the story is nevertheless a conventional piece of a discursive universe Harman inhabits and to which he repeatedly affirms his allegiance. My reading of this episode is indebted to a conversation with Mary Douglas about sexual discipline and women's solidarity in hierarchical cultures.

23 My sense of the multidirectional instability of the *Caveat* counters Stephen Greenblatt's account of Harman's book as a crude case of authority producing and containing its own subversion, that is, of the "forces of order" making revelations of their own duplicity the paradoxical ground for their suppression of resistance (*Shakespearean Negotiations*, 49–51). Greenblatt's argument depends on the assumption that Harman can be unproblematically identified with the agile but ultimately monolithic and alienated "authority" he describes. Such an assumption conflates the various grounds of Harman's activity – his social position, his enterprising personality, the print trade – ignoring the ways in which they may be in conflict with each other. Thus Greenblatt makes the disruptions and slippages which he notes in the text (including the dignity the text accords to the voice of the walking mort in the episode I analyze above) arise from a single discursive activity, the production of "authority" rather than, as I think is in fact the case, from the heterogeneity of the text's discursive activity that produces Harman, not as "authority" but as an author.

24 Beier, *Masterless Men*, 117, provides corroboration for this episode from assize records. See also Carroll, *Fat King, Lean Beggar*, 83. Whatever the origin of the story, however, its deep mythological resonance for capitalist life is indicated by the reappearance of this scenario in Arthur Conan Doyle's "The Man with the Twisted Lip," in which a man with a wife and house in the suburbs travels to the City every day in business clothes to pursue a secret but lucrative career as a beggar (*The Adventures of Sherlock Holmes* [London, 1892], 128–55).

25 Greenblatt also comments on Harman's thematization of print, although he seems to take the episode at face value, arguing that the role of the printer in the Jennings episode "literalizes the power of the book to hunt down vagabonds and bring them to justice" (*Shakespearean Negotiations*, 50–1).

26 The printer of the first three editions of the *Caveat* was William Griffith, a founding member of the Stationers' Company, who printed between 1552 and 1572. I have found no evidence of his age which might suggest his physical condition in 1566. The printer of the fourth edition was Henry Middleton.

27 The naivety of this belief is revealed in the subsequent history of the *Caveat* itself, for at least two printers, Henry Binneman and Gerard Dewes, were fined for attempts to pirate a copy called "the boke of Rogges" belonging to the *Caveat*'s printer William Griffith (*Transcripts of the Registers of the Company of Stationers*, ed. Edward Arber, vol. I [New York, 1950], 345, 369).

28 In this regard, Harman's nimble printer can be seen as an ironic prefiguration of the Marprelate printers and their literally moving press that forced the Elizabethan authorities into pursuit.

29 The Jennings episode begins when the first edition is being printed and apparently is closed "while this second impression was in printing," as a tag

appended to that edition asserts, but is not completely told until the fourth edition of the *Caveat*, the final one to appear in Harman's lifetime (Judges, *Elizabethan Underworld*, 117–18).

30 For a more developed account of this "logic of print" from the consumer's point of view, see Halasz, *Marketplace of Print.*

31 Citing Bakhtin's account of the "alcove realism" of seventeenth-century French depictions of the lower orders, Agnew also notes the way these lexicons frame the reader's experience as eavesdropping (*Worlds Apart*, 67). See also Mikhail Bakhtin, *Rabelais and His World*, trans. Helene Iswolsky (Bloomington, 1984), 105–6.

32 The ambivalent relationship between printed text and oral exchange in Harman's text is pointed up in a brief digression on spelling in the Epistle to the Reader that prefaced the second edition. "Is there no diversity," he asks, "between a *gardein* and a *garden, mayntenaunce* and *maintenance, streytes* and *stretes*?" (66), an apparently gratuitous aside that shows Harman's interest in the mid-sixteenth-century movement to reform English orthography along phonetic lines in an effort to make the written word a transparent mediation of the spoken. What makes plain terms plain is their ability to embody speech, a concern, however, that already presumes that the knowledge he offers can be gleaned only through reading. Ironically, the reason for the Epistle seems to be that readers of the first edition found some of Harman's terms (like "cursitor") as outlandish as cant. For an account of the mid-sixteenth-century orthographic reform see Richard Foster Jones, *The Triumph of the English Language* (Stanford, 1953), 142–67. For an analysis of the political and epistemic subtleties of the debate in a Derridean context, see Jonathan Goldberg, *Writing Matter: From the Hands of the English Renaissance* (Stanford, 1990), 190–200. Lucien Febvre and and Henri-Jean Martin argue that a burgeoning orthographic consciousness in sixteenth-century Europe was a function of printing (*The Coming of the Book: The Impact of Printing, 1450–1800*, trans. David Gerard, ed. Geoffrey Nowell Smith and David Wootton [London, 1976], 319–21). Despite the context of this broader movement, however, the *OED* suggests that Harman's question was by no means rhetorical. In the mid-sixteenth century there was a semantic difference between a guardian and a garden, maintenance (upkeep) and maintenance (deportment), streets and straits, but not an orthographic one.

33 In subordinating its textuality to a putative anterior orality, Harman's book anticipates the epistemological concerns of subsequent ethnography. See Margaret Hodgen, *Early Anthropology in the Sixteenth and Seventeenth Centuries* (Philadelphia, 1964), both for a fascinating and complex account of the epistemological development of ethnography, and for an example of ethnographic suspicion of textuality. For theoretical examinations of this suspicion see James Clifford and George E. Marcus, eds., *Writing Culture: The Poetics and Politics of Ethnography* (Berkeley and Los Angeles, 1986), and Johannes Fabian, "Presence and Representation: The Other and Anthropological Writing," *Critical Inquiry* 16 (1990): 753–93. Fabian recognizes a lexically contradictory attempt to produce "a disjunction between ethnography and writing" in a methodology that insists on the spatial separation of

"research" and "write-up" (759). Harman, as I suggest below, tries to suppress writing altogether.

34 Greenblatt notes that this moment is "not encouraging" to credence in the text's empirical claims (*Shakespearean Negotiations*, 50). A version of this joke recurs in the first French redaction of the vagabond material, *La vie genereuse des mercelots, gueuz, et boesmiens . . . Mis en lumiere par Monsieur Pechon de Ruby, Gentil'homme Breton . . .* (Lyons, 1596). See Roger Chartier, *The Cultural Uses of Print in Early Modern France*, trans. Lydia G. Cochrane (Princeton, 1987), 265–80. In the lexicon appended to the text the reader learns that "pechon de ruby" means "alert child." As in the *Caveat*, the joke calls into question the truth claims of the narrative, but Chartier's account of this text points up the ways in which the effect of "harmans" is more radically destabilizing. Embedded in Spanish picaresque as well as German vagabond-book tradition, *La vie* presents itself not as the fruit of investigation but as a rogue's autobiography – a fiction that is not only obvious but which it does not sustain, and, in any case, a device that already places the narrator on the dubious side of the lexical divide. Harman's text, with its use of the ordinary proper names of verifiably historical persons (including that of the upright author), positions itself far more plausibly in the real world, insisting as well on its moral and analytic distance from the culture it discovers.

35 Edward Said, *Beginnings: Intention and Method* (New York, 1975), 83.

36 Agnew, *Worlds Apart*, 69.

37 The discussion of spelling and diction described in note 32 above arguably constitutes a representation of the task of writing. But, as I explain in that note, the orthographic arguments Harman makes are part of a project to make writing a transparent record of speech.

38 Barry Taylor also offers a reading of the *Caveat* that focuses on Harman's position as writer, arguing that insofar as it implicates him in "vagrant semiois" it is at odds with his desire to uphold traditional forms of authority (*Vagrant Writing* [New York and London, 1991], 1–24). While I share Taylor's sense that the *Caveat*'s ostensible subject-matter also furnishes a kind of allegory about the conditions of the text's production, I differ from Taylor both in what I mean by writing and how I understand Harman's position in relation to it. Taylor intends "writing" in the Derridean sense, as a tissue of signifiers in constant play, which become all the more unstable in a world undergoing deep structural changes in the social order. In this analysis, Harman is the representative of authority whose own text is unwittingly implicated in the semiotic instability it would quell. Following Weimann, I would want to supplement this account by also construing writing as a form of work, and Harman as a subject who engages in it, and thereby develops interests that are at odds with those of the authority he defends.

39 In addition to the use of Harman's material in new books, there were the two attempts to pirate the *Caveat*, mentioned at note 27 above. Moreover, the uses of Harman's name and text were not limited to conycatching pamphlets. William Harrison, in his "Description of England" prefixed to *Holinshed's Chronicles* (1586), cites as an authority "a gentleman [who] also of late hath taken great paines to search out the secret practises of this ungratious

rabble," and places "Thomas Harman" in the margin (cited in Viles and Furnivall, *Rogues and Vagabonds*, xii).

40 The title page also tells the reader that "Therein are handled the practices of the Visiter, the fetches of the shifter and Rufflar, the deceits of their doxies, the devises of Priggers, the names of the base loytering losels etc.," suggesting that Harman's material still had market value of its own, in addition to that which it derived from the fashion started by Greene. Nevertheless, Viles and Furnivall tell us that the "author" of the *Groundworke* had been assumed to be Greene and that the pamphlet was "bound up in the 2nd vol. of Greene's *Works*, among George III's books in the British Museum, as if it really was Greene's" (*Rogues and Vagabonds*, xiv).

41 S. R. has been identified either as Samuel Rid or Samuel Rowlands. For the various arguments for each identification see Judges, *Elizabethan Underworld*, 514. It should be noted that the plagiarism entailed in the production of this literature is not confined to uses of Harman. For example, Greene borrows both from Harman and more extensively from Gilbert Walker's *A Manifest Detection of Dice Play* (1552); Dekker borrows from Greene and Samuel Rowlands as well as Harman. Yet it seems to be only Harman whose rights as original author of specific material ever becomes a subject for comment, a fact which I would link to his writing from a position partially outside the book trade and to his extensive self-representation in the *Caveat*.

42 The story of Bathyllus, who presented verses by Virgil to Augustus under his own name, verses to which Virgil supposedly appended the line "I made the verses, another has born away the honor" was the *locus classicus* on theft of authorial labor, frequently accompanying invocations of Aesop's Crow. See White, *Plagiarism and Imitation*, 15–16, 99, 160 for uses of the anecdote.

43 All quotations except where otherwise noted are from Judges, *Elizabethan Underworld*.

44 Laurence Manly usefully remarks that in Dekker's pamphlets "the most orthodox and creditworthy uses of the word [are] revealed as matters of production and reproduction" (*Literature and Culture in Early Modern London* [Cambridge, 1995], 352).

45 These accounts can be found in Richard A. Burt, *Licensed by Authority: Ben Jonson and the Discourses of Censorship* (Ithaca and London, 1993); David Riggs, *Ben Jonson: A Life* (Cambridge, Mass., 1989); Timothy Murray, *Theatrical Legitimation* (Oxford, 1987) and "From Foul Sheets to Legitimate Model: Antitheater, Text, Ben Jonson," *New Literary History* 14 (1983): 641–64; Joseph Loewenstein, "The Script in the Marketplace," *Representations* 12 (1985), 101–14; Peter Stallybrass and Allon White, "The Fair, the Pig, Authorship," in *The Politics and Poetics of Transgression* (Ithaca, 1986); and Annabel Patterson, *Censorship and Interpretation* (Madison, 1984), although the list could be considerably expanded. The terms in which the opposition is framed vary: in Stallybrass and White they are Bakhtinian classical and grotesque while in Riggs they are the Foucauldian ones of authorization and transgression. And the dynamic of opposition differs: where Patterson makes Jonson the agent of an ethically informed opposition, most of the other readings make Jonson the site of a dialectical encounter between censoring and transgressing impulses which produces the formation

of authorship. All these readings, however, make the relationship between authority, with which Jonson seeks to align himself, and his tendency to go out of bounds the central issue for an understanding of Jonson's career.

46 All quotations are from *Bartholmew Fair*, ed. G. R. Hibbard (London and New York, 1977).

47 See Judges, *Elizabethan Underworld*, 189–90.

48 My argument here is indebted to one Joseph Loewenstein makes, citing Jonson's initial printing of the masque texts as a resistance on his part to the pre-emptive *occasion* of the masque. That Loewenstein can make this argument about Jonson's most courtly works powerfully suggests that the threat posed by the theatre to Jonson arises not merely from its low status but also from its overwhelming force of occasion. "The Script in the Market-place," 108.

5   FRANCIS BACON AND THE DISCOVERING SUBJECT

1 All quotations from the *New Atlantis* are from Francis Bacon, *The Advancement of Learning and New Atlantis*, ed. Arthur Johnston (Oxford, 1974).

2 See E. J. Dijksterhuis, *The Mechanization of the World Picture*, trans. C. Dikshoorn (Princeton, 1986), 396–403. For useful summaries of the fortunes of Bacon's reputation see Antonio Perez-Ramos, *Francis Bacon's Idea of Science and the Maker's Knowledge Tradition* (Oxford, 1988), 7–31; Fulton H. Anderson, *Francis Bacon: His Career and Thought* (Los Angeles, 1962), 3–18.

3 See, for example, Merchant, *Death of Nature*; Reiss, *Discourse of Modernism*, 168–225; Charles Whitney, "Merchants of Light: Science as Colonization in the *New Atlantis*," in William A. Sessions, ed., *Francis Bacon's Legacy of Texts* (New York, 1990), 255–68; Denise Albanese, *New Science, New World* (Durham, NC, 1996), 92–120. All quotations of Bacon's works, except where otherwise noted, are from Spedding *et al.*, *Works of Francis Bacon*, and throughout the chapter citations to Bacon's works will be noted by the initial letters of the title and page numbers referring to the edition of that text I have used.

4 Reiss, *Discourse of Modernism*, 216.

5 I am generally indebted to Charles Whitney, *Francis Bacon and Modernity* (New Haven, 1986) for its account of the role of the revolutionary stance in Bacon's writing.

6 Of course, Bacon's claim to begin anew from the very foundations is also framed as a return, an instauration of the Temple, a restoration of Adam's original dominion over creation, so that Bacon's revolutionary voice is aligned with biblical prophecy. See Whitney, *Francis Bacon and Modernity*, esp. 23–78, and Charles Webster, *The Great Instauration: Science, Medicine and Reform 1626–1660* (London, 1975), 1–31. Whitney productively notes that Bacon's account of his project as an instauration and as a revolution are not, in fact, congruent with each other, that his claim to begin anew is not fully covered, as it were, by his claim to restore. Neither stance, in any case, evinces the ideological loyalty to existing institutions that characterizes the discourse, if not the practices, of other discoverers we have encountered.

7 On the complicated relationship between Bacon's philosophical project and

seventeenth-century political reconfigurations see Webster, *The Great In-stauration*; Margaret C. Jacob, *The Radical Enlightenment* (London, 1981), 65–86; Reiss, *Discourse of Modernism*, 193–4, 198–201.

8 See Merchant, *Death of Nature*, and Archer, *Sovereignty and Intelligence*, 150.

9 Kenneth Cardwell, "Francis Bacon, Inquisitor," in *Francis Bacon's Legacy of Texts*, ed. Sessions, 269–89.

10 See Reiss, *Discourse of Modernism*, 185–94, for a discussion of the role that secrecy plays in defining the superiority of the discovering subject in *The New Atlantis*. Reiss argues that Bacon's concern with secrecy anticipates both possessive individualism and science as a for-profit operation. He does not note, however, that secrecy is not the exclusive property of the discoverer, that it also belongs to nature and thus serves to deconstruct the differences on which the discoverer's mastery depends.

11 The difficulty of locating agency in this passage is complicated by Bacon's old-fashioned use of "discover" as a synonym of "confess," a usage which makes the subject of the verb the initial possessor of a secret rather than the person who uncovers it for the first time. We find this older usage in the torture warrants' instruction to "draw [the victims] to discover their know-ledge" (Heath, *Torture and English Law*, 222). But the modern usage of "to discover" (as the action of someone encountering a new truth for the first time) is also emerging in this period and Bacon uses the verb both ways. In the *New Atlantis*, for example, the explorers pray to God "that he might discover land" (215) to them, but hear of "Columbus that discovered the West Indies" (246). Examples in the *OED* suggest that the discovery of the New World was responsible for making available the modern usage.

12 The *OED* gives as a sample of contemporary usage of "impart" a passage from "Of Counsel" in the *Essays* of 1625: "King Henry the Seventh of England . . . imparted himself to none except it were to Morton and Fox" (VI:425). Thus "imparting" implies a judicious maintaining of secrecy even in disclosure, confirming the connection for Bacon between secrecy and the ability to be a subject, rather than simply a mouthpiece, of one's discourse.

13 This formulation, it should be stressed, is overly schematic since Bacon's imagery can on occasion completely collapse inwardness and outwardness into each other. How, for example, would we map inward and outward in the case of the image, in the *Masculine Birth of Time*, of the island of truth, surrounded by a stormy ocean of illusion (III:536)?

14 Bacon cites the same passage from Heraclitus in the *New Organon* when discussing the Idols of the Cave (IV:54).

15 Julian Martin, *Francis Bacon, the State and the Reform of Natural Philosophy* (Cambridge, 1992).

16 See also Anthony F. C. Wallace, *The Social Context of Innovation* (Princeton, 1982), 3–31.

17 See chapter 2, note 9, above.

18 On the role that personal gain plays in Bacon's discourse, see Reiss, *Discourse of Modernism*, 190–1.

19 Albanese, *New Science, New World*, 111–12, argues persuasively that mon-archical authority is subtly superseded in the *New Atlantis* by the work of science. See also Archer, *Sovereignty and Intelligence*, 145. Wallace makes the

useful point that in the *New Atlantis* Bacon effectively conceals the impli- cations of his project by making the work of innovation be scientific and technological rather than political or social (*The Social Context of Innovation*, 14–15).

20 For the circumstances of Bacon's downfall see Anderson, *Francis Bacon*, 213–30.

21 For a provocative reading of the Feast of the Family see Archer, *Sovereignty and Intelligence*, 148–9. I am indebted to Archer for his observation that the mother's position here is a privileged one, although I would hesitate to align her, as Archer does, with a surveying monarch. The powerful gaze in the Feast seems to belong to the father beholding his offspring.

22 There is, of course, one quasi-allegorical dimension to this relation: the names, such as "Merchants of Light" or "Dowry-men," which are given to the various research functions. However, these serve to make clear the moral value of the actual research practices, not to invite us to read the research practices as something else.

23 See Ronald Levao, "Francis Bacon and the Mobility of Science," *Representa- tions* 40 (1992): 1–32, for another account of the relation between "mobility" and Bacon's conception of the subject. I concur with Levao's assertion that the purpose of Bacon's method is "to discipline the refractory individual" (16) and that this relation between method and mind results in a sense of the dynamism of the subject in Bacon's writing. I would argue, however, that dynamism is not only a characteristic of the subject himself, but of Bacon's multiple, contradictory figurations of the subject, which produce constant conceptual friction.

24 Steven Shapin and Simon Schaffer, *Leviathan and the Air Pump* (Princeton, 1985).

25 *History of the Royal Society of London, for the Improving of Natural Knowledge* (London, 1667), 84. Cited in Shapin and Schaffer, *Leviathan and the Air Pump*, 58.

26 "A Proemial Essay . . . with Some Considerations touching Experimental Essays in General," in *The Works of the Honourable Robert Boyle*, ed. Thomas Birch, 2nd ed. (London, 1772), I:312. Cited in Shapin and Schaffer, *Leviathan and the Air Pump*, 73.

27 Boyle to Moray, July 1662, in Christiaan Huygens, *Œuvres complètes de Christiaan Huygens* (The Hague, 1888–1950), IV:220. Cited in Shapin and Schaffer, *Leviathan and the Air Pump*, 77.

28 Steven Shapin, *A Social History of Truth* (Chicago and London, 1994).

29 Boyle, "Epistolical Discourse . . . Inviting All True Lovers of Vertue and Mankind to a Free and Generous Communication of their Secrets and Receits in Physick," reprinted in Margaret E. Rowbotham, "The Earliest Published Writing of Robert Boyle," *Annals of Science* 6 (1950): 381. Cited in Shapin, *A Social History of Truth*, 175.

30 Boyle Papers, *Commonplace Book*, 189, f. 13r. Cited in Shapin, *A Social History of Truth*, 403.

31 *The Moral and Historical Works of Lord Bacon, Including his Essays . . .*, ed. Joseph Devey (London, 1852), 28. Cited in Shapin, *A Social History of Truth*, 100.

32 Lorraine Daston and Peter Galison, "The Image of Objectivity," *Representations* 40 (1992): 81–128.

33 *History and Bibliography of Anatomic Illustration* (1852), ed. and trans. Mortimer Frank (Chicago, 1920), 23. Cited by Daston and Galison, "The Image of Objectivity," 91.

34 Francis Galton, "Composite Portraits," *Nature* 18 (1878), 97–100. Cited by Daston and Galison, "The Image of Objectivity,"103.

35 (Leipzig, 1927), 18. Cited by Daston and Galison, "The Image of Objectivity," 113.

36 Quoted in Karl Pearson, *The Grammar of Science* (London, 1892), 38. Cited by Daston and Galison, "The Image of Objectivity," (118).

Select bibliography

PRIMARY SOURCES

Allen, William. *A Briefe Historie of the Glorious Martyrdom of the xii Reverend Priests.* Edited by J. H. Pollen. London, 1908.

    A Treatise Made in Defence of the Lawful Power and Authoritie of Priesthood to Remitte Sinnes. Louvain, 1567.

    A True, Sincere and Modest Defence of English Catholics. Edited by Robert M. Kingdon. Ithaca, 1965.

Arber, Edward. *A Transcript of the Registers of the Stationers Company of London, 1554–1640.* New York, 1950.

Askew, Anne. *The Examination of Anne Askew* (1546), and *The Lattre Examination of Anne Askew* (1547). Transcribed and edited by John Bale in *Select Works of John Bale.* Edited by Henry Christmas. London, 1849.

Awdeley, John. *The Fraternity of Vagabonds* (1561) in *The Elizabethan Underworld.* Edited by A. V. Judges.

Bacon, Francis. *The Advancement of Learning and New Atlantis.* Edited by Arthur Johnston. Oxford, 1974.

    The Letters and Life of Francis Bacon. Edited by James Spedding, Robert Ellis, and Douglas Heath. 7 vols. London, 1868–90.

    The Works of Francis Bacon. Edited by James Spedding, Robert Ellis, and Douglas Heath. 7 vols. London, 1878–92.

The Book of Vagabonds and Beggars: With a Vocabulary of their Language. Edited by Martin Luther. Translated and edited by John Camden Hotten. London, 1860.

[Burghley, Sir William Cecil, Baron.] *A Declaration of the Favourable Dealing of Her Majesty's Commissioners.* In William Allen, *A True Sincere and Modest Defence of English Catholics.*

    The Execution of Justice in England. In William Allen, A True Sincere and Modest Defence of English Catholics.

Calendar of Assize Records, Elizabeth I, Kent Indictments. Edited by J. S. Cockburn. London, 1975.

Calendar of Assize Records, James I, Hertfordshire Indictments. Edited by J. S. Cockburn. London, 1975.

Cobbet's Complete Collection of State Trials, vol. I. Edited by T. B. Howell. 34 vols. London, 1811.

Coke, Edward. *The Third Part of the Institutes of the Laws of England*. London, 1797.

Cotta, John. *The Trial of Witchcraft*. London, 1616.

Dalton, Michael. *The Countrey Justice*. London, 1618.

Dekker, Thomas. *Lantern and Candlelight*, in *The Elizabethan Underworld*. Edited by A. V. Judges.

Fortescue, John. *De Laudibus Legum Angliae*. Translated S. B. Chrimes. Cambridge, 1942.

Gerard, John. *The Autobiography of an Elizabethan*. Translated by Philip Caraman. London and New York, 1951.

Greene, Robert. *Notable Discovery of Cozenage*, in *The Elizabethan Underworld*. Edited by A. V. Judges.

Third Part of Cony-Catching, in *The Elizabethan Underworld*. Edited by A. V. Judges.

The Groundworke of Conny-catching. London, 1592.

Harman, Thomas. *A Caveat for Common Cursitors*, in *The Elizabethan Underworld*. Edited by A. V. Judges.

The Horrible Murther of a Young Boy . . . London, 1606.

Jonson, Ben. *Bartholmew Fair*. Edited by G. R. Hibbard. London and New York, 1977.

Lambarde, William. *Eirenarchia*. London, 1588.

Loyola, St. Ignatius. *The Autobiography of St. Ignatius*. Edited by J. F. X. O'Conor. New York, 1900.

The Most Cruell and Bloody Murther . . . London, 1606.

Munday, Anthony. *The English-Romayne Life*. Edited by G. B. Harrison. London, 1925.

Persons, Robert. *An Epistle of the Persecution of Catholickes in Englande*. Douai, 1582.

The Jesuit's Memorial for the Intended Reformation of England under Their First Popish Prince. London, 1690.

A Treatise Tending to Mitigation Towards Catholick Subjects. St. Omer, 1607.

Publications of the Catholic Record Society, Vol. V. Edited by J. H. Pollen. London, 1908.

R. S. *Martin Markall, Beadle of Bridewell*, in A. V. Judges (ed.), *The Elizabethan Underworld*.

Rymer, Thomas. *A Short View of Tragedy*. 1693. Reprint. Menston, Yorkshire, 1970.

Scott, William. *An Essay of Drapery*. London, 1635; *An Essay of Drapery*. Edited by Sylvia Thrupp. Cambridge, Mass., 1953.

Selden, John. *Table Talk of John Selden*. Edited by Frederick Pollock. London, 1927.

Shakespeare, William. *Hamlet*. Edited by Harold Jenkins. London, 1982.

Measure for Measure. Edited by J. W. Lever. London, 1965.

Merchant of Venice. Edited by John Russell Brown. London, 1955.

Othello. Edited by M. R. Ridley. London, 1958.

Smith, Thomas. *De Republica Anglorum*. Edited by Mary Dewar. Cambridge and New York, 1982.

Southwell, Robert. *An Epistle of Comfort to the Reverend Priests*. St. Omer, 1616.

An Humble Supplication to Her Majestie. Edited by R. C. Bald. Cambridge, 1953.

SECONDARY SOURCES

Aers, David. "A Whisper in the Ear of Early Modernists," in *Culture and History 1350–1600.* Edited by David Aers. London, 1992.

Agnew, Jean-Christophe. *Worlds Apart: The Market and the Theater in Anglo-American Thought, 1550–1750.* Cambridge, 1986.

Albanese, Denise. *New Science, New World.* Durham, NC, 1996.

Altman, Joel B. "Preposterous Conclusions: Eros, *Enargeia*, and the Composition of *Othello*," *Representations* 18 (1987), 129–57.

Anderson, Fulton H. *Francis Bacon: His Career and His Thought.* Los Angeles, 1962.

Archer, John Michael. *Sovereignty and Intelligence: Spying and Court Culture in the English Renaissance.* Stanford, 1993.

Aydelotte, Frank. *Elizabethan Rogues and Vagabonds.* Oxford, 1913.

Baker, Herschel. *The Wars of Truth.* Cambridge, Mass., 1952.

Bakhtin, Mikhail. *Rabelais and His World.* Translated by Helene Iswolsky. Bloomington, 1984.

Barker, Francis. *The Culture of Violence: Tragedy and History.* Manchester, 1993.
  The Tremulous Private Body: Essays in Subjection. London and New York, 1984.

Bartlett, Robert. *Trial by Fire and Water.* Oxford, 1986.

Beecher, Donald. "The Lover's Body: The Somatogenesis of Love in Renaissance Medical Treatises." *Renaissance and Reformation*, 24 (n.s.12) (1988), 1–12.

Beier, A. L. *Masterless Men: The Vagrancy Problem in Early Modern England.* London and New York, 1985.

Belsey, Catherine. *The Subject of Tragedy.* London, 1985.

Bossy, John. "The Character of Elizabethan Catholicism," *Past and Present*, 21 (1962), 39–59.
  "The Social History of Confession in the Age of the Reformation," *Transactions of the Royal Historical Society.* 5th series, 25 (1975), 21–38.

Bray, Alan. *Homosexuality in Renaissance England.* London, 1982.

Breight, Curtis. " 'Treason Doth Never Prosper': *The Tempest* and the Discourse of Treason," *Shakespeare Quarterly* 41 (1990), 1–28.

Burckhardt, Jacob. *The Civilization of the Renaissance in Italy.* Translated by S. G. C. Middlemore. New York, 1958.

Burt, Richard A. *Licensed by Authority: Ben Jonson and the Discourses of Censorship.* Ithaca and London, 1993.

Cardwell, Kenneth. "Francis Bacon, Inquisitor," in *Francis Bacon's Legacy of Texts: "The Art of Discovery Grows with Discovery.* Edited by William A. Sessions. New York, 1990.

Carroll, William C. *Fat King, Lean Beggar: Representations of Poverty in the Age of Shakespeare.* Ithaca and London, 1996.

Challoner, Richard. *Complete Modern British Martyrology.* London, 1836.

Chartier, Roger. *Cultural History: Between Practices and Representations.* Translated by Lydia G. Cochrane. Ithaca, 1988.

The Cultural Uses of Print in Early Modern France. Translated by Lydia G. Cochrane. Princeton, 1987.

Clancy, Thomas. H. *Papist Pamphleteers: The Allen–Persons Party and the Political Thought of the Counter-Reformation in England, 1572–1615*. Chicago, 1964.

Clifford, James and George E. Marcus, eds. *Writing Culture: The Poetics and Politics of Ethnography*. Berkeley and Los Angeles, 1986.

Cockburn, J. S. "Trial by the Book: Fact and Theory in the Criminal Process, 1558–1625," in *Legal Records and the Historian*. Edited by J. H. Baker. London, 1978.

Cooper, William Durant. "Further Particulars of Thomas Norton, and of State Proceedings in Matters of Religion, in the Years 1581 and 1582," *Archaelogica* 36 (1855), 105–19.

Copeland, Rita. "William Thorpe and his Lollard Community: Intellectual Labor and the Representation of Dissent," in *Bodies and Disciplines: Intersections of Literature and History in Fifteenth-Century England*. Edited by Barbara Hanawalt and David Wallace.

Corthell, Richard J. " 'The secrecy of man': Recusant Discourse and the Elizabethan Subject," *English Literary Renaissance* 19 (1989), 272–90.

Crane, Mary Thomas. *Framing Authority*. Princeton, 1993.

Curtis, Mark H. "The Alienated Intellectuals of Early Stuart England," *Past and Present*, 23 (1962), 25–43.

Daston, Lorraine and Galison, Peter. "The Image of Objectivity," *Representations* 40 (1992), 81–128.

Davis, Lennard. *Factual Fictions: The Origins of the English Novel*. New York, 1983.

Devlin, Christopher. *The Life of Robert Southwell*. London, 1967.

Dijksterhuis, Eduard Jan. *The Mechanization of the World Picture: Pythagoras to Newton*. Translated by C. Dikshoorn. Oxford, 1961. Reprint. Princeton, 1986

Dolan, Frances. *Dangerous Familiars: Representations of Domestic Crime in England 1550–1700*. Ithaca and London, 1994.

DuBois, Page. *Torture and Truth*, New York and London, 1991.

Eaton, Sara. "Defacing the Feminine in Renaissance Tragedy," in *The Matter of Difference*. Edited by Valerie Wayne. Ithaca, 1991.

Empson, William. *The Structure of Complex Words*. London, 1951.

Fabian, Johannes. "Presence and Representation: The Other and Anthropological Writing," *Critical Inquiry* 16 (1990), 753–93.

Febvre, Lucien and Martin, Henri-Jean. *The Coming of the Book: The Impact of Printing, 1450–1800*. Translated by David Gerard. Edited by Geoffrey Nowell-Smith and David Wootton. London, 1976.

Felperin, Howard. *Uses of the Canon*. Oxford, 1990.

Foucault, Michel. *Discipline and Punish: The Birth of the Prison*. Translated by Alan Sheridan. New York, 1979.

The History of Sexuality: Volume One, An Introduction. Translated by Robert M. Hurley. New York, 1978.

The Order of Things: An Archaeology of the Human Sciences. A translation of *Les Mots et les Choses*. 1970. Reprint. New York, 1973.

"What is an Author?" in *Textual Strategies*. Edited by Josue V. Harari. Ithaca, 1979.

Gallagher, Lowell. *Medusa's Gaze: Casuistry and Conscience in the Renaissance*. Stanford, 1991.

Genster, Julia. "Lieutenancy, Standing In, and *Othello*," *ELH* 57 (1990), 785–809.

Goldberg, Jonathan. *James I and the Politics of Literature*. Baltimore, 1983.
Writing Matter: From the Hands of the English Renaissance. Stanford, 1990.

Green, Thomas. *Verdict According to Conscience: Perspectives on the English Trial Jury 1200–1800*. Chicago, 1985.

Greenblatt, Stephen. *Shakespearean Negotiations*. Berkeley and Los Angeles, 1988.

Halasz, Alexandra. *The Marketplace of Print: Pamphlets, Printing and the Early Modern Public Sphere*. Cambridge, 1997.

Hanawalt, Barbara and Wallace, David (eds.). *Bodies and Disciplines: Intersections of Literature and History in Fifteenth-Century England*. Minneapolis, 1996.

Haydn, Hiram. *The Counter Renaissance*. New York, 1950.

Haynes, Alan. *Invisible Power: The Elizabethan Secret Services 1570–1603*. Stroud, Gloucestershire, 1992.

Haynes, Jonathan. *The Social Relations of Jonson's Theater*. Cambridge, 1992.

Heath, James. *Torture and English Law*. Westport, Conn., 1983.

Hodgen, Margaret. *Early Anthropology in the Sixteenth and Seventeenth Centuries*. Philadelphia, 1964.

Hodges, Devon. *Renaissance Fictions of Anatomy*. Amherst, Mass., 1985.

Ingram, Martin. *Church Courts, Sex and Marriage in England, 1570–1640*. Cambridge, 1987.

Jacob, Margaret C. *The Radical Enlightenment: Pantheists, Freemasons and Republicans*. London, 1981.

Johnson, Paul. *Elizabeth I: A Study in Power and Intellect*. London, 1964.

Jones, Richard Foster. *The Triumph of the English Language*. Stanford, 1953.

Judges, A. V. (ed.). *The Elizabethan Underworld*. London, 1930.

Knafla, Louis A. "John at Love Killed Her: The Assizes and Criminal Law in Early Modern England," *University of Toronto Law Journal*. 35 (1985), 305–20.

Langbein, John. *Prosecuting Crime in the Renaissance*. Cambridge, Mass., 1974.
Torture and the Law of Proof. Chicago, 1976.

Leggatt, Alexander. *Jacobean Public Stage*. London and New York, 1992.
"Substitution in *Measure for Measure*," *Shakespeare Quarterly* 39 (1988), 342–59.

Leonard, Nancy J. "Substitution in Shakespeare's Problem Comedies," *English Literary Renaissance* 9 (1979), 281–301.

Lerer, Seth. " 'Representyd now in yower syght': The Culture of Spectatorship in Late Fifteenth-Century England," in Barbara Hanawalt and David Wallace, *Bodies and Disciplines: Intersections of Literature and History in Fifteenth-Century England*.

Levao, Ronald. "Francis Bacon and the Mobility of Science," *Representations* 40 (1992), 1–32.

Levy, Leonard W. *Origins of the Fifth Amendment*. New York, 1968.

Lezra, Jacques. "Pirating Reading: The Appearance of History in *Measure for Measure*," *ELH* 56 (1989), 255–92.

Loewenstein, Joseph. "The Script in the Marketplace," *Representations* 12 (1985), 101–14.

McKeon, Michael. *The Origins of the English Novel*. Baltimore, 1987.

McPherson, David C. *Shakespeare, Jonson and the Myth of Venice*. Newark, 1990.

Manly, Laurence. *Literature and Culture in Early Modern London*. Cambridge, 1995.

Marcus, Leah. *Puzzling Shakespeare: Local Reading and Its Discontents*. Berkeley, 1988.

Martin, Julian. *Francis Bacon, the State and the Reform of Natural Philosophy*. Cambridge, 1992.

Maus, Katherine Eisaman. "Horns of a Dilemma: Jealousy, Gender and Spectatorship in English Drama." *ELH* 54 (1987), 561–83.

Inwardness and Theater in the English Renaissance. Chicago, 1995.

Merchant, Carolyn. *The Death of Nature: Women, Ecology and the Scientific Revolution*. San Francisco, 1980.

Mikalachki, Jodi. "Popular Fictions, Court Records and Female Vagrants in Late Sixteenth and Early Seventeenth-Century England." Paper delivered to the Seminar on Women and Early Modern Culture, Center for Literary and Cultural Studies, Harvard University, September 30, 1992.

Miller, Edwin Haviland. *The Professional Writer in Elizabethan England*. Cambridge, Mass., 1959.

Mullaney, Steven. *The Place of the Stage*. Chicago, 1988.

Murray, Timothy. "From Foul Sheets to Legitimate Model: Antitheatre, Text, Ben Jonson." *New Literary History* 14 (1983), 641–64.

Theatrical Legitimation: Allegories of Genius in Seventeenth-Century England and France. New York and Oxford, 1987.

Neill, Michael. "Improper Beds: Race, Adultery and Hideous in *Othello*," *Shakespeare Quarterly* 40 (1989), 383–412.

Newman, Karen. *Fashioning Femininity and English Renaissance Drama*. Chicago, 1991.

Oestreich, Gerhard. *Neostoicism and the Early Modern State*. Edited by Brigitta Oestreich and H. G. Koenigsberger. Translated by David McLintock. Cambridge, 1982.

Orgel, Stephen. "The Renaissance Artist as Plagiarist." *ELH* 48 (1981), 476–95.

Orlin, Lena Cowen. *Private Matters and Public Culture in Post-Reformation England*. Ithaca and London, 1994.

Parker, Patricia. "*Othello* and *Hamlet*: Dilation, Spying and the 'Secret Place' of Woman," *Representations* 44 (1993), 60–95.

"Shakespeare and Rhetoric: 'Dilation' and 'Delation' in *Othello*," *Shakespeare and the Question of Theory*. Edited by Patricia Parker and Geoffrey Hartman. London, 1985.

Patterson, Annabel. *Censorship and Interpretation*. Madison, 1984.

Perez-Ramos, Antonio. *Francis Bacon's Idea of Science and the Maker's Knowledge Tradition*. Oxford, 1988.

Select bibliography 185

Peters, Edward. *Torture*. Oxford, 1985.
Plowden, Alison. *The Elizabethan Secret Service*. Hampstead, Hertfordshire, and New York, 1991.
Pye, Christopher. *The Regal Phantasm: Shakespeare and the Politics of Spectacle*. London and New York, 1990.
Rambuss, Richard. *Spenser's Secret Career*. Cambridge, 1993.
Reiss, Timothy. *The Discourse of Modernism*. Ithaca, 1982.
Riggs, David. *Ben Jonson: A Life*. Cambridge, Mass., 1989.
Said, Edward. *Beginnings: Intention and Method*. New York, 1975.
Salgado, Gamini. *The Elizabethan Underworld*. London and New York, 1977·
Scarry, Elaine. *The Body in Pain*. New York and Oxford, 1985.
Sedgwick, Eve. *Between Men: English Literature and Male Homosocial Desire*. New York, 1985.
Shapin, Steven. *A Social History of Truth*. Chicago and London, 1994.
Shapin, Steven and Schaffer, Simon. *Leviathan and the Air Pump*. Princeton, 1985.
Shapiro, Barbara. *Probability and Certainty in Seventeenth-Century England*. Princeton, 1983.
Shapiro, James. "'Tragedies naturally performed': Kyd's Representation of Violence," in *Staging the Renaissance*. Edited by David Scott Kastan and Peter Stallybrass. London and New York, 1991.
Sharpe, J. A. *Crime in Early Modern England: 1550–1750*. London and New York, 1974.
Shell, Marc. *The End of Kinship: "Measure for Measure," Incest and the Ideal of Universal Siblinghood*. Stanford, 1988.
Simpson, Richard. *Edmund Campion: A Biography*. London, 1896.
Sinfield, Alan. *Faultlines: Cultural Materialism and the Politics of Dissident Reading*. Oxford, 1992.
Skura, Meredith. "New Interpretations for Interpretation in *Measure for Measure*," *boundary 2* 7 (1979), 39–58.
Slights, Camille. *The Casuistical Tradition*. Princeton, 1981.
Stallybrass, Peter. "Patriarchal Territories: The Body Enclosed," in *Rewriting the Renaissance: The Discourses of Sexual Difference in Early Modern Europe*. Edited by Margaret W. Ferguson, Maureen Quilligan, and Nancy J. Vickers. Chicago, 1986.
Stallybrass, Peter and White, Allon. *The Politics and Poetics of Transgression*. Ithaca, 1986.
Stone, Lawrence and Stone, Jeanne C. Fawtier. *An Open Elite?* Oxford and New York, 1984.
Strype, John. *Life and Acts of John Whitgift*. 3 vols. Oxford, 1822.
Taylor, Charles. *Sources of the Self: The Making of the Modern Identity*. Cambridge, 1989.
Tennenhouse, Leonard. "Representing Power: *Measure for Measure* in its Time," in *The Power of Forms in the English Rennaissance*. Edited by Stephen Greenblatt. Norman, Oklahoma, 1982.
Tentler, Thomas. *Sin and Confession on the Eve of the Reformation*. Princeton, 1977.
Thomas, Keith. "Literacy in Early Modern England," in *The Written Word:*

Literacy in Transition. Edited by Gerd Baumann. Oxford: Clarendon Press, 1986.

Religion and the Decline of Magic. Harmondsworth, 1971.

Viles, Edward and Furnivall, Frederick James, eds. *Rogues and Vagabonds of Shakespeare's Youth.* Early English Text Society Extra Series, vol. 9. London: N. Trubner for the Early English Text Society, 1869.

Wallace, Anthony F. C. *The Social Context of Innovation: Bureaucrats, Families, and Heroes in the Early Industrial Revolution as Foreseen in Bacon's New Atlantis.* Princeton, 1982.

Webster, Charles. *The Great Instauration: Science, Medicine, and Reform, 1626–1660.* London, 1975.

Weimann, Robert. "'Appropriation' and Modern History in Renaissance Prose Narrative," *New Literary History,*14 (1983), 459–95.

Westen, Peter. "The Compulsory Process Clause," *Michigan Law Review* 73 (1974), 73–184.

White, Harold Ogden. *Plagiarism and Imitation During the English Renaissance.* New York, 1965.

Whitney, Charles. *Francis Bacon and Modernity.* New Haven, 1986.

"Merchants of Light: Science as Colonization in the *New Atlantis*," in *Francis Bacon's Legacy of Texts: "The Art of Discovery Grows with Discovery.* Edited by William A. Sessions. New York, 1990.

Wigmore, John Henry. *Evidence in Trials at Common Law.* Revised by John T. McNaughton. 11 vols. Boston, 1961.

Wilson, Luke. "William Harvey's *Prelectiones:*The Performance of the Body in the Renaissance Theater of Anatomy." *Representations* 17 (1987), 62–95.

Index

Cambridge Studies in Renaissance Literature and Culture

General editor
STEPHEN ORGEL
Jackson Eli Reynolds Professor of Humanities, Stanford University